A Casebook on
RALPH ELLISON'S
INVISIBLE MAN

A Casebook on RALPH ELLISON'S INVISIBLE MAN

edited by
Joseph F. Trimmer

Ball State University

THOMAS Y. CROWELL
NEW YORK
ESTABLISHED 1834

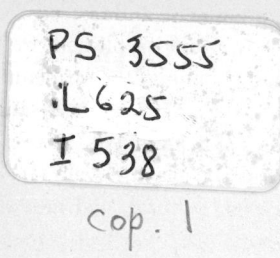

Copyright © 1972 by
Thomas Y. Crowell Company, Inc.
All Rights Reserved

Except for use in a review, the reproduction or utilization of this work in any form or by any electronic, mechanical, or other means, now known or hereafter invented, including photocopying and recording, and in any information storage and retrieval system is forbidden without the written permission of the publisher.

L. C. Card 75–179779
ISBN 0–690–17921–9

Manufactured in the United States of America

Finally, I have included a wide spectrum of critical reactions to *Invisible Man,* Ellison's acceptance speech for the National Book Award, a bibliography to facilitate further study of the novel, and some suggested discussion questions and research topics.

I would like to acknowledge the secretarial staff of the English Department of Ball State University, and, in particular, Jeannine Ellsworth, for providing valuable assistance in the preparation of this manuscript.

J.F.T.

Preface

Ralph Ellison's *Invisible Man* certainly needs no formal introduction. Winner of the 1953 National Book Award for fiction, and acclaimed by a 1965 *Book Week* poll of prominent authors, critics, and editors as "the most distinguished single work published in the last twenty years," the novel is gradually gaining the critical reputation of a classic. And that reputation is being arrived at by three separate and yet finally interlocking standards of judgment. In the first place *Invisible Man* is often mentioned as *the* black novel. There are immensely complex and controversial racial, cultural, and aesthetic problems involved in making that judgment. But the fact remains that no other single work of art gives us so abundant and intricately diverse a vision of the black experience in America. Secondly, *Invisible Man* has achieved the stature of an American classic. In the great tradition of novels like *The Scarlet Letter*, *Moby Dick*, and *The Adventures of Huckleberry Finn*, *Invisible Man* deals with the question of man's personal moral responsibility in a democratic society. And, like all great American documents, the novel strikes at the axis of the American experience—the dilemma that always exists when we try to gauge what we are by what we say we are or aspire to be. Finally, *Invisible Man* may be seen as a classic of modern fiction. Employing the aesthetic principles of Eliot, exploiting the technical innovations of Joyce, and confronting the condition of man that Camus called the Absurd, *Invisible Man* emerges as a novel that, "on the lower frequencies," speaks to all of us in the modern world.

A novel of such richness makes enormous demands on a critic. One of those demands is that the critic should know the complex traditions that inform an individual work of art. As Ellison says in "The World and the Jug," "for the critic there simply exists no substitute for the knowledge of history and literary tradition." For this reason I have decided to devote a major portion of this book to the historical tradition. Initially this means that as critics we must be aware of the racial heritage, which serves as the experiential core of the novel. Secondly, we must be aware of the artistic heritage. The racial heritage is merely inherited, but the artistic heritage is chosen, earned, created by the individual artist. Some of the elements contributing to Ellison's artistic heritage are included in the second part of the first major division of the book. In the second major division of the book it is appropriate to present Ellison in dialogue with the tradition.

Contents

THE HISTORICAL TRADITION — 1

The Racial Heritage — 1

Atlanta Exposition Address — 4
 Booker T. Washington

Of Mr. Booker T. Washington and Others — 8
 W. E. B. DuBois

The New Negro — 20
 Alain Locke

An Appeal to the Conscience of the Black Race to See Itself — 32
 Marcus Garvey

I Tried to Be a Communist — 37
 Richard Wright

The Artistic Heritage — 79

The Poet — 82
 Ralph Waldo Emerson

Tradition and the Individual Talent — 103
 T. S. Eliot

Negro Character as Seen by White Authors — 111
 Sterling A. Brown

Black Boys and Native Sons — 150
 Irving Howe

ELLISON IN DIALOGUE WITH THE TRADITION — 171

The World and the Jug — 171
 Ralph Ellison

CRITICAL REACTIONS TO INVISIBLE MAN — 201

- Ralph Ellison and the Uses of Imagination — 203
  Robert Bone

- Ralph Ellison and the Birth of the Anti-Hero — 225
  William J. Schafer

- The Rebirth of the Artist — 238
  Ellin Horowitz

- Ralph Ellison and the American Comic Tradition — 254
  Earl H. Rovit

- Sight Imagery in Invisible Man — 264
  Alice Bloch

- Whitman and Ellison: Older Symbols in a Modern Mainstream — 269
  Marvin E. Mengeling

- Ralph Ellison's Modern Version of Brer Bear and Brer Rabbit in Invisible Man — 273
  Floyd R. Horowitz

- The Politics of Ellison's Booker: Invisible Man as Symbolic History — 281
  Richard Kostelanetz

EPILOGUE — 307

- Brave Words for a Startling Occasion — 307
  Ralph Ellison

BIBLIOGRAPHY — 311

POSSIBLE DISCUSSION QUESTIONS OR RESEARCH TOPICS — 317

A Casebook on
RALPH ELLISON'S
INVISIBLE MAN

THE HISTORICAL TRADITION

The Racial Heritage

As Richard Kostelanetz points out, *Invisible Man* is the "most comprehensive one-volume fictional—symbolic—treatment of the history of the American Negro in the twentieth century." The novel charts the journey of a nameless protagonist as he searches for self, visibility, in the shadow world of modern America. But this protagonist is simultaneously Noman and Everyman; in the very process of his search for an individual identity he symbolically recapitulates a major portion of the history of black America.

Each of the selections in this part is a key document in that history. Taken together these documents form a fairly coherent intellectual history running parallel to, and helping to explain and confirm, the symbolic history rendered in the novel. The novel proper begins in the South where the Reconstruction mentality and the ideological heritage of Booker T. Washington still reign. In the second paragraph of the first chapter the narrator tells us that his grandparents believed that "they were free, united with others of our country in everything pertaining to the common good, and in everything social, separate like the fingers of the hand." [1] This obvious allusion to Washington's "Atlanta Exposition Address" is the first of many in the Southern segment of the novel. After the Battle Royal, the narrator delivers a carbon copy of Washington's speech. The picture we get of the Southern Negro College and of its Founder is remarkably similar to Washington's descriptions of Tuskegee in *Up from Slavery*. (For a fuller discussion of the references to Washington see Richard Kostelanetz's "The Politics of Ellison's Booker: *Invisible Man* as Symbolic History," pp. 281–305 in this book.)

The novel certainly points to the limitations and deficiencies in Washington's ideology in many symbolic ways—for example, Homer

---

1. Ralph Ellison, *Invisible Man* (New York: Random House, 1952), p. 19. All further quotations from *Invisible Man* in the introductory matter of this text will be documented by page references in parentheses.

2 HISTORICAL TRADITION: THE RACIAL HERITAGE

A. Barbee's blindness, and the less than glorious future awaiting those who believe in the rite of the black Horatio Alger at the Golden Day. Historically, it was W. E. B. DuBois who launched a full-scale attack on the Washington ideology near the turn of the century. The selection from *Souls of Black Folk* shows that DuBois' criticism had its origin in a debate over educational philosophy. DuBois was unwilling to settle for vocational education since that implied accepting the "alleged inferiority of the Black race." Dubois was also convinced that any true meaning for the word *vocation* could only come once the black man acquired the legal and political equipment necessary to defend his vocation. For both Washington and DuBois, however, a necessary ingredient in any move toward social progress was the white man: Washington needed the financial patronage of men like the fictional Norton to keep his educational machine going, while DuBois placed his hope in the possible allegiance of the enlightened white man, perhaps a man like young Emerson in Ellison's novel, and "the talented tenth" of the black race. Such dependence on the white man, the veteran tells the narrator, leads nowhere—or more appropriately it leads to The Golden Day. As the narrator leaves for the North the veteran counsels independence, "Be your own father" (p. 139).

"The Great Migration" North in search of freedom and independence, particularly in the first decades of the twentieth century, was one of the major events in black history. Harlem especially was seen as a potential race capital where for the first time blacks could begin to have some sense of themselves as a community. Such a feeling of community, of race consciousness, would produce a "New Negro" who would in turn initiate a black Renaissance. Certainly this was the visionary impetus behind Alain Locke's 1925 introduction to a collection of Negro writing called "The New Negro." For the black man there was some value in moving from the medieval world of the South to the modern world of the North; but though "history is born in his brain," the frustrations remain the same. Locke's optimism now seems pitifully ironic. As the invisible man discovered, migration North produced no true mobility,

Independence and the cultivation of a racial consciousness are also the themes of Marcus Garvey. In the speech included in this section Garvey argues that black progress can only come through black independence. Dependence on the white man for progress produces, at best, a society of "good slaves." What is needed is black organization, and the migration to a black country. Locke and DuBois certainly recognize the limitations of a man like Garvey, but as Tod Clifton says in Ellison's novel, "on the inside he's dangerous" (p. 327). The message of black independence and categorical distrust of the white man because he will ultimately be discovered as a betrayer does have psychological validity "on the inside." Unfortunately, as the novel suggests, black nationalism is a closed street. Ras is driven from Exhorter to Destroyer, but for all his efforts he becomes merely another victim of white exploitation.

The alternative to the black organization that Garvey offered to Harlem in the 1920s was the communist party. Dedicated to the liberation of the oppressed people of the world, the party had no better potential converts, particularly with the onset of the Depression, than the black American community. But ideological rigidity and a more sophisticated kind of racism prevented the party from understanding the human reality it attempted to exploit. The history of the Negro and the communist party is long and extremely complex—witness the proportional amount of space devoted to it in Ellison's novel. Richard Wright's lengthy essay, "I Tried to Be a Communist," confirms many of the conclusions arrived at in *Invisible Man*. For both the narrator and Wright, the ideology of history-making prevents man from seeing himself and the true historical reality of the "inexpressibly human."

ATLANTA EXPOSITION ADDRESS
Booker T. Washington

MR. PRESIDENT AND GENTLEMEN OF THE BOARD OF DIRECTORS AND CITIZENS.

One-third of the population of the South is of the Negro race., No enterprise seeking the material, civil, or moral welfare of this section can disregard this element of our population and reach the highest success. I but convey to you, Mr. President and Directors, the sentiment of the masses of my race when I say that in no way have the value and manhood of the American Negro been more fittingly and generously recognized than by the managers of this magnificent Exposition at every stage of its progress. It is a recognition that will do more to cement the friendship of the two races than any occurrence since the dawn of our freedom.

Not only this, but the opportunity here afforded will awaken among us a new era of industrial progress. Ignorant and inexperienced, it is not strange that in the first years of our new life we began at the top instead of at the bottom; that a seat in Congress or the state legislature was more sought than real estate or industrial skill; that the political [218] * convention of stump speaking had more attractions than starting a dairy farm or truck garden.

A ship lost at sea for many days suddenly sighted a friendly vessel. From the mast of the unfortunate vessel was seen a signal, "Water, water; we die of thirst!" The answer from the friendly vessel at once came back, "Cast down your bucket where you are." A second time the signal, "Water, water; send us water!" ran up from the distressed vessel, and was answered, "Cast down your bucket where you are." And a third and fourth signal for water was answered, "Cast down your bucket where you are." The captain of the distressed vessel, at last heeding the injunction, cast down his bucket, and it came up full of fresh, sparkling water from the mouth of the Amazon River. To those of my race who depend on bettering their condition in a foreign

SOURCE: Booker T. Washington, "Atlanta Exposition Address," *Up from Slavery: An Autobiography* (New York: Doubleday Page and Co., 1901). Doubleday, Doran & Co., 1938, pp. 218–25.

* In the texts of the selections, bracketed numbers indicate the pagination of the original sources. When a page in the original ends with a hyphenated word, we have indicated the original pagination after the entire word.

land or who underestimate the importance of cultivating friendly relations with the Southern white man, who is their next-door neighbour, I would say: "Cast down your bucket where you are"—cast it down in making friends in every manly way of the people of all races by whom we are surrounded.

Cast it down in agriculture, mechanics, in commerce, in domestic service, and in the professions. And in this connection it is well to bear in mind that whatever other sins the South may be called to [219] bear, when it comes to business, pure and simple, it is in the South that the Negro is given a man's chance in the commercial world, and in nothing is this Exposition more eloquent than in emphasizing this chance. Our greatest danger is that in the great leap from slavery to freedom we may overlook the fact that the masses of us are to live by the productions of our hands, and fail to keep in mind that we shall prosper in proportion as we learn to dignify and glorify common labour and put brains and skill into the common occupations of life; shall prosper in proportion as we learn to draw the line between the superficial and the substantial, the ornamental gewgaws of life and the useful. No race can prosper till it learns that there is as much dignity in tilling a field as in writing a poem. It is at the bottom of life we must begin, and not at the top. Nor should we permit our grievances to overshadow our opportunities.

To those of the white race who look to the incoming of those of foreign birth and strange tongue and habits for the prosperity of the South, were I permitted I would repeat what I say to my own race, "Cast down your bucket where you are." Cast it down among the eight millions of Negroes whose habits you know, whose fidelity and love you have tested in days when to have proved treacherous [220] meant the ruin of your firesides. Cast down your bucket among these people who have, without strikes and labour wars, tilled your fields, cleared your forests, built your railroads and cities, and brought forth treasures from the bowels of the earth, and helped make possible this magnificent representation of the progress of the South. Casting down your bucket among my people, helping and encouraging them as you are doing on these grounds, and to education of head, hand, and heart, you will find that they will buy your surplus land, make blossom the waste places in your fields, and run your factories. While doing this, you can be sure in the future, as in the past, that you and your families will be surrounded by the most patient, faithful, law-abiding, and unresentful people that the world has seen. As we have proved our loyalty to you in the past, in nursing your children, watching by the sick-bed of your mothers and fathers, and often following them with tear-dimmed eyes to their graves, so in the future, in our humble way, we shall stand by you with a devotion that no foreigner can approach, ready to lay down our lives, if need be, in defence of yours, interlacing our industrial, commercial, civil, and religious life with yours in a way that shall make the interests of both races one. In all things that are purely social we can be as separate [221] as the fingers, yet one as the hand in all things essential to mutual progress.

There is no defence or security for any of us except in the highest intelligence and development of all. If anywhere there are efforts tending to curtail the fullest growth of the Negro, let these efforts be turned into stimulating, encouraging, and making him the most useful and intelligent citizen. Effort or means so invested will pay a thousand per cent. interest. These efforts will be twice blessed—"blessing him that gives and him that takes."

There is no escape through law of man or God from the inevitable:—

> The laws of changeless justice bind
> Oppressor with oppressed;
> And close as sin and suffering joined
> We march to fate abreast.

Nearly sixteen millions of hands will aid you in pulling the load upward, or they will pull against you the load downward. We shall constitute one-third and more of the ignorance and crime of the South, or one-third its intelligence and progress; we shall contribute one-third to the business and industrial prosperity of the South, or we shall prove a veritable body of death, stagnating, depressing, retarding every effort to advance the body politic. [222]

Gentlemen of the Exposition, as we present to you our humble effort at an exhibition of our progress, you must not expect overmuch. Starting thirty years ago with ownership here and there in a few quilts and pumpkins and chickens (gathered from miscellaneous sources), remember the path that has led from these to the inventions and production of agricultural implements, buggies, steam-engines, newspapers, books, statuary, carving, paintings, the management of drugstores and banks, has not been trodden without contact with thorns and thistles. While we take pride in what we exhibit as a result of our independent efforts, we do not for a moment forget that our part in this exhibition would fall far short of your expectations but for the constant help that has come to our educational life, not only from the Southern states, but especially from Northern philanthropists, who have made their gifts a constant stream of blessing and encouragement.

The wisest among my race understand that the agitation of questions of social equality is the extremest folly, and that progress in the enjoyment of all the privileges that will come to us must be the result of severe and constant struggle rather than of artificial forcing. No race that has anything to contribute to the markets of the world is long in any degree ostracized. It is important and [223] right that all privileges of the law be ours, but it is vastly more important that we be prepared for the exercises of these privileges. The opportunity to earn a dollar in a factory just now is worth infinitely more than the opportunity to spend a dollar in an opera-house.

In conclusion, may I repeat that nothing in thirty years has given us more hope and encouragement, and drawn us so near to you of the white race, as this opportunity offered by the Exposition; and here bending, as it were, over the altar that represents the results of the struggles of your race and mine, both starting practically empty-handed three decades ago, I pledge that in your effort to work out the great and intricate problem which God has laid at the doors of the South, you shall have at all times the patient, sympathetic help of my race; only let this be constantly in mind, that, while from representations in these buildings of the product of field, of forest, of mine, of factory, letters, and art, much good will come, yet far above and beyond material benefits will be that higher good, that, let us pray God, will come, in a blotting out of sectional differences and racial animosities and suspicions, in a determination to administer absolute justice, in a willing obedience among all classes to the mandates of law. This, this, coupled with our [224] material prosperity, will bring into our beloved South a new heaven and a new earth. [225]

OF MR. BOOKER T. WASHINGTON AND OTHERS
W. E. B. DuBois

From birth till death enslaved; in word, in deed, unmanned!

. . . .

Hereditary bondsmen! Know ye not
Who would be free themselves must strike the blow?

BYRON

Easily the most striking thing in the history of the American Negro since 1876 is the ascendancy of Mr. Booker T. Washington. It began at the time when war memories and ideals were rapidly passing; a day of astonishing commercial development was dawning; a sense of doubt and hesitation overtook the freedmen's sons,—then it was that his leading began. Mr. Washington came, with a simple definite programme, at the psychological moment when the nation was a little ashamed of having bestowed so much sentiment on Negroes, and [41] was concentrating its energies on Dollars. His programme of industrial education, conciliation of the South, and submission and silence as to civil and political rights, was not wholly original; the Free Negroes from 1830 up to war-time had striven to build industrial schools, and the American Missionary Association had from the first taught various trades; and Price and others had sought a way of honorable alliance with the best of the Southerners. But Mr. Washington first indissolubly linked these things; he put enthusiasm, unlimited energy, and perfect faith into this programme, and changed it from a by-path into a veritable Way of Life. And the tale of the methods by which he did this is a fascinating study of human life.

It startled the nation to hear a Negro advocating such a programme after many decades of bitter complaint; it startled and won the applause of the South, it interested and won the admiration of the North; and after a confused murmur of protest, it silenced if it did not convert the Negroes themselves.

To gain the sympathy and coöperation of the various elements

SOURCE: W. E. B. DuBois, "Of Mr. Booker T. Washington and Others," *The Souls of Black Folk* (Chicago: A. C. McClurg & Co., 1903), pp. 41–59.

comprising the white South was Mr. Washington's first task; and this, at the time Tuskegee was founded, seemed, for a black man, well-nigh impossible. And yet ten years later it was done in the word spoken at Atlanta: "In all things purely social we can be as separate as the five fingers, and yet one as the hand in all things essential to mutual progress." This "Atlanta Compromise" is by all odds the most notable thing in Mr. Washington's career. The South interpreted it in [42] different ways: the radicals received it as a complete surrender of the demand for civil and political equality; the conservatives, as a generously conceived working basis for mutual understanding. So both approved it, and to-day its author is certainly the most distinguished Southerner since Jefferson Davis, and the one with the largest personal following.

Next to this achievement comes Mr. Washington's work in gaining place and consideration in the North. Others less shrewd and tactful had formerly essayed to sit on these two stools and had fallen between them; but as Mr. Washington knew the heart of the South from birth and training, so by singular insight he intuitively grasped the spirit of the age which was dominating the North. And so thoroughly did he learn the speech and thought of triumphant commercialism, and the ideals of material prosperity, that the picture of a lone black boy poring over a French grammar amid the weeds and dirt of a neglected home soon seemed to him the acme of absurdities. One wonders what Socrates and St. Francis of Assisi would say to this.

And yet this very singleness of vision and thorough oneness with his age is a mark of the successful man. It is as though Nature must needs make men narrow in order to give them force. So Mr. Washington's cult has gained unquestioning followers, his work has wonderfully prospered, his friends are legion, and his enemies are confounded. To-day he stands as the one recognized spokesman of his ten million fellows, and one of the most notable figures in a nation of seventy millions. One hesitates, therefore, to criticise [43] a life which, beginning with so little, has done so much. And yet the time is come when one may speak in all sincerity and utter courtesy of the mistakes and shortcomings of Mr. Washington's career, as well as of his triumphs, without being thought captious or envious, and without forgetting that it is easier to do ill than well in the world.

The criticism that has hitherto met Mr. Washington has not always been of this broad character. In the South especially has he had to walk warily to avoid the harshest judgments,—and naturally so, for he is dealing with the one subject of deepest sensitiveness to that section. Twice—once when at the Chicago celebration of the Spanish-American War he alluded to the color-prejudice that is "eating away the vitals of the South," and once when he dined with President Roosevelt—has the resulting Southern criticism been violent enough to threaten seriously his popularity. In the North the feeling has several times forced itself into words, that Mr. Washington's counsels of submission overlooked certain elements of true manhood, and that his educational programme was unnecessarily narrow. Usually, however, such criticism has not found open expression, although, too, the spiritual sons of the Abolitionists have not been prepared to acknowledge that the schools founded before Tuskegee, by men of broad ideals and self-sacrificing spirit, were wholly failures or worthy of ridicule. While, then, criticism has not failed to follow Mr. Washington, yet the prevailing public opinion of the land has been but too willing to deliver the solution of a wearisome [44] problem into his hands, and say, "If that is all you and your race ask, take it."

Among his own people, however, Mr. Washington has encountered the strongest and most lasting opposition, amounting at times to bitterness, and even to-day continuing strong and insistent even though largely silenced in outward expression by the public opinion of the nation. Some of this opposition is, of course, mere envy; the disappointment of displaced demagogues and the spite of narrow minds. But aside from this, there is among educated and thoughtful colored men in all parts of the land a feeling of deep regret, sorrow, and apprehension at the wide currency and ascendancy which some of Mr. Washington's theories have gained. These same men admire his sincerity of purpose, and are willing to forgive much to honest endeavor which is doing something worth the doing. They coöperate with Mr. Washington as far as they conscientiously can; and, indeed, it is no ordinary tribute to this man's tact and power that, steering as he must between so many diverse interests and opinions, he so largely retains the respect of all.

But the hushing of the criticism of honest opponents is a dangerous thing. It leads some of the best of the critics to unfortunate silence and paralysis of effort, and others to burst into speech so passionately and intemperately as to lose listeners. Honest and earnest criticism from those whose interests are most nearly touched,—criticism of writers by readers, of government by those governed, of leaders by those led,—this is the soul of democracy and the safeguard [45] of modern society. If the best of the American Negroes receive by outer pressure a leader whom they had not recognized before, manifestly there is here a certain palpable gain. Yet there is also irreparable loss,—a loss of that peculiarly valuable education which a group receives when by search and criticism it finds and commissions its own leaders. The way in which this is done is at once the most elementary and the nicest problem of social growth. History is but the record of such group-leadership; and yet how infinitely changeful is its type and character! And of all types and kinds, what can be more instructive than the leadership of a group within a group?—that curious double movement where real progress may be negative and actual advance be relative retrogression. All this is the social student's inspiration and despair.

Now in the past the American Negro has had instructive experience in the choosing of group leaders, founding thus a peculiar dynasty which in the light of present conditions is worth while studying. When sticks and stones and beasts form the sole environment of a people, their attitude is largely one of determined opposition to and conquest of natural forces. But when to earth and brute is added an environment of men and ideas, then the attitude of the imprisoned group may take three main forms,—a feeling of revolt and revenge; an attempt to adjust all thought and action to the will of the greater group or, finally, a determined effort at self-realization and self-development despite environing opinion. The influence of all these [46] attitudes at various times can be traced in the history of the American Negro, and in the evolution of his successive leaders.

Before 1750, while the fire of African freedom still burned in the veins of the slaves, there was in all leadership or attempted leadership but the one motive of revolt and revenge,—typified in the terrible Maroons, the Danish blacks, and Cato of Stono, and veiling all the Americas in fear of insurrection. The liberalizing tendencies of the latter half of the eighteenth century brought, along with kindlier relations between black and white, thoughts of ultimate adjustment and assimilation. Such aspiration was especially voiced in the earnest songs of Phyllis, in the martyrdom of Attucks, the fighting of Salem and Poor, the intellectual accomplishments of Banneker and Derham, and the political demands of the Cuffes.

Stern financial and social stress after the war cooled much of the previous humanitarian ardor. The disappointment and impatience of the Negroes at the persistence of slavery and serfdom voiced itself in two movements. The slaves in the South, aroused undoubtedly by vague rumors of the Haytian revolt, made three fierce attempts at insurrection,—in 1800 under Gabriel in Virginia, in 1822 under Vesey in Carolina, and in 1831 again in Virginia under the terrible Nat Turner. In the Free States, on the other hand, a new and curious attempt at self-development was made. In Philadelphia and New York color-prescription led to a withdrawal of Negro communicants from white churches and the formation [47] of a peculiar socio-religious institution among the Negroes known as the African Church,—an organization still living and controlling in its various branches over a million of men.

Walker's wild appeal against the trend of the times showed how the world was changing after the coming of the cotton-gin. By 1830 slavery seemed hopelessly fastened on the South, and the slaves thoroughly cowed into submission. The free Negroes of the North, inspired by the mulatto immigrants from the West Indies, began to change the basis of their demands; they recognized the slavery of slaves, but insisted that they themselves were freemen, and sought assimilation and amalgamation with the nation on the same terms with other men. Thus, Forten and Purvis of Philadelphia, Shad of Wilmington, Du Bois of New Haven, Barbadoes of Boston, and others, strove singly and together as men, they said, not as slaves; as "people of color," not as "Negroes." The trend of the times, however, refused them recognition save in individual and exceptional cases, considered them as one with all the despised blacks, and they soon found themselves striving to keep even the rights they formerly had of voting and working and moving as freemen. Schemes of migration and colonization arose among them; but these they refused to entertain, and they eventually turned to the Abolition movement as a final refuge.

Here, led by Remond, Nell, Wells-Brown, and Douglass, a new period of self-assertion and self-development dawned. To be sure, ultimate freedom [48] and assimilation was the ideal before the leaders, but the assertion of the manhood rights of the Negro by himself was the main reliance, and John Brown's raid was the extreme of its logic. After the war and emancipation, the great form of Frederick Douglass, the greatest of American Negro leaders, still led the host. Self-assertion, especially in political lines, was the main programme, and behind Douglass came Elliot, Bruce, and Langston, and the Reconstruction politicians, and, less conspicuous but of greater social significance Alexander Crummell and Bishop Daniel Payne.

Then came the Revolution of 1876, the suppression of the Negro votes, the changing and shifting of ideals, and the seeking of new lights in the great night. Douglass, in his old age, still bravely stood for the ideals of his early manhood,—ultimate assimilation *through* self-assertion, and on no other terms. For a time Price arose as a new leader, destined, it seemed, not to give up, but to re-state the old ideals in a form less repugnant to the white South. But he passed away in his prime. Then came the new leader. Nearly all the former ones had become leaders by the silent suffrage of their fellows, had sought to lead their own people alone, and were usually, save Douglass, little known outside their race. But Booker T. Washington arose as essentially the leader not of one race but of two,—a compromiser between the South, the North, and the Negro. Naturally the Negroes resented, at first bitterly, signs of compromise which surrendered their civil and political rights, even though this was to be [49] exchanged for larger chances of economic development. The rich and dominating North, however, was not only weary of the race problem, but was investing largely in Southern enterprises, and welcomed any method of peaceful coöperation. Thus, by national opinion, the Negroes began to recognize Mr. Washington's leadership; and the voice of criticism was hushed.

Mr. Washington represents in Negro thought the old attitude of adjustment and submission; but adjustment at such a peculiar time as to make his programme unique. This is an age of unusual economic development, and Mr. Washington's programme naturally takes an economic cast, becoming a gospel of Work and Money to such an extent as apparently almost completely to overshadow the higher aims of life. Moreover, this is an age when the more advanced races are coming in closer contact with the less developed races, and the race-feeling is therefore intensified; and Mr. Washington's programme practically accepts the alleged inferiority of the Negro races. Again, in our own land, the reaction from the sentiment of war time has given impetus to race-prejudice against Negroes, and Mr. Washington withdraws many of the high demands of Negroes as men and American citizens. In other periods of intensified prejudice all the Negro's tendency to self-assertion has been called forth; at this period a policy of submission is advocated. In the history of nearly all other races and peoples the doctrine preached at such crises has been that manly self-respect is worth more than lands and houses, and that a people who [50] voluntarily surrender such respect, or cease striving for it, are not worth civilizing.

In answer to this, it has been claimed that the Negro can survive only through submission. Mr. Washington distinctly asks that black people give up, at least for the present, three things,—

First, political power,

Second, insistence on civil rights,

Third, higher education of Negro youth,—

and concentrate all their energies on industrial education, the accumulation of wealth, and the conciliation of the South. This policy has been courageously and insistently advocated for over fifteen years, and has been triumphant for perhaps ten years. As a result of this tender of the palm-branch, what has been the return? In these years there have occurred:

1. The disfranchisement of the Negro.

2. The legal creation of a distinct status of civil inferiority for the Negro.

3. The steady withdrawal of aid from institutions for the higher training of the Negro.

These movements are not, to be sure, direct results of Mr. Washington's teachings; but his propaganda has, without a shadow of doubt, helped their speedier accomplishment. The question then comes: Is it possible, and probable, that nine millions of men can make effective progress in economic lines if they are deprived of political rights, made a servile caste, and allowed only the most meagre chance for developing their exceptional men? If history and reason give any distinct answer to these questions, it is an emphatic [51] *No*. And Mr. Washington thus faces the triple paradox of his career:

1. He is striving nobly to make Negro artisans business men and property-owners; but it is utterly impossible, under modern competitive methods, for workingmen and property-owners to defend their rights and exist without the right of suffrage.

2. He insists on thrift and self-respect, but at the same time

counsels a silent submission to civic inferiority such as is bound to sap the manhood of any race in the long run.

3. He advocates common-school and industrial training, and depreciates institutions of higher learning; but neither the Negro common-schools, nor Tuskegee itself, could remain open a day were it not for teachers trained in Negro colleges, or trained by their graduates.

This triple paradox in Mr. Washington's position is the object of criticism by two classes of colored Americans. One class is spiritually descended from Toussaint the Savior, through Gabriel, Vesey, and Turner, and they represent the attitude of revolt and revenge; they hate the white South blindly and distrust the white race generally, and so far as they agree on definite action, think that the Negro's only hope lies in emigration beyond the borders of the United States. And yet, by the irony of fate, nothing has more effectually made this programme seem hopeless than the recent course of the United States toward weaker and darker peoples in the West Indies, Hawaii, and the Philippines,—for where in the world may we go and be safe from lying and brute force? [52]

The other class of Negroes who cannot agree with Mr. Washington has hitherto said little aloud. They deprecate the sight of scattered counsels, of internal disagreement; and especially they dislike making their just criticism of a useful and earnest man an excuse for a general discharge of venom from small-minded opponents. Nevertheless, the questions involved are so fundamental and serious that it is difficult to see how men like the Grimkes, Kelly Miller, J. W. E. Bowen, and other representatives of this group, can much longer be silent. Such men feel in conscience bound to ask of this nation three things:

1. The right to vote.
2. Civic equality.
3. The education of youth according to ability.

They acknowledge Mr. Washington's invaluable service in counselling patience and courtesy in such demands; they do not ask that ignorant black men vote when ignorant whites are debarred, or that any reasonable restrictions in the suffrage should not be applied; they know that the low social level of the mass of the race is responsible for much discrimination against it, but they also know, and the nation knows, that relentless color-prejudice is more often a cause than a result of the Negro's degradation; they seek the abatement of this relic of barbarism, and not its systematic encouragement and pampering by all agencies of social power from the Associated Press to the Church of Christ. They advocate, with Mr. Washington, a broad system of Negro common schools supplemented by thorough industrial training; but they are surprised that a man of Mr. Washington's [53] insight cannot see that no such educational system ever has rested or can rest on any other basis than that of the well-equipped college and university, and they insist that there is a demand for a few such institutions throughout the South to train the best of the Negro youth as teachers, professional men, and leaders.

This group of men honor Mr. Washington for his attitude of conciliation toward the white South; they accept the "Atlanta Compromise" in its broadest interpretation; they recognize, with him, many signs of promise, many men of high purpose and fair judgment, in this section; they know that no easy task has been laid upon a region already tottering under heavy burdens. But, nevertheless, they insist that the way to truth and right lies in straightforward honesty, not in indiscriminate flattery; in praising those of the South who do well and criticising uncompromisingly those who do ill; in taking advantage of the opportunities at hand and urging their fellows to do the same, but at the same time in remembering that only a firm adherence to their higher ideals and aspirations will ever keep those ideals within the realm of possibility. They do not expect that the free right to vote, to enjoy civic rights, and to be educated, will come in a moment; they do not expect to see the bias and prejudices of years disappear at the blast of a trumpet; but they are absolutely certain that the way for a people to gain their reasonable rights is not by voluntarily throwing them away and insisting that they do not want them; that the way for a people to gain respect is not by continually [54] belittling and ridiculing themselves; that, on the contrary, Negroes must insist continually, in season and out of season, that voting is necessary to modern manhood, that color discrimination is barbarism, and that black boys need education as well as white boys.

In failing thus to state plainly and unequivocally the legitimate demands of their people, even at the cost of opposing an honored leader, the thinking classes of American Negroes would shirk a heavy responsibility,—a responsibility to themselves, a responsibility to the struggling masses, a responsibility to the darker races of men whose future depends so largely on this American experiment, but especially a responsibility to this nation,—this common Fatherland. It is wrong to encourage a man or a people in evil-doing; it is wrong to aid and abet a national crime simply because it is unpopular not to do so. The growing spirit of kindliness and reconciliation between the North and South after the frightful differences of a generation ago ought to be a source of deep congratulation to all, and especially to those whose mistreatment caused the war; but if that reconciliation is to be marked by the industrial slavery and civic death of those same black men, with permanent legislation into a position of inferiority, then those black men, if they are really men, are called upon by every consideration of patriotism and loyalty to oppose such a course by all civilized methods, even though such opposition involves disagreement with Mr. Booker T. Washington. We have no right to sit silently by while the inevitable seeds are sown [55] for a harvest of disaster to our children, black and white.

First, it is the duty of black men to judge the South discriminatingly. The present generation of Southerners are not responsible for the past, and they should not be blindly hated or blamed for it. Furthermore, to no class is the indiscriminate endorsement of the recent course of the South toward Negroes more nauseating than to the best thought of the South. The South is not "solid"; it is a land in the ferment of social change, wherein forces of all kinds are fighting for supremacy; and to praise the ill the South is to-day perpetrating is just as wrong as to condemn the good. Discriminating and broad-minded criticism is what the South needs,—needs it for the sake of her own white sons and daughters, and for the insurance of robust, healthy mental and moral development.

To-day even the attitude of the Southern whites toward the blacks is not, as so many assume, in all cases the same; the ignorant Southerner hates the Negro, the workingmen fear his competition, the money-makers wish to use him as a laborer, some of the educated see a menace in his upward development, while others—usually the sons of the masters—wish to help him to rise. National opinion has enabled this last class to maintain the Negro common schools, and to protect the Negro partially in property, life, and limb. Through the pressure of the money-makers, the Negro is in danger of being reduced to semi-slavery, especially in the country districts; the workingmen, and those of the educated [56] who fear the Negro, have united to disfranchise him, and some have urged his deportation; while the passions of the ignorant are easily aroused to lynch and abuse any black man. To praise this intricate whirl of thought and prejudice is nonsense; to inveigh indiscriminately against "the South" is unjust; but to use the same breath in praising Governor Aycock, exposing Senator Morgan, arguing with Mr. Thomas Nelson Page, and denouncing Senator Ben Tillman, is not only sane, but the imperative duty of thinking black men.

It would be unjust to Mr. Washington not to acknowledge that in several instances he has opposed movements in the South which were unjust to the Negro; he sent memorials to the Louisiana and Alabama constitutional conventions, he has spoken against lynching, and in other ways has openly or silently set his influence against sinister schemes and unfortunate happenings. Notwithstanding this, it is equally true to assert that on the whole the distinct impression left by Mr. Washington's propaganda is, first, that the South is justified in its present attitude toward the Negro because of the Negro's degradation; secondly, that the prime cause of the Negro's failure to rise more quickly is his wrong education in the past, and, thirdly, that his future rise depends primarily on his own efforts. Each of these propositions is a dangerous half-truth. The supplementary truths must never be lost sight of: first, slavery and race-prejudice are potent if not sufficient causes of the Negro's position; second, industrial and common-school training were necessarily slow in [57] planting because they had to await the black teachers trained by higher institutions,—it being extremely doubtful if any essentially different development was possible, and certainly a Tuskegee was unthinkable before 1880; and, third, while it is a great truth to say that the Negro must strive and strive mightily to help himself, it is equally true that unless his striving be not simply seconded, but rather aroused and encouraged, by the initiative of the richer and wiser environing group, he cannot hope for great success.

In his failure to realize and impress this last point, Mr. Washington is especially to be criticised. His doctrine has tended to make the whites, North and South, shift the burden of the Negro problem to the Negro's shoulders and stand aside as critical and rather pessimistic spectators; when in fact the burden belongs to the nation, and the hands of none of us are clean if we bend not our energies to righting these great wrongs.

The South ought to be led, by candid and honest criticism, to assert her better self and do her full duty to the race she has cruelly wronged and is still wronging. The North—her co-partner in guilt—cannot salve her conscience by plastering it with gold. We cannot settle this problem by diplomacy and suaveness, by "policy" alone. If worse come to worst, can the moral fibre of this country survive the slow throttling and murder of nine millions of men?

The black men of America have a duty to perform, a duty stern and delicate,—a forward movement to [58] oppose a part of the work of their greatest leader. So far as Mr. Washington preaches Thrift, Patience, and Industrial Training for the masses, we must hold up his hands and strive with him, rejoicing in his honors and glorying in the strength of this Joshua called of God and of man to lead the headless host. But so far as Mr. Washington apologizes for injustice, North or South, does not rightly value the privilege and duty of voting, belittles the emasculating effects of caste distinctions, and opposes the higher training and ambition of our brighter minds,—so far as he, the South, or the Nation, does this,—we must unceasingly and firmly oppose them. By every civilized and peaceful method we must strive for the rights which the world accords to men, clinging unwaveringly to those great words which the sons of the Fathers would fain forget: "We hold these truths to be self-evident: That all men are created equal; that they are endowed by their Creator with certain unalienable rights; that among these are life, liberty, and the pursuit of happiness." [59]

THE NEW NEGRO
Alain Locke

In the last decade something beyond the watch and guard of statistics has happened in the life of the American Negro and the three norns who have traditionally presided over the Negro problem have a changeling in their laps. The Sociologist, the Philanthropist, the Race-leader are not unaware of the New Negro, but they are at a loss to account for him. He simply cannot be swathed in their formulæ. For the younger generation is vibrant with a new psychology; the new spirit is awake in the masses, and under the very eyes of the professional observers is transforming what has been a perennial problem into the progressive phases of contemporary Negro life.

Could such a metamorphosis have taken place as suddenly as it has appeared to? The answer is no; not because the New Negro is not here, but because the Old Negro had long become more of a myth than a man. The Old Negro, we must remember, was a creature of moral debate and historical controversy. His has been a stock figure perpetuated as an historical fiction partly in innocent sentimentalism, partly in deliberate reactionism. The Negro himself has contributed his share to this through a sort of protective social mimicry forced upon him by the adverse circumstances of dependence. So for generations in the mind of America, the Negro has been more of a formula than a human being—a something to be argued about, condemned or defended, to be "kept down," or "in his place," or "helped up," to be worried with or worried over, harassed or patronized, a social bogey or a social burden. The thinking Negro even has been induced to share this same general attitude, [3] to focus his attention on controversial issues, to see himself in the distorted perspective of a social problem. His shadow, so to speak, has been more real to him than his personality. Through having had to appeal from the unjust stereotypes of his oppressors and traducers to those of his liberators, friends and benefactors he has had to subscribe to the traditional positions from which his case has been viewed. Little true social or self-understanding has or could come from such a situation.

SOURCE: Alain Locke, "The New Negro," *The New Negro, An Interpretation*, ed. Alain Locke (New York: Albert and Charles Boni, 1925). Reprinted by Atheneum, 1969. Pp. 3–16.

But while the minds of most of us, black and white, have thus burrowed in the trenches of the Civil War and Reconstruction, the actual march of development has simply flanked these positions, necessitating a sudden reorientation of view. We have not been watching in the right direction; set North and South on a sectional axis, we have not noticed the East till the sun has us blinking.

Recall how suddenly the Negro spirituals revealed themselves; suppressed for generations under the stereotypes of Wesleyan hymn harmony, secretive, half-ashamed, until the courage of being natural brought them out—and behold, there was folk-music. Similarly the mind of the Negro seems suddenly to have slipped from under the tyranny of social intimidation and to be shaking off the psychology of imitation and implied inferiority. By shedding the old chrysalis of the Negro problem we are achieving something like a spiritual emancipation. Until recently, lacking self-understanding, we have been almost as much of a problem to ourselves as we still are to others. But the decade that found us with a problem has left us with only a task. The multitude perhaps feels as yet only a strange relief and a new vague urge, but the thinking few know that in the reaction the vital inner grip of prejudice has been broken.

With this renewed self-respect and self-dependence, the life of the Negro community is bound to enter a new dynamic phase, the buoyancy from within compensating for whatever pressure there may be of conditions from without. The migrant masses, shifting from countryside to city, hurdle several generations of experience at a leap, but more important, the same thing happens spiritually in the life-attitudes and [4] self-expression of the Young Negro, in his poetry, his art, his education and his new outlook, with the additional advantage, of course, of the poise and greater certainty of knowing what it is all about. From this comes the promise and warrant of a new leadership. As one of them has discerningly put it:

> We have tomorrow
> Bright before us
> Like a flame.
>
> Yesterday, a night-gone thing
> A sun-down name.

And dawn today
Broad arch above the road we came.
We march!

This is what, even more than any "most creditable record of fifty years of freedom," requires that the Negro of to-day be seen through other than the dusty spectacles of past controversy. The day of "aunties," "uncles" and "mammies" is equally gone. Uncle Tom and Sambo have passed on, and even the "Colonel" and "George" play barnstorm roles from which they escape with relief when the public spotlight is off. The popular melodrama has about played itself out, and it is time to scrap the fictions, garret the bogeys and settle down to a realistic facing of facts.

First we must observe some of the changes which since the traditional lines of opinion were drawn have rendered these quite obsolete. A main change has been, of course, that shifting of the Negro population which has made the Negro problem no longer exclusively or even predominantly Southern. Why should our minds remain sectionalized, when the problem itself no longer is? Then the trend of migration has not only been toward the North and the Central Midwest, but city-ward and to the great centers of industry—the problems of adjustment are new, practical, local and not peculiarly racial. Rather they are an integral part of the large industrial and social problems of our present-day democracy. And finally, with the Negro rapidly in process [5] of class differentiation, if it ever was warrantable to regard and treat the Negro *en masse* it is becoming with every day less possible, more unjust and more ridiculous.

In the very process of being transplanted, the Negro is becoming transformed.

The tide of Negro migration, northward and city-ward, is not to be fully explained as a blind flood started by the demands of war industry coupled with the shutting off of foreign migration, or by the pressure of poor crops coupled with increased social terrorism in certain sections of the South and Southwest. Neither labor demand, the boll-weevil nor the Ku Klux Klan is a basic factor, however contributory any or all of them may have been. The wash and rush of this human tide on the beach line of the northern city centers is to be explained primarily in terms of a new vision of opportunity, of social and economic freedom, of a spirit to seize, even in the face of an extortionate and heavy toll, a chance for the improvement of conditions. With each successive wave of it, the movement of the Negro becomes more and more a mass movement toward the larger and the more democratic chance—in the Negro's case a deliberate flight not only from countryside to city, but from medieval America to modern.

Take Harlem as an instance of this. Here in Manhattan is not merely the largest Negro community in the world, but the first concentration in history of so many diverse elements of Negro life. It has attracted the African, the West Indian, the Negro American; has brought together the Negro of the North and the Negro of the South; the man from the city and the man from the town and village; the peasant, the student, the business man, the professional man, artist, poet, musician, adventurer and worker, preacher and criminal, exploiter and social outcast. Each group has come with its own separate motives and for its own special ends, but their greatest experience has been the finding of one another. Proscription and prejudice have thrown these dissimilar elements into a common area of contact and interaction. Within this area, race sympathy and unity have determined a further fusing of sentiment [6] and experience. So what began in terms of segregation becomes more and more, as its elements mix and react, the laboratory of a great race-welding. Hitherto, it must be admitted that American Negroes have been a race more in name than in fact, or to be exact, more in sentiment than in experience. The chief bond between them has been that of a common condition rather than a common consciousness; a problem in common rather than a life in common. In Harlem, Negro life is seizing upon its first chances for group expression and self-determination. It is—or promises at least to be—a race capital. That is why our comparison is taken with those nascent centers of folk-expression and self-determination which are playing a creative part in the world to-day. Without pretense to their political significance, Harlem has the same rôle to play for the New Negro as Dublin has had for the New Ireland or Prague for the New Czechoslovakia.

Harlem, I grant you, isn't typical—but it is significant, it is prophetic. No sane observer, however sympathetic to the new trend, would contend that the great masses are articulate as yet, but they stir, they move, they are more than physically restless. The challenge of the new intellectuals among them is clear enough—the "race radicals" and realists who have broken with the old epoch of philanthropic guidance, sentimental appeal and protest. But are we after all only reading into the stirrings of a sleeping giant the dreams of an agitator? The answer is in the migrating peasant. It is the "man farthest down" who is most active in getting up. One of the most characteristic symptoms of this is the professional man, himself migrating to recapture his constituency after a vain effort to maintain in some Southern corner what for years back seemed an established living and clientele. The clergyman following his errant flock, the physician or lawyer trailing his clients, supply the true clues. In a real sense it is the rank and file who are leading, and the leaders who are following. A transformed and transforming psychology permeates the masses.

When the racial leaders of twenty years ago spoke of developing race-pride and stimulating race-consciousness, and of the desirability of race solidarity, they could not in any accurate [7] degree have anticipated the abrupt feeling that has surged up and now pervades the awakened centers. Some of the recognized Negro leaders and a powerful section of white opinion identified with "race work" of the older order have indeed attempted to discount this feeling as a "passing phase," an attack of "race nerves" so to speak, an "aftermath of the war," and the like. It has not abated, however, if we are to gauge by the present tone and temper of the Negro press, or by the shift in popular support from the officially recognized and orthodox spokesmen to those of the independent, popular, and often radical type who are unmistakable symptoms of a new order. It is a social disservice to blunt the fact that the Negro of the Northern centers has reached a stage where tutelage, even of the most interested and well-intentioned sort, must give place to new relationships, where positive self-direction must be reckoned with in ever increasing measure. The American mind must reckon with a fundamentally changed Negro.

The Negro too, for his part, has idols of the tribe to smash. If on the one hand the white man has erred in making the Negro appear to be that which would excuse or extenuate his treatment of him, the Negro, in turn, has too often unnecessarily excused himself because of the way he has been treated. The intelligent Negro of today is resolved not to make discrimination an extenuation for his shortcomings in performance, individual or collective; he is trying to hold himself at par, neither inflated by sentimental allowances nor depreciated by current social discounts. For this he must know himself and be known for precisely what he is, and for that reason he welcomes the new scientific rather than the old sentimental interest. Sentimental interest in the Negro has ebbed. We used to lament this as the falling off of our friends; now we rejoice and pray to be delivered both from self-pity and condescension. The mind of each racial group has had a bitter weaning, apathy or hatred on one side matching disillusionment or resentment on the other; but they face each other today with the possibility at least of entirely new mutual attitudes.

It does not follow that if the Negro were better known, he would be better liked or better treated. But mutual understanding [8] is basic for any subsequent cooperation and adjustment. The effort toward this will at least have the effect of remedying in large part what has been the most unsatisfactory feature of our present stage of race relationships in America, namely the fact that the more intelligent and representative elements of the two race groups have at so many points got quite out of vital touch with one another.

The fiction is that the life of the races is separate, and increasingly so. The fact is that they have touched too closely at the unfavorable and too lightly at the favorable levels.

While inter-racial councils have sprung up in the South, drawing on forward elements of both races, in the Northern cities manual laborers may brush elbows in their everyday work, but the community and business leaders have experienced no such interplay or far too little of it. These segments must achieve contact or the race situation in America becomes desperate. Fortunately this is happening. There is a growing realization that in social effort the co-operative basis must supplant long-distance philanthropy, and that the only safeguard for mass relations in the future must be provided in the carefully maintained contacts of the enlightened minorities of both race groups. In the intellectual realm a renewed and keen curiosity is replacing the recent apathy; the Negro is being carefully studied, not just talked about and discussed. In art and letters, instead of being wholly caricatured, he is being seriously portrayed and painted.

To all of this the New Negro is keenly responsive as an augury of a new democracy in American culture. He is contributing his share to the new social understanding. But the desire to be understood would never in itself have been sufficient to have opened so completely the protectively closed portals of the thinking Negro's mind. There is still too much possibility of being snubbed or patronized for that. It was rather the necessity for fuller, truer self-expression, the realization of the unwisdom of allowing social discrimination to segregate him mentally, and a counter-attitude to cramp and fetter his own living—and so the "spite-wall" that the intellectuals built over the "color-line" has happily been taken [9] down. Much of this reopening of intellectual contacts has centered in New York and has been richly fruitful not merely in the enlarging of personal experience, but in the definite enrichment of American art and letters and in the clarifying of our common vision of the social tasks ahead.

The particular significance in the re-establishment of contact between the more advanced and representative classes is that it promises to offset some of the unfavorable reactions of the past, or at least to re-surface race contacts somewhat for the future. Subtly the conditions that are molding a New Negro are molding a new American attitude.

However, this new phase of things is delicate; it will call for less charity but more justice; less help, but infinitely closer understanding. This is indeed a critical stage of race relationships because of the likelihood, if the new temper is not understood, of engendering sharp group antagonism and a second crop of more calculated prejudice. In some quarters, it has already done so. Having weaned the Negro, public opinion cannot continue to paternalize. The Negro today is inevitably moving forward under the control largely of his own objectives. What are these objectives? Those of his outer life are happily already well and finally formulated, for they are none other than the ideals of American institutions and democracy. Those of his inner life are yet in process of formation, for the new psychology at present is more of a consensus of feeling than of opinion, of attitude rather than of program. Still some points seem to have crystallized.

Up to the present one may adequately describe the Negro's "inner objectives" as an attempt to repair a damaged group psychology and reshape a warped social perspective. Their realization has required a new mentality for the American Negro. And as it matures we begin to see its effects; at first, negative, iconoclastic, and then positive and constructive. In this new group psychology we note the lapse of sentimental appeal, then the development of a more positive self-respect and self-reliance; the repudiation of social dependence, and then the gradual recovery from hyper-sensitiveness and "touchy" nerves, the repudiation of the double standard of [10] judgment with its special philanthropic allowances and then the sturdier desire for objective and scientific appraisal; and finally the rise from social disillusionment to race pride, from the sense of social debt to the responsibilities of social contribution, and offsetting the necessary working and commonsense acceptance of restricted conditions, the belief in ultimate esteem and recognition. Therefore the Negro to-day wishes to be known for what he is, even in his faults and shortcomings, and scorns a craven and precarious survival at the price of seeming to be what he is not. He resents being spoken of as a social ward or minor, even by his own, and to being regarded a chronic patient for the sociological clinic, the sick man of American Democracy. For the same reasons, he himself is through with those social nostrums and panaceas, the so-called "solutions" of his "problem," with which he and the country have been so liberally dosed in the past. Religion, freedom, education, money—in turn, he has ardently hoped for and peculiarly trusted these things; he still believes in them, but not in blind trust that they alone will solve his life-problem.

Each generation, however, will have its creed, and that of the present is the belief in the efficacy of collective effort, in race co-operation. This deep feeling of race is at present the mainspring of Negro life. It seems to be the outcome of the reaction to proscription and prejudice; an attempt, fairly successful on the whole, to convert a defensive into an offensive position, a handicap into an incentive. It is radical in tone, but not in purpose and only the most stupid forms of opposition, misunderstanding or persecution could make it otherwise. Of course, the thinking Negro has shifted a little toward the left with the world-trend, and there is an increasing group who affiliate with radical and liberal movements. But fundamentally for the present the Negro is radical on race matters, conservative on others, in other words, a "forced radical," a social protestant rather than a genuine radical. Yet under further pressure and injustice iconoclastic thought and motives will inevitably increase. Harlem's quixotic radicalisms call for their ounce of democracy to-day lest to-morrow they be beyond cure.

The Negro mind reaches out as yet to nothing but American wants, American ideas. But this forced attempt to build his Americanism on race values is a unique social experiment, and its ultimate success is impossible except through the fullest sharing of American culture and institutions. There should be no delusion about this. American nerves in sections unstrung with race hysteria are often fed the opiate that the trend of Negro advance is wholly separatist, and that the effect of its operation will be to encyst the Negro as a benign foreign body in the body politic. This cannot be—even if it were desirable. The racialism of the Negro is no limitation or reservation with respect to American life; it is only a constructive effort to build the obstructions in the stream of his progress into an efficient dam of social energy and power. Democracy itself is obstructed and stagnated to the extent that any of its channels are closed. Indeed they cannot be selectively closed. So the choice is not between one way for the Negro and another way for the rest, but between American institutions frustrated on the one hand and American ideals progressively fulfilled and realized on the other.

There is, of course, a warrantably comfortable feeling in being on the right side of the country's professed ideals. We realize that we cannot be undone without America's undoing. It is within the gamut of this attitude that the thinking Negro faces America, but with variations of mood that are if anything more significant than the attitude itself. Sometimes we have it taken with the defiant ironic challenge of McKay:

> Mine is the future grinding down to-day
> Like a great landslip moving to the sea,
> Bearing its freight of débris far away
> Where the green hungry waters restlessly
> Heave mammoth pyramids, and break and roar
> Their eerie challenge to the crumbling shore.

Sometimes, perhaps more frequently as yet, it is taken in the fervent and almost filial appeal and counsel of Weldon Johnson's:

> O Southland, dear Southland!
> Then why do you still cling
> To an idle age and a musty page,
> To a dead and useless thing? [12]

But between defiance and appeal, midway almost between cynicism and hope, the prevailing mind stands in the mood of the same author's *To America,* an attitude of sober query and stoical challenge:

How would you have us, as we are?
  Or sinking 'neath the load we bear,
Our eyes fixed forward on a star,
  Or gazing empty at despair?

Rising or falling? Men or things?
  With dragging pace or footsteps fleet?
Strong, willing sinews in your wings,
  Or tightening chains about your feet?

More and more, however, an intelligent realization of the great discrepancy between the American social creed and the American social practice forces upon the Negro the taking of the moral advantage that is his. Only the steadying and sobering effect of a truly characteristic gentleness of spirit prevents the rapid rise of a definite cynicism and counter-hate and a defiant superiority feeling. Human as this reaction would be, the majority still deprecate its advent, and would gladly see it forestalled by the speedy amelioration of its causes. We wish our race pride to be a healthier, more positive achievement than a feeling based upon a realization of the shortcomings of others. But all paths toward the attainment of a sound social attitude have been difficult; only a relatively few enlightened minds have been able as the phrase puts it "to rise above" prejudice. The ordinary man has had until recently only a hard choice between the alternatives of supine and humiliating submission and stimulating but hurtful counterprejudice. Fortunately from some inner, desperate resourcefulness has recently sprung up the simple expedient of fighting prejudice by mental passive resistance, in other words by trying to ignore it. For the few, this manna may perhaps be effective, but the masses cannot thrive upon it.

Fortunately there are constructive channels opening out into which the balked social feelings of the American Negro can flow freely.

Without them there would be much more pressure and danger than there is. These compensating interests are racial but in a new and enlarged way. One is the consciousness of acting as the advance-guard of the African peoples in their contact with Twentieth Century civilization; the other, the sense of a mission of rehabilitating the race in world esteem from that loss of prestige for which the fate and conditions of slavery have so largely been responsible. Harlem, as we shall see, is the center of both these movements; she is the home of the Negro's "Zionism." The pulse of the Negro world has begun to beat in Harlem. A Negro newspaper carrying news material in English, French and Spanish, gathered from all quarters of America, the West Indies and Africa has maintained itself in Harlem for over five years. Two important magazines, both edited from New York, maintain their news and circulation consistently on a cosmopolitan scale. Under American auspices and backing, three pan-African congresses have been held abroad for the discussion of common interests, colonial questions and the future co-operative development of Africa. In terms of the race question as a world problem, the Negro mind has leapt, so to speak, upon the parapets of prejudice and extended its cramped horizons. In so doing it has linked up with the growing group consciousness of the dark-peoples and is gradually learning their common interests. As one of our writers has recently put it: "It is imperative that we understand the white world in its relations to the non-white world." As with the Jew, persecution is making the Negro international.

As a world phenomenon this wider race consciousness is a different thing from the much asserted rising tide of color. Its inevitable causes are not of our making. The consequences are not necessarily damaging to the best interests of civilization. Whether it actually brings into being new Armadas of conflict or argosies of cultural exchange and enlightenment can only be decided by the attitude of the dominant races in an era of critical change. With the American Negro, his new internationalism [14] is primarily an effort to recapture contact with the scattered peoples of African derivation. Garveyism may be a transient, if spectacular, phenomenon, but the possible rôle of the American Negro in the future development of Africa is one of the most constructive and universally helpful missions that any modern people can lay claim to.

Constructive participation in such causes cannot help giving the Negro valuable group incentives, as well as increased prestige at home and abroad. Our greatest rehabilitation may possibly come through such channels, but for the present, more immediate hope rests in the revaluation by white and black alike of the Negro in terms of his artistic endowments and cultural contributions, past and prospective. It must be increasingly recognized that the Negro has already made very substantial contributions, not only in his folk-art, music especially, which has always found appreciation, but in larger, though humbler and less acknowledged ways. For generations the Negro has been the peasant matrix of that section of America which has most undervalued him, and here he has contributed not only materially in labor and in social patience, but spiritually as well. The South has unconsciously absorbed the gift of his folk-temperament. In less than half a generation it will be easier to recognize this, but the fact remains that a leaven of humor, sentiment, imagination and tropic nonchalance has gone into the making of the South from a humble, unacknowledged source. A second crop of the Negro's gifts promises still more largely. He now becomes a conscious contributor and lays aside the status of a beneficiary and ward for that of a collaborator and participant in American civilization. The great social gain in this is the releasing of our talented group from the arid fields of controversy and debate to the productive fields of creative expression. The especially cultural recognition they win should in turn prove the key to that revaluation of the Negro which must precede or accompany any considerable further betterment of race relationships. But whatever the general effect, the present generation will have added the motives of self-expression and spiritual development to the old and still unfinished task of making material [15] headway and progress. No one who understandingly faces the situation with its substantial accomplishment or views the new scene with its still more abundant promise can be entirely without hope. And certainly, if in our lifetime the Negro should not be able to celebrate his full initiation into American democracy, he can at least, on the warrant of these things, celebrate the attainment of a significant and satisfying new phase of group development, and with it a spiritual Coming of Age. [16]

AN APPEAL TO THE CONSCIENCE OF THE BLACK RACE TO SEE ITSELF
Marcus Garvey

It is said to be a hard and difficult task to organize and keep together large numbers of the Negro race for the common good. Many have tried to congregate us, but have failed, the reason being that our characteristics are such as to keep us more apart than together.

The evil of internal divison is wrecking our existence as a people, and if we do not seriously and quickly move in the direction of a readjustment it simply means that our doom becomes imminently conclusive.

For years the Universal Negro Improvement Association has been working for the unification of our race, not on domestic-national lines only, but universally. The success which we have met in the course of our effort is rather encouraging, considering the time consumed and the environment surrounding the object of our concern.

It seems that the whole world of sentiment is against the Negro, and the difficulty of our generation is to extricate ourselves from the prejudice that hides itself beneath, as well as above, the action of an international environment.

Prejudice is conditional on many reasons, and it is apparent that the Negro supplies, consciously or unconsciously, all the reasons by which the world seems to ignore and avoid him. No one cares for a leper, for lepers are infectious persons, and all are afraid of the disease, so, because the Negro keeps himself poor, helpless and undemonstrative, it is natural also that no one wants to be of him or with him.

Progress and Humanity

Progress is the attraction that moves humanity, and to whatever people or race this "modern virtue" attaches itself, there will you find the

SOURCE: Marcus Garvey, "An Appeal to the Conscience of the Black Race to See Itself," *The Philosophy and Opinions of Marcus Garvey*, ed. Amy Jacques-Garvey, 2 vols. (Kingsport, Tenn.: Kingsport Press, Inc., 1923). Reprinted in *Studies in American Negro Life* (New

splendor of pride and self-esteem that never fail to win the respect and admiration of all.

It is the progress of the Anglo-Saxons that singles them out for the respect of all the world. When their race had no progress or achievement to its credit, then, like all other inferior peoples, they paid the price in slavery, bondage, as well as through prejudice. We cannot forget the time when even the ancient Briton was regarded as being too dull to make a good Roman slave, yet today the influence of that race rules the world.

It is the industrial and commercial progress of America that causes Europe and the rest of the world to think appreciatively of the Anglo-American race. It is not because one hundred and [22] ten million people live in the United States that the world is attracted to the republic with so much reverence and respect—a reverence and respect not shown to India with its three hundred millions, or to China with its four hundred millions. Progress of and among any people will advance them in the respect and appreciation of the rest of their fellows. It is such a progress that the Negro must attach to himself if he is to rise above the prejudice of the world.

The reliance of our race upon the progress and achievements of others for a consideration in sympathy, justice and rights is like a dependence upon a broken stick, resting upon which will eventually consign you to the ground.

Self-Reliance and Respect

The Universal Negro Improvement Association teaches our race self-help and self-reliance, not only in one essential, but in all those things that contribute to human happiness and well-being. The disposition of the many to depend upon the other races for a kindly and sympathetic consideration of their needs, without making the effort to do for themselves, has been the race's standing disgrace by which we have

---

York: Atheneum, 1969), Vol. II, pp. 22–26. Reprinted by permission of Amy Jacques-Garvey.

been judged and through which we have created the strongest prejudice against ourselves.

There is no force like success, and that is why the individual makes all efforts to surround himself throughout life with the evidence of it. As of the individual, so should it be of the race and nation. The glittering success of Rockefeller makes him a power in the American nation; the success of Henry Ford suggests him as an object of universal respect, but no one knows and cares about the bum or hobo who is Rockefeller's or Ford's neighbor. So, also, is the world attracted by the glittering success of races and nations, and pays absolutely no attention to the bum or hobo race that lingers by the wayside.

The Negro must be up and doing if he will break down the prejudice of the rest of the world. Prayer alone is not going to improve our condition, nor the policy of watchful waiting. We must strike out for ourselves in the course of material achievement, and by our own effort and energy present to the world those forces by which the progress of man is judged.

A Nation and Country

The Negro needs a nation and a country of his own, where he can best show evidence of his own ability in the art of human progress. Scattered as an unmixed and unrecognized part of alien nations and civilizations is but to demonstrate his imbecility, [23] and point him out as an unworthy derelict, fit neither for the society of Greek, Jew nor Gentile.

It is unfortunate that we should so drift apart, as a race, as not to see that we are but perpetuating our own sorrow and disgrace in failing to appreciate the first great requisite of all peoples—organization.

Organization is a great power in directing the affairs of a race or nation toward a given goal. To properly develop the desires that are uppermost, we must first concentrate through some system or method, and there is none better than organization. Hence, the Universal Negro Improvement Association appeals to each and every Negro to throw in his lot with those of us who, through organization, are working for the universal emancipation of our race and the redemption of our common country, Africa.

No Negro, let him be American, European, West Indian or

African, shall be truly respected until the race as a whole has emancipated itself, through self-achievement and progress, from universal prejudice. The Negro will have to build his own government, industry, art, science, literature and culture, before the world will stop to consider him. Until then, we are but wards of a superior race and civilization, and the outcasts of a standard social system.

The race needs workers at this time, not plagiarists, copyists and mere imitators; but men and women who are able to create, to originate and improve, and thus make an independent racial contribution to the world and civilization.

Monkey Apings of "Leaders"

The unfortunate thing about us is that we take the monkey apings of our "so-called leading men" for progress. There is no progress in Negroes aping white people and telling us that they represent the best in the race, for in that respect any dressed monkey would represent the best of its species, irrespective of the creative matter of the monkey instinct. The best in a race is not reflected through or by the action of its apes, but by its ability to create of and by itself. It is such a creation that the Universal Negro Improvement Association seeks.

Let us not try to be the best or worst of others, but let us make the effort to be the best of ourselves. Our own racial critics criticise us as dreamers and "fanatics," and call us "benighted" and "ignorant," because they lack racial backbone. They are unable to see themselves creators of their own needs. The slave instinct has not yet departed from them. They still believe that [24] they can only live or exist through the good graces of their "masters." The good slaves have not yet thrown off their shackles; thus, to them, the Universal Negro Improvement Association is an "impossibility."

It is the slave spirit of dependence that causes our "so-called leading men" (apes) to seek the shelter, leadership, protection and patronage of the "master" in their organization and so-called advancement work. It is the spirit of feeling secured as good servants of the master, rather than as independents, why our modern Uncle Toms take pride in laboring under alien leadership and becoming surprised at the audacity of the Universal Negro Improvement Association in proclaiming for racial liberty and independence.

But the world of white and other men, deep down in their hearts, have much more respect for those of us who work for our racial salvation under the banner of the Universal Negro Improvement Association, than they could ever have, in all eternity, for a group of helpless apes and beggars who make a monopoly of undermining their own race and belittling themselves in the eyes of self-respecting people, by being "good boys" rather than able men.

Surely there can be no good will between apes, seasoned beggars and independent minded Negroes who will at least make an effort to do for themselves. Surely, the "dependents" and "wards" (and may I not say racial imbeciles?) will rave against and plan the destruction of movements like the Universal Negro Improvement Association that expose them to the liberal white minds of the world as not being representative of the best in the Negro, but, to the contrary, the worst. The best of a race does not live on the patronage and philanthropy of others, but makes an effort to do for itself. The best of the great white race doesn't fawn before and beg black, brown or yellow men; they go out, create for self and thus demonstrate the fitness of the race to survive; and so the white race of America and the world will be informed that the best in the Negro race is not the class of beggars who send out to other races piteous appeals annually for donations to maintain their coterie, but the groups within us that are honestly striving to do for themselves with the voluntary help and appreciation of that class of other races that is reasonable, just and liberal enough to give to each and every one a fair chance in the promotion of those ideals that tend to greater human progress and human love.

The work of the Universal Negro Improvement Association is clear and clean-cut. It is that of inspiring an unfortunate race [25] with pride in self and with the determination of going ahead in the creation of those ideals that will lift them to the unprejudiced company of races and nations. There is no desire for hate or malice, but every wish to see all mankind linked into a common fraternity of progress and achievement that will wipe away the odor of prejudice, and elevate the human race to the height of real godly love and satisfaction. [26]

I TRIED TO BE A COMMUNIST
Richard Wright

One Thursday night I received an invitation from a group of white boys I had known when I was working in the post office to meet in one of Chicago's South Side hotels and argue the state of the world. About ten of us gathered, and ate salami sandwiches, drank beer, and talked. I was amazed to discover that many of them had joined the Communist Party. I challenged them by reciting the antics of the Negro Communists I had seen in the parks, and I was told that those antics were "tactics" and were all right. I was dubious.

Then one Thursday night Sol, a Jewish chap, startled us by announcing that he had had a short story accepted by a little magazine called the *Anvil*, edited by Jack Conroy, and that he had joined a revolutionary artist organization, the John Reed Club. Sol repeatedly begged me to attend the meetings of the club.

"You'd like them," Sol said.

"I don't want to be organized," I said.

"They can help you to write," he said.

"Nobody can tell me how or what to write," I said.

"Come and see," he urged. "What have you to lose?"

I felt that Communists could not possibly have a sincere interest in Negroes. I was cynical and I would rather have heard a white man say that he hated Negroes, which I could have readily believed, than to have heard him say that he respected Negroes, which would have made me doubt him.

One Saturday night, bored with reading, I decided to appear at the John Reed Club in the capacity of an amused spectator. I rode to the Loop and found the number. A dark stairway led upwards; it did not look welcoming. What on earth of importance could happen in so dingy a place? Through the windows above me I saw vague murals along the walls. I mounted the stairs to a door that was lettered: THE CHICAGO JOHN REED CLUB.

SOURCE: Richard Wright, "I Tried to Be a Communist," *Atlantic Monthly*, 174 (August, 1944), 61–70; (September, 1944), 48–56. Copyright © 1944 The Atlantic Monthly Company, Boston, Mass. Reprinted by permission of Paul R. Reynolds, Inc., 599 Fifth Avenue, New York, N.Y.

I opened it and stepped into the strangest room I had ever seen. Paper and cigarette butts lay on the floor. A few benches ran along the walls, above which were vivid colors depicting colossal figures of workers carrying streaming banners. The mouths of the workers gaped in wild cries; their legs were sprawled over cities.

"Hello."

I turned and saw a white man smiling at me.

"A friend of mine, who's a member of this club, asked me to visit here. His name is Sol ———," I told him.

"You're welcome here," the white man said. "We're not having an affair tonight. We're holding an editorial meeting. Do you paint?" He was slightly gray and he had a mustache.

"No," I said. "I try to write."

"Then sit in on the editorial meeting of our magazine, *Left Front*," he suggested.

"I know nothing of editing," I said.

"You can learn," he said.

I stared at him, doubting.

"I don't want to be in the way here," I said.

"My name's Grimm," he said.

I told him my name and we shook hands. He went to a closet and returned with an armful of magazines.

"Here are some back issues of the *Masses*," he said. "Have you ever read it?"

"No," I said.

"Some of the best writers in America publish in it," he explained. He also gave me copies of a magazine called *International Literature*. "There's stuff here from Gide, Gorky—"

I assured him that I would read them. He took me to an office and introduced me to a Jewish boy [61] who was to become one of the nation's leading painters, to a chap who was to become one of the eminent composers of his day, to a writer who was to create some of the best novels of his generation, to a young Jewish boy who was destined to film the Nazi occupation of Czechoslovakia. I was meeting men and women whom I should know for decades to come, who were to form the first sustained relationships in my life.

I sat in a corner and listened while they discussed their magazine, *Left Front*. Were they treating me courteously because I was a Negro? I must let cold reason guide me with these people, I told myself. I was asked to contribute something to the magazine, and I said vaguely that I would consider it. After the meeting I met an Irish girl who worked for an advertising agency, a girl who did social work, a schoolteacher, and the wife of a prominent university professor. I had once worked as a servant for people like these and I was skeptical. I tried to fathom their motives, but I could detect no condescension in them.

2

I went home full of reflection, probing the sincerity of the strange white people I had met, wondering how they *really* regarded Negroes. I lay on my bed and read the magazines and was amazed to find that there did exist in this world an organized search for the truth of the lives of the oppressed and the isolated. When I had begged bread from the officials, I had wondered dimly if the outcasts could become united in action, thought, and feeling. Now I knew. It was being done in one sixth of the earth already. The revolutionary words leaped from the printed page and struck me with tremendous force.

It was not the economics of Communism, nor the great power of trade unions, nor the excitement of underground politics that claimed me; my attention was caught by the similarity of the experiences of workers in other lands, by the possibility of uniting scattered but kindred peoples into a whole. It seemed to me that here at last, in the realm of revolutionary expression, Negro experience could find a home, a functioning value and role. Out of the magazines I read came a passionate call for the experiences of the disinherited, and there were none of the lame lispings of the missionary in it. It did not say: "Be like us and we will like you, maybe." It said: "If you possess enough courage to speak out what you are, you will find that you are not alone." It urged life to believe in life.

I read on into the night; then, toward dawn, I swung from bed and inserted paper into the typewriter. Feeling for the first time that I could speak to listening ears, I wrote a wild, crude poem in free verse, coining images of black hands playing, working, holding bayonets, stiffening finally in death. I felt that in a clumsy way it linked white life with black, merged two streams of common experience.

I heard someone poking about the kitchen.

"Richard, are you ill?" my mother called.

"No. I'm reading."

My mother opened the door and stared curiously at the pile of magazines that lay upon my pillow.

"You're not throwing away money buying those magazines, are you?" she asked.

"No. They were given to me."

She hobbled to the bed on her crippled legs and picked up a copy of the *Masses* that carried a lurid May Day cartoon. She adjusted her glasses and peered at it for a long time.

"My God in heaven," she breathed in horror.

"What's the matter, Mama?"

"What is this?" she asked, extending the magazine to me, pointing to the cover. "What's wrong with that man?"

With my mother standing at my side, lending me her eyes, I stared at a cartoon drawn by a Communist artist; it was the figure of a worker clad in ragged overalls and holding aloft a red banner. The man's eyes bulged; his mouth gaped as wide as his face; his teeth showed; the muscles of his neck were like ropes. Following the man was a horde of nondescript men, women, and children, waving clubs, stones, and pitchforks.

"What are those people going to do?" my mother asked.

"I don't know," I hedged.

"Are these Communist magazines?"

"Yes."

"And do they want people to act like this?"

"Well—" I hesitated.

My mother's face showed disgust and moral loathing. She was a gentle woman. Her ideal was Christ upon the cross. How could I tell her that the Communist Party wanted her to march in the streets, chanting, singing?

"What do Communists think people are?" she asked.

"They don't quite mean what you see there," I said, fumbling with my words.

"Then what do they mean?"

"This is symbolic," I said.

"Then why don't they speak out what they mean?"

"Maybe they don't know how."

"Then why do they print this stuff?"

"They don't quite know how to appeal to people [62] yet," I admitted, wondering whom I could convince of this if I could not convince my mother.

"That picture's enough to drive a body crazy," she said, dropping the magazine, turning to leave, then pausing at the door. "You're not getting mixed up with those people?"

"I'm just reading, Mama," I dodged.

My mother left and I brooded upon the fact that I had not been able to meet her simple challenge. I looked again at the cover of the *Masses* and I knew that the wild cartoon did not reflect the passions of the common people. I reread the magazine and was convinced that much of the expression embodied what the *artists* thought would appeal to others, what they thought would gain recruits. They had a program, an ideal, but they had not yet found a language.

Here, then, was something that I could do, reveal, say. The Communists, I felt, had oversimplified the experience of those whom they sought to lead. In their efforts to recruit masses, they had missed the meaning of the lives of the masses, had conceived of people in too abstract a manner. I would try to put some of that meaning back. I would tell Communists how common people felt, and I would tell common people of the self-sacrifice of Communists who strove for unity among them.

The editor of *Left Front* accepted two of my crude poems for publication, sent two of them to Jack Conroy's *Anvil*, and sent another to the *New Masses*, the successor of the *Masses*. Doubts still lingered in my mind.

"Don't send them if you think they aren't good enough," I said to him.

"They're good enough," he said.

"Are you doing this to get me to join up?" I asked.

"No," he said. "Your poems are crude, but good for us. You see, we're all new in this. We write articles about Negroes, but we never see any Negroes. We need your stuff."

I sat through several meetings of the club and was impressed by the scope and seriousness of its activities. The club was demanding that the government create jobs for unemployed artists; it planned and organized art exhibits; it raised funds for the publication of *Left Front*; and it sent scores of speakers to trade-union meetings. The members were fervent, democratic, restless, eager, self-sacrificing. I was convinced, and my response was to set myself the task of making Negroes know what Communists were. I got the notion of writing a series of biographical sketches of Negro Communists. I told no one of my intentions, and I did not know how fantastically naïve my ambition was.

3

I had attended but a few meetings before I realized that a bitter factional fight was in progress between two groups of members of the club. Sharp arguments rose at every meeting. I noticed that a small group of painters actually led the club and dominated its policies. The group of writers that centered in *Left Front* resented the leadership of the painters. Being primarily interested in *Left Front*, I sided in simple loyalty with the writers.

Then came a strange development. The *Left Front* group declared that the incumbent leadership did not reflect the wishes of the club. A special meeting was called and a motion was made to re-elect an executive secretary. When nominations were made for the office, my name was included. I declined the nomination, telling the members that I was too ignorant of their aims to be seriously considered. The debate lasted all night. A vote was taken in the early hours of morning by a show of hands, and I was elected.

Later I learned what had happened: the writers of the club had decided to use me to oust the painters, who were party members, from the leadership of the club. Without my knowledge and consent, they confronted the members of the party with a Negro, knowing that it would be difficult for Communists to refuse to vote for a man representing the largest single racial minority in the nation, inasmuch as Negro equality was one of the main tenets of Communism.

As the club's leader, I soon learned the nature of the fight. The Communists had secretly organized a "fraction" in the club; that is, a small portion of the club's members were secret members of the Communist Party. They would meet outside of the club and decide what policies the club should follow; in club meetings the sheer strength of their arguments usually persuaded non-party members to vote with them. The crux of the fight was that the non-party members resented the excessive demands made upon the club by the local party authorities through the fraction.

The demands of the local party authorities for money, speakers, and poster painters were so great that the publication of *Left Front* was in danger. Many young writers had joined the club because of their hope of publishing in *Left Front*, and when the Communist Party sent word through the fraction that the magazine should be dissolved, the writers rejected the decision, an act which was interpreted as hostility toward party authority.

I pleaded with the party members for a more liberal [63] program for the club. Feelings waxed violent and bitter. Then the showdown came. I was informed that if I wanted to continue as secretary of the club I should have to join the Communist Party. I stated that I favored a policy that allowed for the development of writers and artists. My policy was accepted. I signed the membership card.

One night a Jewish chap appeared at one of our meetings and introduced himself as Comrade Young of Detroit. He told us that he was a member of the Communist Party, a member of the Detroit John Reed Club, that he planned to make his home in Chicago. He was a short, friendly, black-haired, well-read fellow with hanging lips and bulging eyes. Shy of forces to execute the demands of the Communist Party, we welcomed him. But I could not make out Young's personality; whenever I asked him a simple question, he looked off and stammered a confused answer. I decided to send his references to the Communist Party for checking and forthwith named him for membership in the club. He's O.K., I thought. Just a queer artist.

After the meeting Comrade Young confronted me with a problem. He had no money, he said, and asked if he could sleep temporarily on the club's premises. Believing him loyal, I gave him permission. Straightway Young became one of the most ardent members of our organization, admired by all. His paintings—which I did not understand—impressed our best artists. No report about Young had come from the Communist Party, but since Young seemed a conscientious worker, I did not think the omission serious in any case.

At a meeting one night Young asked that his name be placed upon the agenda; when his time came to speak, he rose and launched into one of the most violent and bitter political attacks in the club's history upon Swann, one of our best young artists. We were aghast. Young accused Swann of being a traitor to the workers, an opportunist, a collaborator with the police, and an adherent of

Trotsky. Naturally most of the club's members assumed that Young, a member of the party, was voicing the ideas of the party. Surprised and baffled, I moved that Young's statement be referred to the executive committee for decision. Swann rightfully protested; he declared that he had been attacked in public and would answer in public.

It was voted that Swann should have the floor. He refuted Young's wild charges, but the majority of the club's members were bewildered, did not know whether to believe him or not. We all liked Swann, did not believe him guilty of any misconduct; but we did not want to offend the party. A verbal battle ensued. Finally the members who had been silent in deference to the party rose and demanded of me that the foolish charges against Swann be withdrawn. Again I moved that the matter be referred to the executive committee, and again my proposal was voted down. The membership had now begun to distrust the party's motives. They were afraid to let an executive committee, the majority of whom were party members, pass upon the charges made by party member Young.

A delegation of members asked me later if I had anything to do with Young's charges. I was so hurt and humiliated that I disavowed all relations with Young. Determined to end the farce, I cornered Young and demanded to know who had given him authority to castigate Swann.

"I've been asked to rid the club of traitors."

"But Swann isn't a traitor," I said.

"We must have a purge," he said, his eyes bulging, his face quivering with passion.

I admitted his great revolutionary fervor, but I felt that his zeal was a trifle excessive. The situation became worse. A delegation of members informed me that if the charges against Swann were not withdrawn, they would resign in a body. I was frantic. I wrote to the Communist Party to ask why orders had been issued to punish Swann, and a reply came back that no such orders had been issued. Then what was Young up to? Who was prompting him? I finally begged the club to let me place the matter before the leaders of the Communist Party. After a violent debate, my proposal was accepted.

One night ten of us met in an office of a leader of the party to hear Young restate his charges against Swann. The party leader, aloof and amused, gave Young the signal to begin. Young unrolled a sheaf of papers and declaimed a list of political charges that excelled in viciousness his previous charges. I stared at Young, feeling that he was making a dreadful mistake, but fearing him because he had, by his own account, the sanction of high political authority.

When Young finished, the party leader asked, "Will you allow me to read these charges?"

"Of course," said Young, surrendering a copy of his indictment. "You may keep that copy. I have ten carbons."

"Why did you make so many carbons?" the leader asked.

"I didn't want anyone to steal them," Young said.

"If this man's charges against me are taken seriously," Swann said, "I'll resign and publicly denounce the club."

"You see!" Young yelled. "He's with the police!" [64]

I was sick. The meeting ended with a promise from the party leader to read the charges carefully and render a verdict as to whether Swann should be placed on trial or not. I was convinced that something was wrong, but I could not figure it out. One afternoon I went to the club to have a long talk with Young; but when I arrived, he was not there. Nor was he there the next day. For a week I sought Young in vain. Meanwhile the club's members asked his whereabouts and they would not believe me when I told them that I did not know. Was he ill? Had he been picked up by the police?

One afternoon Comrade Grimm and I sneaked into the club's headquarters and opened Young's luggage. What we saw amazed and puzzled us. First of all, there was a scroll of paper twenty yards long —one page pasted to another—which had drawings depicting the history of the human race from a Marxist point of view. The first page read: *A Pictorial Record of Man's Economic Progress.*

"This is terribly ambitious," I said.

"He's very studious," Grimm said.

There were long dissertations written in longhand; some were political and others dealt with the history of art. Finally we found a letter with a Detroit return address and I promptly wrote asking news of our esteemed member. A few days later a letter came which said in part:—

Dear Sir:
In reply to your letter, we beg to inform you that Mr. Young, who was a patient in our institution and who escaped from our

custody a few months ago, has been apprehended and returned to this institution for mental treatment.

I was thunderstruck. Was this true? Undoubtedly it was. Then what kind of club did we run that a lunatic could step into it and help run it? Were we all so mad that we could not detect a madman when we saw one?

I made a motion that all charges against Swann be dropped, which was done. I offered Swann an apology, but as the leader of the Chicago John Reed Club I was a sobered and chastened Communist.

4

The Communist Party fraction in the John Reed Club instructed me to ask my party cell—or "unit," as it was called—to assign me to full duty in the work of the club. I was instructed to give my unit a report of my activities, writing, organizing, speaking. I agreed and wrote the report.

A unit, membership in which is obligatory for all Communists, is the party's basic form of organization. Unit meetings are held on certain nights which are kept secret for fear of police raids. Nothing treasonable occurs at these meetings; but once one is a Communist, one does not have to be guilty of wrongdoing to attract the attention of the police.

I went to my first unit meeting—which was held in the Black Belt of the South Side—and introduced myself to the Negro organizer.

"Welcome, comrade," he said, grinning. "We're glad to have a writer with us."

"I'm not much of a writer," I said.

The meeting started. About twenty Negroes were gathered. The time came for me to make my report and I took out my notes and told them how I had come to join the party, what few stray items I had published, what my duties were in the John Reed Club. I finished and waited for comment. There was silence. I looked about. Most of the comrades sat with bowed heads. Then I was surprised to catch a twitching smile on the lips of a Negro woman. Minutes passed. The

Negro woman lifted her head and looked at the organizer. The organizer smothered a smile. Then the woman broke into unrestrained laughter, bending forward and burying her face in her hands. I stared. Had I said something funny?

"What's the matter?" I asked.

The giggling became general. The unit organizer, who had been dallying with his pencil, looked up.

"It's all right, comrade," he said. "We're glad to have a writer in the party."

There was more smothered laughter. What kind of people were these? I had made a serious report and now I heard giggles.

"I did the best I could," I said uneasily. "I realize that writing is not basic or important. But, given time, I think I can make a contribution."

"We know you can, comrade," the black organizer said.

His tone was more patronizing than that of a Southern white man. I grew angry. I thought I knew these people, but evidently I did not. I wanted to take issue with their attitude, but caution urged me to talk it over with others first.

During the following days I learned through discreet questioning that I had seemed a fantastic element to the black Communists. I was shocked to hear that I, who had been only to grammar school, had been classified as an *intellectual*. What was an intellectual? I had never heard the word used in the sense in which it was applied to me. I had thought that they might refuse me on the ground that I was not politically advanced; I had thought they might say I would have to be investigated. But they had simply laughed. [65]

I learned, to my dismay, that the black Communists in my unit had commented upon my shined shoes, my clean shirt, and the tie I had worn. Above all, my manner of speech had seemed an alien thing to them.

"He talks like a book," one of the Negro comrades had said. And that was enough to condemn me forever as bourgeois.

5

In my party work I met a Negro Communist, Ross, who was under indictment for "inciting to riot." Ross typified the effective street agitator. Southern-born, he had migrated north and his life reflected the crude hopes and frustrations of the peasant in the city. Distrustful but aggressive, he was a bundle of the weaknesses and virtues of a man struggling blindly between two societies, of a man living on the margin of a culture. I felt that if I could get his story I could make known some of the difficulties inherent in the adjustment of a folk people to an urban environment; I should make his life more intelligible to others than it was to himself.

I approached Ross and explained my plan. He was agreeable. He invited me to his home, introduced me to his Jewish wife, his young son, his friends. I talked to Ross for hours, explaining what I was about, cautioning him not to relate anything that he did not want to divulge.

"I'm after the things that made you a Communist," I said.

Word spread in the Communist Party that I was taking notes on the life of Ross, and strange things began to happen. A quiet black Communist came to my home one night and called me out to the street to speak to me in private. He made a prediction about my future that frightened me.

"Intellectuals don't fit well into the party, Wright," he said solemnly.

"But I'm not an intellectual," I protested. "I sweep the streets for a living." I had just been assigned by the relief system to sweep the streets for thirteen dollars a week.

"That doesn't make any difference," he said. "We've kept records of the trouble we've had with intellectuals in the past. It's estimated that only 13 per cent of them remain in the party."

"Why do they leave, since you insist upon calling me an intellectual?" I asked.

"Most of them drop out of their own accord."

"Well, I'm not dropping out," I said.

"Some are expelled," he hinted gravely.

"For what?"

"General opposition to the party's policies," he said.

"But I'm not opposing anything in the party."

"You'll have to prove your revolutionary loyalty."

"How?"

"The party has a way of testing people."

"Well, talk. What is this?"

"How do you react to police?"

"I don't react to them," I said. "I've never been bothered by them."

"Do you know Evans?" he asked, referring to a local militant Negro Communist.

"Yes. I've seen him; I've met him."

"Did you notice that he was injured?"

"Yes. His head was bandaged."

"He got that wound from the police in a demonstration," he explained. "That's proof of revolutionary loyalty."

"Do you mean that I must get whacked over the head by cops to prove that I'm sincere?" I asked.

"I'm not suggesting anything," he said. "I'm explaining."

"Look. Suppose a cop whacks me over the head and I suffer a brain concussion. Suppose I'm nuts after that. Can I write then? What shall I have proved?"

He shook his head. "The Soviet Union has had to shoot a lot of intellectuals," he said.

"Good God!" I exclaimed. "Do you know what you're saying? You're not in Russia. You're standing on a sidewalk in Chicago. You talk like a man lost in a fantasy."

"You've heard of Trotsky, haven't you?" he asked.

"Yes."

"Do you know what happened to him?"

"He was banished from the Soviet Union," I said.

"Do you know why?"

"Well," I stammered, trying not to reveal my ignorance of politics, for I had not followed the details of Trotsky's fight against the Communist Party of the Soviet Union, "it seems that after a decision had been made, he broke that decision by organizing against the party."

"It was for counter-revolutionary activity," he snapped impatiently; I learned afterwards that my answer had not been satisfactory, had not been couched in the acceptable phrases of bitter, anti-Trotsky denunciation.

"I understand," I said. "But I've never read Trotsky. What's his stand on minorities?"

"Why ask me?" he asked. "I don't read Trotsky." [66]

"Look," I said. "If you found me reading Trotsky, what would that mean to you?"

"Comrade, you don't understand," he said in an annoyed tone.

That ended the conversation. But that was not the last time I was to hear the phrase: "Comrade, you don't understand." I had not been aware of holding wrong ideas. I had not read any of Trotsky's works; indeed, the very opposite had been true. It had been Stalin's *National and Colonial Question* that had captured my interest.

Of all the developments in the Soviet Union, the way scores of backward peoples had been led to unity on a national scale was what had enthralled me. I had read with awe how the Communists had sent phonetic experts into the vast regions of Russia to listen to the stammering dialects of peoples oppressed for centuries by the tsars. I had made the first total emotional commitment of my life when I read how the phonetic experts had given these tongueless people a language, newspapers, institutions. I had read how these forgotten folk had been encouraged to keep their old cultures, to see in their ancient customs meanings and satisfactions as deep as those contained in supposedly superior ways of living. And I had exclaimed to myself how different this was from the way in which Negroes were sneered at in America.

Then what was the meaning of the warning I had received from the black Communist? Why was I a suspected man because I wanted to reveal the vast physical and spiritual ravages of Negro life, the profundity latent in these rejected people, the dramas as old as man and the sun and the mountains and the seas that were taking place in the poverty of black America? What was the danger in showing the kinship between the sufferings of the Negro and the sufferings of other people?

6

I sat one morning in Ross's home with his wife and child. I was scribbling furiously upon my yellow sheets of paper. The doorbell rang and Ross's wife admitted a black Communist, one Ed Green. He was tall, taciturn, soldierly, square-shouldered. I was introduced to him and he nodded stiffly.

"What's happening here?" he asked bluntly.

Ross explained my project to him, and as Ross talked I could see Ed Green's face darken. He had not sat down and when Ross's wife offered him a chair he did not hear her.

"What're you going to do with these notes?" he asked me.

"I hope to weave them into stories," I said.

"What're you asking the party members?"

"About their lives in general."

"Who suggested this to you?" he asked.

"Nobody. I thought of it myself."

"Were you ever a member of any other political group?"

"I worked with the Republicans once," I said.

"I mean, revolutionary organizations?" he asked.

"No. Why do you ask?"

"What kind of work do you do?"

"I sweep the streets for a living."

"How far did you go in school?"

"Through the grammar grades."

"You talk like a man who went further than that," he said.

"I've read books. I taught myself."

"I don't know," he said, looking off.

"What do you mean?" I asked. "What's wrong?"

"To whom have you shown this material?"

"I've shown it to no one yet."

What was the meaning of his questions? Naïvely I thought that he himself would make a good model for a biographical sketch.

"I'd like to interview you next," I said.

"I'm not interested," he snapped.

His manner was so rough that I did not urge him. He called Ross into a rear room. I sat feeling that I was guilty of something. In a few minutes Ed Green returned, stared at me wordlessly, then marched out.

"Who does he think he is?" I asked Ross.

"He's a member of the Central Committee," Ross said.

"But why does he act like that?"

"Oh, he's always like that," Ross said uneasily.

There was a long silence.

"He's wondering what you're doing with this material," Ross said finally.

I looked at him. He, too, had been captured by suspicion. He was trying to hide the fear in his face.

"You don't have to tell me anything you don't want to," I said.

That seemed to soothe him for a moment. But the seed of doubt had already been planted. I felt dizzy. Was I mad? Or were these people mad?

"You see, Dick," Ross's wife said, "Ross is under an indictment. Ed Green is the representative of the International Labor Defense for the South Side. It's his duty to keep track of the people he's trying to defend. He wanted to know if Ross has given you anything that could be used against him in court."

I was speechless.

"What does he think I am?" I demanded. [67]

There was no answer.

"You lost people!" I cried, and banged my fist on the table.

Ross was shaken and ashamed. "Aw, Ed Green's just supercautious," he mumbled.

"Ross," I asked, "do you trust me?"

"Oh, yes," he said uneasily.

We two black men sat in the same room looking at each other in fear. Both of us were hungry. Both of us depended upon public charity to eat and for a place to sleep. Yet we had more doubt in our hearts of each other than of the men who had cast the mold of our lives.

I continued to take notes on Ross's life, but each successive morning found him more reticent. I pitied him and did not argue with him, for I knew that persuasion would not nullify his fears. Instead I sat and listened to him and his friends tell tales of Southern Negro experience, noting them down in my mind, not daring to ask questions for fear they would become alarmed.

In spite of their fears, I became drenched in the details of their lives. I gave up the idea of the biographical sketches and settled finally upon writing a series of short stories, using the material I had got from Ross and his friends, building upon it, inventing. I wove a tale of a group of black boys trespassing upon the property of a white man and the lynching that followed. The story was published in an anthology under the title of "Big Boy Leaves Home," but its appearance came too late to influence the Communists who were questioning the use to which I was putting their lives.

My fitful work assignments from the relief officials ceased and I looked for work that did not exist. I borrowed money to ride to and fro on the club's business. I found a cramped attic for my mother and aunt and brother behind some railroad tracks. At last the relief authorities placed me in the South Side Boys' Club and my wages were just enough to provide a bare living for my family.

Then political problems rose to plague me. Ross, whose life I had tried to write, was charged by the Communist Party with "anti-leadership tendencies," "class collaborationist attitudes," and "ideological factionalism"—phrases so fanciful that I gaped when I heard them. And it was rumored that I, too, would face similar charges. It was believed that I had been politically influenced by him.

One night a group of black comrades came to my house and ordered me to stay away from Ross.

"But why?" I demanded.

"He's an unhealthy element," they said. "Can't you accept a decision?"

"Is this a decision of the Communist Party?"

"Yes," they said.

"If I were guilty of something, I'd feel bound to keep your decision," I said. "But I've done nothing."

"Comrade, you don't understand," they said. "Members of the party do not violate the party's decisions."

"But your decision does not apply to me," I said. "I'll be damned if I'll act as if it does."

"Your attitude does not merit our trust," they said.

I was angry.

"Look," I exploded, rising and sweeping my arms at the bleak attic in which I lived. "What is it here that frightens you? You know where I work. You know what I earn. You know my friends. Now, what in God's name is wrong?"

They left with mirthless smiles which implied that I would soon know what was wrong.

But there was relief from these shadowy political bouts. I found my work in the South Side Boys' Club deeply engrossing. Each day black boys between the ages of eight and twenty-five came to swim, draw, and read. They were a wild and homeless lot, culturally lost, spiritually disinherited, candidates for the clinics, morgues, prisons, reformatories, and the electric chair of the state's death house. For hours I listened to their talk of planes, women, guns, politics, and crime. Their figures of speech were as forceful and colorful as any ever used by English-speaking people. I kept pencil and paper in my pocket to jot down their word-rhythms and reactions. These boys did not fear people to the extent that every man looked like a spy. The Communists who doubted my motives did not know these boys, their twisted dreams, their all too clear destinies; and I doubted if I should ever be able to convey to them the tragedy I saw here.

7

Party duties broke into my efforts at expression. The club decided upon a conference of all the left-wing writers in the Middle West. I supported the idea and argued that the conference should deal with craft problems. My arguments were rejected. The conference, the club decided, would deal with political questions. I asked for a definition of what was expected from the writers—books or political activity. Both, was the answer. Write a few hours a day and march on the picket line the other hours.

The conference convened with a leading Communist attending as adviser. The question debated [68] was: What does the Communist Party expect from the club? The answer of the Communist leader ran from organizing to writing novels. I argued that either a man organized or he wrote novels. The party leader said that both must be done. The attitude of the party leader prevailed and *Left Front*, for which I had worked so long, was voted out of existence.

I knew now that the club was nearing its end, and I rose and stated my gloomy conclusions, recommending that the club dissolve. My "defeatism," as it was called, brought upon my head the sharpest disapproval of the party leader. The conference ended with the passing of a multitude of resolutions dealing with China, India, Germany, Japan, and conditions afflicting various parts of the earth. But not one idea regarding writing had emerged.

The ideas I had expounded at the conference were linked with the suspicions I had roused among the Negro Communists on the South

Side, and the Communist Party was now certain that it had a dangerous enemy in its midst. It was whispered that I was trying to lead a secret group in opposition to the party. I had learned that denial of accusations was useless. It was now painful to meet a Communist, for I did not know what his attitude would be.

Following the conference, a national John Reed Club congress was called. It convened in the summer of 1934 with left-wing writers attending from all states. But as the sessions got under way there was a sense of looseness, bewilderment, and dissatisfaction among the writers, most of whom were young, eager, and on the verge of doing their best work. No one knew what was expected of him, and out of the congress came no unifying idea.

As the congress drew to a close, I attended a caucus to plan the future of the clubs. Ten of us met in a Loop hotel room, and to my amazement the leaders of the clubs' national board confirmed my criticisms of the manner in which the clubs had been conducted. I was excited. Now, I thought, the clubs will be given a new lease on life.

Then I was stunned when I heard a nationally known Communist announce a decision to dissolve the clubs. Why? I asked. Because the clubs do not serve the new People's Front policy, I was told. That can be remedied; the clubs can be made healthy and broad, I said. No; a bigger and better organization must be launched, one in which the leading writers of the nation could be included, they said. I was informed that the People's Front policy was now the correct vision of life and that the clubs could no longer exist. I asked what was to become of the young writers whom the Communist Party had implored to join the clubs and who were ineligible for the new group, and there was no answer. "This thing is cold!" I exclaimed to myself. To effect a swift change in policy, the Communist Party was dumping one organization, then organizing a new scheme with entirely new people!

I found myself arguing alone against the majority opinion and then I made still another amazing discovery. I saw that even those who agreed with me would not support me. At that meeting I learned that when a man was informed of the wish of the party he submitted, even though he knew with all the strength of his brain that the wish was not a wise one, was one that would ultimately harm the party's interests.

It was not courage that made me oppose the party. I simply did not know any better. It was inconceivable to me, though bred in the lap of Southern hate, that a man could not have his say. I had spent a third of my life traveling from the place of my birth to the North just to talk freely, to escape the pressure of fear. And now I was facing fear again.

Before the congress adjourned, it was decided that another congress of American writers would be called in New York the following summer, 1935. I was lukewarm to the proposal and tried to make up my mind to stand alone, write alone. I was already afraid that the stories I had written would not fit into the new, official mood. Must I discard my plot-ideas and seek new ones? No. I could not. My writing was my way of seeing, my way of living, my way of feeling; and who could change his sight, his sense of direction, his senses?

8

The spring of 1935 came and the plans for the writers' congress went on apace. For some obscure reason—it might have been to "save" me —I was urged by the local Communists to attend and I was named as a delegate. I got time off from my job at the South Side Boys' Club and, along with several other delegates, hitchhiked to New York.

We arrived in the early evening and registered for the congress sessions. The opening mass meeting was being held at Carnegie Hall. I asked about housing accommodations, and the New York John Reed Club members, all white members of the Communist Party, looked embarrassed. I waited while one white Communist called another white Communist to one side and discussed what could be done to get me, a black Chicago Communist, housed. During the trip I had not thought of myself as a Negro; I had been mulling over the problems of the young left-wing writers I knew. Now, as I stood watching one white comrade talk frantically to another about the color of my skin, I felt disgusted. The white comrade returned.

"Just a moment, comrade," he said to me. "I'll get a place for you."

"But haven't you places already?" I asked. "Matters of this sort are ironed out in advance."

"Yes," he admitted in an intimate tone. "We have some addresses here, but we don't know the people. You understand?"

"Yes, I understand," I said, gritting my teeth.

"But just wait a second," he said, touching my arm to reassure me. "I'll find something."

"Listen, don't bother," I said, trying to keep anger out of my voice.

"Oh, no," he said, shaking his head determinedly. "This is a problem and I'll solve it."

"It oughtn't to be a problem," I could not help saying.

"Oh, I didn't mean that," he caught himself.

I cursed under my breath. Several people standing near-by observed the white Communist trying to find a black Communist a place to sleep. I burned with shame. A few minutes later the white Communist returned, frantic-eyed, sweating.

"Did you find anything?" I asked.

"No, not yet," he said, panting. "Just a moment. I'm going to call somebody I know. Say, give me a nickel for the phone."

"Forget it," I said. My legs felt like water. "I'll find a place. But I'd like to put my suitcase somewhere until after the meeting tonight."

"Do you really think you can find a place?" he asked, trying to keep a note of desperate hope out of his voice.

"Of course I can," I said.

He was still uncertain. He wanted to help me, but he did not know how. He locked my bag in a closet and I stepped to the sidewalk wondering where I would sleep that night. I stood on the sidewalks of New York with a black skin and practically no money, absorbed, not with the burning questions of the left-wing literary movement in the United States, but with the problem of how to get a bath. I presented my credentials at Carnegie Hall. The building was jammed with people. As I listened to the militant speeches, I found myself wondering why in hell I had come.

I went to the sidewalk and stood studying the faces of the people. I met a Chicago club member.

"Didn't you find a place yet?" he asked.

"No," I said. "I'd like to try one of the hotels, but, God, I'm in no mood to argue with a hotel clerk about my color."

"Oh, hell, wait a minute," he said.

He scooted off. He returned in a few moments with a big, heavy white woman. He introduced us.

"You can sleep in my place tonight," she said.

I walked with her to her apartment and she introduced me to her husband. I thanked them for their hospitality and went to sleep on a cot in the kitchen. I got up at six, dressed, tapped on their door, and bade them good-bye. I went to the sidewalk, sat on a bench, took out pencil and paper, and tried to jot down notes for the argument I wanted to make in defense of the John Reed Clubs. But the problem of the clubs did not seem important. What did seem important was: Could a Negro ever live halfway like a human being in this goddamn country?

That day I sat through the congress sessions, but what I heard did not touch me. That night I found my way to Harlem and walked pavements filled with black life. I was amazed, when I asked passersby, to learn that there were practically no hotels for Negroes in Harlem. I kept walking. Finally I saw a tall, clean hotel; black people were passing the doors and no white people were in sight. Confidently I entered and was surprised to see a white clerk behind the desk. I hesitated.

"I'd like a room," I said.

"Not here," he said.

"But isn't this Harlem?" I asked.

"Yes, but this hotel is for white only," he said.

"Where is a hotel for colored?"

"You might try the Y," he said.

Half an hour later I found the Negro Young Men's Christian Association, that bulwark of Jim Crowism for young black men, got a room, took a bath, and slept for twelve hours. When I awakened, I did not want to go to the congress. I lay in bed thinking, "I've got to go it alone . . . I've got to learn how again . . ."

I dressed and attended the meeting that was to make the final decision to dissolve the clubs. It started briskly. A New York Communist writer summed up the history of the clubs and made a motion for their dissolution. Debate started and I rose and explained what the clubs had meant to young writers and begged for their continuance. I sat down amid silence. Debate was closed. The vote was called. The room filled with uplifted hands to dissolve. Then came a call for those who disagreed and my hand went up alone. I knew that my stand would be interpreted as one of opposition to the Communist Party, but I thought: "The hell with it." [70]

9

With the John Reed clubs now dissolved, I was free of all party relations. I avoided unit meetings for fear of being subjected to discipline. Occasionally a Negro Communist—defying the code that enjoined him to shun suspect elements—came to my home and informed me of the current charges that Communists were bringing against one another. To my astonishment I heard that Buddy Nealson had branded me a "smuggler of reaction."

Buddy Nealson was the Negro who had formulated the Communist position for the American Negro; he had made speeches in the Kremlin; he had spoken before Stalin himself.

"Why does Nealson call me that?" I asked.

"He says that you are a petty bourgeois degenerate," I was told.

"What does that mean?"

"He says that you are corrupting the party with your ideas."

"How?"

There was no answer. I decided that my relationship with the party was about over; I should have to leave it. The attacks were growing worse, and my refusal to react incited Nealson into coining more absurd phrases. I was termed a "bastard intellectual," an "incipient Trotskyite"; it was claimed that I possessed an "anti-leadership attitude" and that I was manifesting "seraphim tendencies"—a phrase meaning that one has withdrawn from the struggle of life and considers oneself infallible.

Working all day and writing half the night brought me down with a severe chest ailment. While I was ill, a knock came at my door one morning. My mother admitted Ed Green, the man who had demanded to know what use I planned to make of the material I was collecting from the comrades. I stared at him as I lay abed and I knew that he considered me a clever and sworn enemy of the party. Bitterness welled up in me.

"What do you want?" I asked bluntly. "You see I'm ill."

"I have a message from the party for you," he said.

I had not said good day, and he had not offered to say it. He had not smiled, and neither had I. He looked curiously at my bleak room.

"This is the home of a bastard intellectual," I cut at him.

He stared without blinking. I could not endure his standing there so stone-like. Common decency made me say, "Sit down."

His shoulders stiffened.

"I'm in a hurry." He spoke like an army officer.

"What do you want to tell me?"

"Do you know Buddy Nealson?" he asked.

I was suspicious. Was this a political trap?

"What about Buddy Nealson?" I asked, committing myself to nothing until I knew the kind of reality I was grappling with.

"He wants to see you," Ed Green said.

"What about?" I asked, still suspicious.

"He wants to talk with you about your party work," he said.

"I'm ill and can't see him until I'm well," I said.

Ed Green stood for a fraction of a second, then turned on his heel and marched out of the room.

When my chest healed, I sought an appointment with Buddy Nealson. He was a short, black man with an ever ready smile, thick lips, a furtive manner, and a greasy, sweaty look. His bearing was nervous, self-conscious; he seemed always to be hiding some deep irritation. He spoke in short, jerky sentences, hopping nimbly from thought to thought, as though his mind worked in a free, associational [48] manner. He suffered from asthma and would snort at unexpected intervals. Now and then he would punctuate his flow of words by taking a nip from a bottle of whiskey. He had traveled half around the world and his talk was pitted with vague allusions to European cities. I met him in his apartment, listened to him intently, observed him minutely, for I knew that I was facing one of the leaders of World Communism.

"Hello, Wright," he snorted. "I've heard about you."

As we shook hands he burst into a loud, seemingly causeless laugh; and as he guffawed I could not tell whether his mirth was directed at me or was meant to hide his uneasiness.

"I hope what you've heard about me is good," I parried.

"Sit down," he laughed again, waving me to a chair. "Yes, they tell me you write."

"I try to," I said.

"You can write," he snorted. "I read that article you wrote for the *New Masses* about Joe Louis. Good stuff. First political treatment of sports we've yet had. Ha-ha."

I waited. I had thought that I should encounter a man of ideas, but he was not that. Then perhaps he was a man of action? But that was not indicated either.

"They tell me that you are a friend of Ross," he shot at me.

I paused before answering. He had not asked me directly, but had hinted in a neutral, teasing way. Ross, I had been told, was slated for expulsion from the party on the ground that he was "anti-leadership"; and if a member of the Communist International was asking me if I was a friend of a man about to be expelled, he was indirectly asking me if I was loyal or not.

"Ross is not particularly a friend of mine," I said frankly. "But I know him well; in fact, quite well."

"If he isn't your friend, how do you happen to know him so well?" he asked, laughing to soften the hard threat of his question.

"I was writing an account of his life and I know him as well, perhaps, as anybody," I told him.

"I heard about that," he said. "Wright. Ha-ha. Say, let me call you Dick, hunh?"

"Go ahead," I said.

"Dick," he said, "Ross is a nationalist." He paused to let the weight of his accusation sink in. He meant that Ross's militancy was extreme. "We Communists don't dramatize Negro nationalism," he said in a voice that laughed, accused, and drawled.

"What do you mean?" I asked.

"We're not advertising Ross." He spoke directly now.

"We're talking about two different things," I said. "You seem worried about my making Ross popular because he is your political opponent. But I'm not concerned about Ross's politics at all. The man struck me as one who typified certain traits of the Negro migrant. I've already sold a story based upon an incident in his life."

Nealson became excited.

"What was the incident?" he asked.

"Some trouble he got into when he was thirteen years old," I said.

"Oh, I thought it was political," he said, shrugging.

"But I'm telling you that you are wrong about that," I explained. "I'm not trying to fight you with my writing. I've no political ambitions. You must believe that. I'm trying to depict Negro life."

"Have you finished writing about Ross?"

"No," I said. "I dropped the idea. Our party members were suspicious of me and were afraid to talk." He laughed.

"Dick," he began, "we're short of forces. We're facing a grave crisis."

"The party's always facing a crisis," I said.

His smile left and he stared at me.

"You're not cynical, are you, Dick?" he asked.

"No," I said. "But it's the truth. Each week, each month there's a crisis."

"You're a funny guy," he said, laughing, snorting again. "But we've got a job to do. We're altering our work. Fascism's the danger, the danger now to all people."

"I understand," I said.

"We've got to defeat the Fascists," he said, snorting from asthma. "We've discussed you and know your abilities. We want you to work with us. We've got to crash out of our narrow way of working and get our message to the church people, students, club people, professionals, middle class.

"I've been called names," I said softly. "Is that crashing out of the narrow way?"

"Forget that," he said.

He had not denied the name-calling. That meant that, if I did not obey him, the name-calling would begin again.

"I don't know if I fit into things," I said openly.

"We want to trust you with an important assignment," he said.

"What do you want me to do?"

"We want you to organize a committee against the high cost of living."

"The high cost of living?" I exclaimed. "What do I know about such things?" [49]

"It's easy. You can learn," he said.

I was in the midst of writing a novel and he was calling me from it to tabulate the price of groceries. "He doesn't think much of what I'm trying to do," I thought.

"Comrade Nealson," I said, "a writer who hasn't written anything worth while is a most doubtful person. Now, I'm in that category. Yet I think I can write. I don't want to ask for special favors, but I'm in the midst of a book which I hope to complete in six months or so.

Let me convince myself that I'm wrong about my hankering to write and then I'll be with you all the way."

"Dick," he said, turning in his chair and waving his hand as though to brush away an insect that was annoying him, "you've got to get to the masses of people."

"You've seen some of my work," I said. "Isn't it just barely good enough to warrant my being given a chance?"

"The party can't deal with your feelings," he said.

"Maybe I don't belong in the party," I stated it in full.

"Oh, no! Don't say that," he said, snorting. He looked at me. "You're blunt."

"I put things the way I feel them," I said. "I want to start in right with you. I've had too damn much crazy trouble in the party."

He laughed and lit a cigarette.

"Dick," he said, shaking his head, "the trouble with you is that you've been around with those white artists on the North Side too much. You even talk like 'em. You've got to know your own people."

"I think I know them," I said, realizing that I could never really talk with him. "I've been inside of three fourths of the Negroes' homes on the South Side."

"But you've got to work with 'em," he said.

"I was working with Ross until I was suspected of being a spy," I said.

"Dick," he spoke seriously now, "the party has decided that you are to accept this task."

I was silent. I knew the meaning of what he had said. A decision was the highest injunction that a Communist could receive from his party, and to break a decision was to break the effectiveness of the party's ability to act. In principle I heartily agreed with this, for I knew that it was impossible for working people to forge instruments of political power until they had achieved unity of action. Oppressed for centuries, divided, hopeless, corrupted, misled, they were cynical—as I had once been—and the Communist method of unity had been found historically to be the only means of achieving discipline. In short, Nealson had asked me directly if I were a Communist or not. I wanted to be a Communist, but my kind of Communist. I wanted to shape people's feelings, awaken their hearts. But I could not tell Nealson that; he would only have snorted.

"I'll organize the committee and turn it over to someone else," I suggested.

"You don't want to do this, do you?" he asked.

"No," I said firmly.

"What would you like to do on the South Side, then?"

"I'd like to organize Negro artists," I said.

"But the party doesn't need that now," he said.

I rose, knowing that he had no intention of letting me go after I had organized the committee. I wanted to tell him that I was through, but I was not ready to bring matters to a head. I went out, angry with myself, angry with him, angry with the party. Well, I had not broken the decision, but neither had I accepted it wholly. I had dodged, trying to save time for writing, time to think.

10

My task consisted in attending meetings until the late hours of the night, taking part in discussions, or lending myself generally along with other Communists in leading the people of the South Side. We debated the housing situation, the best means of forcing the city to authorize open hearings on conditions among Negroes. I gritted my teeth as the daily value of pork chops was tabulated, longing to be at home with my writing.

Nealson was cleverer than I and he confronted me before I had a chance to confront him. I was summoned one night to meet Nealson and a "friend." When I arrived at a South Side hotel I was introduced to a short, yellow man who carried himself like Napoleon. He wore glasses, kept his full lips pursed as though he were engaged in perpetual thought. He swaggered when he walked. He spoke slowly, precisely, trying to charge each of his words with more meaning than the words were able to carry. He talked of trivial things in lofty tones. He said that his name was Smith, that he was from Washington, that he planned to launch a national organization among Negroes to federalize all existing Negro institutions so as to achieve a broad unity of action. The three of us sat at a table, facing one another. I knew that another and last offer was about to be made to me, and if I did not accept it, there would be open warfare.[50]

"Wright, how would you like to go to Switzerland?" Smith asked with dramatic suddenness.

"I'd like it," I said. "But I'm tied up with work now."

"You can drop that," Nealson said. "This is important."

"What would I do in Switzerland?" I asked.

"You'll go as a youth delegate," Smith said. "From there you can go to the Soviet Union."

"Much as I'd like to, I'm afraid I can't make it," I said honestly. "I simply cannot drop the writing I'm doing now."

We sat looking at one another, smoking silently.

"Has Nealson told you how I feel?" I asked Smith.

Smith did not answer. He stared at me a long time, then spat: "Wright, you're a fool!"

I rose. Smith turned away from me. A breath more of anger and I should have driven my fist into his face. Nealson laughed sheepishly, snorting.

"Was that necessary?" I asked, trembling.

I stood recalling how, in my boyhood, I would have fought until blood ran had anyone said anything like that to me. But I was a man now and master of my rage, able to control the surging emotions. I put on my hat and walked to the door. "Keep cool," I said to myself. "Don't let this get out of hand."

"This is good-bye," I said.

I attended the next unit meeting and asked for a place on the agenda, which was readily granted. Nealson was there. Evans was there. Ed Green was there. When my time came to speak, I said:—

"Comrades, for the past two years I've worked daily with most of you. Despite this, I have for some time found myself in a difficult position in the party. What has caused this difficulty is a long story which I do not care to recite now; it would serve no purpose. But I tell you honestly that I think I've found a solution of my difficulty. I am proposing here tonight that my membership be dropped from the party rolls. No ideological differences impel me to say this. I simply do not wish to be bound any longer by the party's decisions. I should like to retain my membership in those organizations in which the party has influence, and I shall comply with the party's program in those organizations. I hope that my words will be accepted in the spirit in which they are said. Perhaps sometime in the future I can meet and talk with the leaders of the party as to what tasks I can best perform."

I sat down amid a profound silence. The Negro secretary of the meeting looked frightened, glancing at Nealson, Evans, and Ed Green.

"Is there any discussion on Comrade Wright's statement?" the secretary asked finally.

"I move that discussion on Wright's statement be deferred," Nealson said.

A quick vote confirmed Nealson's motion. I looked about the silent room, then reached for my hat and rose.

"I should like to go now," I said.

No one said anything. I walked to the door and out into the night and a heavy burden seemed to lift from my shoulders. I was free. And I had done it in a decent and forthright manner. I had not been bitter. I had not raked up a single recrimination. I had attacked no one. I had disavowed nothing.

The next night two Negro Communists called at my home. They pretended to be ignorant of what had happened at the unit meeting. Patiently I explained what had occurred.

"Your story does not agree with what Nealson says," they said, revealing the motive of their visit.

"And what does Nealson say?" I asked.

"He says that you are in league with a Trotskyite group, and that you made an appeal for other party members to follow you in leaving the party."

"What?" I gasped. "That's not true. I asked that my membership be dropped. I raised no political issues." What did this mean? I sat pondering. "Look, maybe I ought to make my break with the party clean. If Nealson's going to act this way, I'll resign."

"You can't resign," they told me.

"What do you mean?" I demanded.

"No one can resign from the Communist Party."

I looked at them and laughed.

"You're talking crazy," I said.

"Nealson would expel you publicly, cut the ground from under your feet if you resigned," they said. "People would think that something was wrong if someone like you quit here on the South Side."

I was angry. Was the party so weak and uncertain of itself that it could not accept what I had said at the unit meeting? Who thought up such tactics? Then, suddenly, I understood. These were the secret, underground tactics of the political movement of the Communists under the tsars of Old Russia! The Communist Party felt that it had to assassinate me morally merely because I did not want to be bound by its decisions. I saw now that my comrades were acting out a fantasy that had no relation whatever to the reality of their environment.

"Tell Nealson that if he fights me, then, by God, I'll fight him," I said. "If he leaves this damn thing where it is, then all right. If he thinks I won't fight him publicly, he's crazy!" [51]

I was not able to know if my statement reached Nealson. There was no public outcry against me, but in the ranks of the party itself a storm broke loose and I was branded a traitor, an unstable personality, and one whose faith had failed.

My comrades had known me, my family, my friends; they, God knows, had known my aching poverty. But they had never been able to conquer their fear of the individual way in which I acted and lived, an individuality which life had seared into my bones.

11

I was transferred by the relief authorities from the South Side Boys' Club to the Federal Negro Theater to work as a publicity agent. There were days when I was acutely hungry for the incessant analyses that went on among the comrades, but whenever I heard news of the party's inner life, it was of charges and countercharges, reprisals and counterreprisals.

The Federal Negro Theater, for which I was doing publicity, had run a series of ordinary plays, all of which had been revamped to "Negro style," with jungle scenes, spirituals, and all. For example, the skinny white woman who directed it, an elderly missionary type, would take a play whose characters were white, whose theme dealt with the Middle Ages, and recast it in terms of Southern Negro life with overtones of African backgrounds. Contemporary plays dealing realistically with Negro life were spurned as being controversial. There were about forty Negro actors and actresses in the theater, lolling about, yearning, disgruntled.

What a waste of talent, I thought. Here was an opportunity for the production of a worth-while Negro drama and no one was aware of it. I studied the situation, then laid the matter before white friends of mine who held influential positions in the Works Progress Administration. I asked them to replace the white woman—including her quaint aesthetic notions—with someone who knew the Negro and the theater. They promised me that they would act.

Within a month the white woman director had been transferred. We moved from the South Side to the Loop and were housed in a first-rate theater. I successfully recommended Charles DeSheim, a talented Jew, as director. DeSheim and I held long talks during which I outlined what I thought could be accomplished. I urged that our first offering should be a bill of three one-act plays, including Paul Green's *Hymn to the Rising Sun,* a grim, poetical, powerful one-acter dealing with chain-gang conditions in the South.

I was happy. At last I was in a position to make suggestions and have them acted upon. I was convinced that we had a rare chance to build a genuine Negro theater. I convoked a meeting and introduced DeSheim to the Negro company, telling them that he was a man who knew the theater, who could lead them toward serious dramatics. DeSheim made a speech wherein he said that he was not at the theater to direct it, but to help the Negroes to direct it. He spoke so simply and eloquently that they rose and applauded him.

I then proudly passed out copies of Paul Green's *Hymn to the Rising Sun* to all members of the company. DeSheim assigned reading parts. I sat down to enjoy adult Negro dramatics. But something went wrong. The Negroes stammered and faltered in their lines. Finally they stopped reading altogether. DeSheim looked frightened. One of the Negro actors rose.

"Mr. DeSheim," he began, "we think this play is indecent. We don't want to act in a play like this before the American public. I don't think any such conditions exist in the South. I lived in the South and I never saw any chain gangs. Mr. DeSheim, we want a play that will make the public love us."

"What kind of play do you want?" DeSheim asked them.

They did not know. I went to the office and looked up their records and found that most of them had spent their lives playing cheap vaudeville. I had thought that they played vaudeville because the legitimate theater was barred to them, and now it turned out they wanted none of the legitimate theater, that they were scared spitless at the prospects of appearing in a play that the public might not like, even though they did not understand that public and had no way of determining its likes or dislikes.

I felt—but only temporarily—that perhaps the whites were right, that Negroes were children and would never grow up. DeSheim informed the company that he would produce any play they liked, and they sat like frightened mice, possessing no words to make known their vague desires.

When I arrived at the theater a few mornings later, I was horrified to find that the company had drawn up a petition demanding the ousting of DeSheim. I was asked to sign the petition and I refused.

"Don't you know your friends?" I asked them.

They glared at me. I called DeSheim to the theater and we went into a frantic conference.

"What must I do?" he asked.

"Take them into your confidence," I said. "Let them know that it is their right to petition for a redress of their grievances." [52]

DeSheim thought my advice sound and, accordingly, he assembled the company and told them that they had a right to petition against him if they wanted to, but that he thought any misunderstandings that existed could be settled smoothly.

"Who told you that we were getting up a petition?" a black man demanded.

DeSheim looked at me and stammered wordlessly.

"There's an Uncle Tom in the theater!" a black girl yelled.

After the meeting a delegation of Negro men came to my office and took out their pocket knives and flashed them in my face.

"You get the hell off this job before we cut your bellybutton out!" they said.

I telephoned my white friends in the Works Progress Administration: "Transfer me at once to another job, or I'll be murdered."

Within twenty-four hours DeSheim and I were given our papers. We shook hands and went our separate ways.

I was transferred to a white experimental theatrical company as a publicity agent and I resolved to keep my ideas to myself, or, better, to write them down and not attempt to translate them into reality.

12

One evening a group of Negro Communists called at my home and asked to speak to me in strict secrecy. I took them into my room and locked the door.

"Dick," they began abruptly, "the party wants you to attend a meeting Sunday."

"Why?" I asked. "I'm no longer a member."

"That's all right. They want you to be present," they said.

"Communists don't speak to me on the street," I said. "Now, why do you want me at a meeting?"

They hedged. They did not want to tell me.

"If you can't tell me, then I can't come," I said.

They whispered among themselves and finally decided to take me into their confidence.

"Dick, Ross is going to be tried," they said.

"For what?"

They recited a long list of political offenses of which they alleged that he was guilty.

"But what has that got to do with me?"

"If you come, you'll find out," they said.

"I'm not that naïve," I said. I was suspicious now. Were they trying to lure me to a trial and expel me? "This trial might turn out to be mine."

They swore that they had no intention of placing me on trial, that the party merely wanted me to observe Ross's trial so that I might learn what happened to "enemies of the working class."

As they talked, my old love of witnessing something new came over me. I wanted to see this trial, but I did not want to risk being placed on trial myself.

"Listen," I told them. "I'm not guilty of Nealson's charges. If I showed up at this trial, it would seem that I am."

"No, it won't. Please come."

"All right. But, listen. If I'm tricked, I'll fight. You hear? I don't trust Nealson. I'm not a politician and I cannot anticipate all the funny moves of a man who spends his waking hours plotting."

Ross's trial took place that following Sunday afternoon. Comrades stood inconspicuously on guard about the meeting hall, at the doors, down the street, and along the hallways. When I appeared, I was ushered in quickly. I was tense. It was a rule that once you had entered a meeting of this kind you could not leave until the meeting was over; it was feared that you might go to the police and denounce them all.

Ross, the accused, sat alone at a table in the front of the hall, his face distraught. I felt sorry for him; yet I could not escape feeling that he enjoyed this. For him, this was perhaps the highlight of an otherwise bleak existence.

In trying to grasp why Communists hated intellectuals, my mind was led back again to the accounts I had read of the Russian Revolution. There had existed in Old Russia millions of poor, ignorant people who were exploited by a few educated, arrogant noblemen, and it became natural for the Russian Communists to associate betrayal with intellectualism. But there existed in the Western world an element that baffled and frightened the Communist Party: the prevalence of self-achieved literacy. Even a Negro, entrapped by ignorance and exploitation,—as I had been,—could, if he had the will and the love for it, learn to read and to understand the world in which he lived. And it was these people that the Communists could not understand.

The trial began in a quiet, informal manner. The comrades acted like a group of neighbors sitting in judgment upon one of their kind who had stolen a chicken. Anybody could ask and get the floor. There was absolute freedom of speech. Yet the meeting had an amazingly formal structure of its own, a structure that went as deep as the desire of men to live together.

A member of the Central Committee of the Communist Party rose and gave a description of the world situation. He spoke without emotion and [53] piled up hard facts. He painted a horrible but masterful picture of Fascism's aggression in Germany, Italy, and Japan.

I accepted the reason why the trial began in this manner. It was imperative that here be postulated against what or whom Ross's crimes had been committed. Therefore there had to be established in the minds of all present a vivid picture of mankind under oppression.

And it was a true picture. Perhaps no organization on earth, save the Communist Party, possessed so detailed a knowledge of how workers lived, for its sources of information stemmed directly from the workers themselves.

The next speaker discussed the role of the Soviet Union as the world's lone workers' state—how the Soviet Union was hemmed in by enemies, how the Soviet Union was trying to industrialize itself, what sacrifices it was making to help workers of the world to steer a path toward peace through the idea of collective security.

The facts presented so far were as true as any facts could be in this uncertain world. Yet no one word had been said of the accused, who sat listening like any other member. The time had not yet come to include him and his crimes in this picture of global struggle. An absolute had first to be established in the minds of the comrades so that they could measure the success or failure of their deeds by it.

Finally a speaker came forward and spoke of Chicago's South Side, its Negro population, their suffering and handicaps, linking all that also to the world struggle. Then still another speaker followed and described the tasks of the Communist Party of the South Side. At last, the world, the national, and the local pictures had been fused into one overwhelming drama of moral struggle in which everybody in the hall was participating. This presentation had lasted for more than three hours, but it had enthroned a new sense of reality in the hearts of those present, a sense of man on earth. With the exception of the church and its myths and legends, there was no agency in the world so capable of making men feel the earth and the people upon it as the Communist Party.

Toward evening the direct charges against Ross were made, not by the leaders of the party, but by Ross's friends, those who knew him best! It was crushing. Ross wilted. His emotions could not withstand the weight of the moral pressure. No one was terrorized into giving information against him. They gave it willingly, citing dates, conversations, scenes. The black mass of Ross's wrongdoing emerged slowly and irrefutably.

The moment came for Ross to defend himself. I had been told that he had arranged for friends to testify in his behalf, but he called upon no one. He stood, trembling; he tried to talk and his words would not come. The hall was as still as death. Guilt was written in every pore of his black skin. His hands shook. He held on to the edge of the table to keep on his feet. His personality, his sense of himself, had been obliterated. Yet he could not have been so humbled unless he had shared and accepted the vision that had crushed him, the common vision that bound us all together.

"Comrades," he said in a low, charged voice, "I'm guilty of all the charges, all of them."

His voice broke in a sob. No one prodded him. No one tortured him. No one threatened him. He was free to go out of the hall and never see another Communist. But he did not want to. He could not. The vision of a communal world had sunk down into his soul and it would never leave him until life left him. He talked on, outlining how he had erred, how he would reform.

I knew, as I sat there, that there were many people who thought they knew life who had been skeptical of the Moscow trials. But they could not have been skeptical had they witnessed this astonishing trial. Ross had not been doped; he had been awakened. It was not a fear of the Communist Party that had made him confess, but a fear of the punishment that he would exact of himself that made him tell of his wrongdoings. The Communists had talked to him until they had given him new eyes with which to see his own crime. And then they sat back and listened to him tell how he had erred. He was one with all the members there, regardless of race or color; his heart was theirs and their hearts were his; and when a man reaches that state of kinship with others, that degree of oneness, or when a trial has made him kin after he has been sundered from them by wrongdoing, then he must rise and say, out of a sense of the deepest morality in the world: "I'm guilty. Forgive me."

This, to me, was a spectacle of glory; and yet, because it had condemned me, because it was blind and ignorant, I felt that it was a spectacle of horror. The blindness of their limited lives—lives truncated and impoverished by the oppression they had suffered long before they had ever heard of Communism—made them think that I was with their enemies. American life had so corrupted their consciousness that they were unable to recognize their friends when they saw them. I knew that if they had held state power I should have been declared guilty of treason and my execution would have followed. And I knew that they felt, with all the strength of their black blindness, that they were right. [54]

I could not stay until the end. I was anxious to get out of the hall and into the streets and shake free from the gigantic tension that had hold of me. I rose and went to the door; a comrade shook his head, warning me that I could not leave until the trial had ended.

"You can't leave now," he said.

"I'm going out of here," I said, my anger making my voice louder than I intended.

We glared at each other. Another comrade came running up. I stepped forward. The comrade who had rushed up gave the signal for me to be allowed to leave. They did not want violence, and neither did I. They stepped aside.

I went into the dark Chicago streets and walked home through the cold, filled with a sense of sadness. Once again I told myself that I must learn to stand alone. I did not feel so wounded by their rejection of me that I wanted to spend my days bleating about what they had done. Perhaps what I had already learned to feel in my childhood saved me from that futile path. I lay in bed that night and said to myself: "I'll be for them, even though they are not for me."

13

From the Federal Experimental Theater I was transferred to the Federal Writers' Project, and I tried to earn my bread by writing guidebooks. Many of the writers on the project were members of the Communist Party and they kept their revolutionary vows that restrained them from speaking to "traitors of the working class." I sat beside them in the office, ate next to them in restaurants, and rode up and down in the elevators with them, but they always looked straight ahead, wordlessly.

After working on the project for a few months, I was made acting supervisor of essays and straightway I ran into political difficulties. One morning the administrator of the project called me into his office.

"Wright, who are your friends on this project?" he asked.

"I don't know," I said. "Why?"

"Well, you ought to find out soon," he said.

"What do you mean?"

"Some people are asking for your removal on the ground that you are incompetent," he said.

"Who are they?"

He named several of my erstwhile comrades. Yes, it had come to that. They were trying to take the bread out of my mouth.

"What do you propose to do about their complaints?" I asked.

"Nothing," he said, laughing. "I think I understand what's happening here. I'm not going to let them drive you off this job."

I thanked him and rose to go to the door. Something in his words had not sounded right. I turned and faced him.

"*This* job?" I repeated. "What do you mean?"

"You mean to say that you don't know?" he asked.

"Know what? What are you talking about?"

"Why did you leave the Federal Negro Theater?"

"I had trouble there. They drove me off the job, the Negroes did."

"And you don't think that they had any encouragement?" he asked me ironically.

I sat again. This was deadly. I gaped at him.

"You needn't fear here," he said. "You work, write."

"It's hard to believe that," I murmured.

"Forget it," he said.

But the worst was yet to come. One day at noon I closed my desk and went down in the elevator. When I reached the first floor of the building, I saw a picket line moving to and fro in the streets. Many of the men and women carrying placards were old friends of mine, and they were chanting for higher wages for Works Progress Administration artists and writers. It was not the kind of picket line that one was not supposed to cross, and as I started away from the door I heard my name shouted:—

"There's Wright, that goddamn Trotskyite!"

"We know you, you——!"

"Wright's a traitor!"

For a moment it seemed that I ceased to live. I had now reached that point where I was cursed aloud in the busy streets of America's second-largest city. It shook me as nothing else had.

Days passed. I continued on my job, where I functioned as the shop chairman of the union which I had helped to organize, though my election as shop chairman had been bitterly opposed by the party. In their efforts to nullify my influence in the union, my old comrades were willing to kill the union itself.

As May Day of 1936 approached, it was voted by the union membership that we should march in the public procession. On the morning of May Day I received printed instructions as to the time and place where our union contingent would assemble to join the parade. At noon I hurried to the spot and found that the parade was already in progress. In vain I searched for the banners of my union local. Where were they? I went up and down the streets, asking for the location of my local.

"Oh, that local's gone fifteen minutes ago," a [55] Negro told me. "If you're going to march, you'd better fall in somewhere."

I thanked him and walked through the milling crowds. Suddenly I heard my name called. I turned. To my left was the Communist Party's South Side section, lined up and ready to march.

"Come here!" an old party friend called to me.

I walked over to him.

"Aren't you marching today?" he asked me.

"I missed my union local," I told him.

"What the hell," he said. "March with us."

"I don't know," I said, remembering my last visit to the headquarters of the party, and my status as an "enemy."

"This is May Day," he said. "Get into the ranks."

"You know the trouble I've had," I said.

"That's nothing," he said. "Everybody's marching today."

"I don't think I'd better," I said, shaking my head.

"Are you scared?" he asked. "This is *May Day*."

He caught my right arm and pulled me into line beside him. I stood talking to him, asking him about his work, about common friends.

"Get out of our ranks!" a voice barked.

I turned. A white Communist, a leader of the district of the Communist Party, Cy Perry, a slender, close-cropped fellow, stood glaring at me.

"I— It's May Day and I want to march," I said.

"Get out!" he shouted.

"I was invited here," I said.

I turned to the Negro Communist who had invited me into the

ranks. I did not want public violence. I looked at my friend. He turned his eyes away. He was afraid. I did not know what to do.

"You asked me to march here," I said to him.

He did not answer.

"Tell him that you did invite me," I said, pulling his sleeve.

"I'm asking you for the last time to get out of our ranks!" Cy Perry shouted.

I did not move. I had intended to, but I was beset by so many impulses that I could not act. Another white Communist came to assist Perry. Perry caught hold of my collar and pulled at me. I resisted. They held me fast. I struggled to free myself.

"Turn me loose!" I said.

Hands lifted me bodily from the sidewalk; I felt myself being pitched headlong through the air. I saved myself from landing on my head by clutching a curbstone with my hands. Slowly I rose and stood. Perry and his assistant were glaring at me. The rows of white and black Communists were looking at me with cold eyes of non-recognition. I could not believe what had happened, even though my hands were smarting and bleeding. I had suffered a public, physical assault by two white Communists with black Communists looking on. I could not move from the spot. I was empty of any idea about what to do. But I did not feel belligerent. I had outgrown my childhood.

Suddenly, the vast ranks of the Communist Party began to move. Scarlet banners with the hammer and sickle emblem of world revolution were lifted, and they fluttered in the May breeze. Drums beat. Voices were chanting. The tramp of many feet shook the earth. A long line of set-faced men and women, white and black, flowed past me.

I followed the procession to the Loop and went into Grant Park Plaza and sat upon a bench. I was not thinking; I could not think. But an objectivity of vision was being born within me. A surging sweep of many odds and ends came together and formed an attitude, a perspective. "They're blind," I said to myself. "Their enemies have blinded them with too much oppression." I lit a cigarette and I heard a song floating out over the sunlit air:—

"Arise you pris'ners of starvation!"

I remembered the stories I had written, the stories in which I had assigned a role of honor and glory to the Communist Party, and I was glad that they were down in black and white, were finished. For I knew in my heart that I should never be able to write that way again, should never be able to feel with that simple sharpness about life, should never again express such passionate hope, should never again make so total a commitment of faith.

"A better world's in birth . . ."

The procession still passed. Banners still floated. Voices of hope still chanted.

I headed toward home alone, really alone now, telling myself that in all the sprawling immensity of our mighty continent the least-known factor of living was the human heart, the least-sought goal of being was a way to live a human life. Perhaps, I thought, out of my tortured feelings I could fling a spark into this darkness. I would try, not because I wanted to but because I felt that I had to if I were to live at all.

I would hurl words into this darkness and wait for an echo; and if an echo sounded, no matter how faintly, I would send other words to tell, to march, to fight, to create a sense of the hunger for life that gnaws in us all, to keep alive in our hearts a sense of the inexpressibly human. [56]

The Artistic Heritage

Ralph Ellison is preoccupied with the question of what it means to be an artist. But this preoccupation is always in a historical context and involves a series of more complex questions. What does it mean to be a black writer? What does it mean to be an American writer? What, in fact, does it mean to be an American? Answering these questions necessitates a constant dialogue with history and culture, the result of which is a highly sophisticated conception of art and the role of the individual artist.

The following selections all contribute significantly to Ellison's concern with the problems of the artistic heritage. This concern begins, as he has said, with the problem of his own identity, and more particularly the problem of his own name. Ralph Waldo Ellison is quite aware of his ancestor Ralph Waldo Emerson and of the significance Emerson gives to the function naming. (For Ellison's own comments on his name see "Hidden Name and Complex Fate" in *Shadow and Act*.) As Robert Bone and Earl Rovit both point out, Ellison has inherited more than a name from Emerson. Emerson's conception of the poet as a celebrator of life, as the sayer who "reattaches things to nature and to the Whole," squares with Ellison's statement that "true novels, even when most pessimistic and bitter, arise out of an impulse to celebrate human life and therefore are ritualistic and ceremonial at their core."[1] The nature of language and symbols, the role of the poet as "liberating god," the conception of America as a poem, the need for the poet to "write his autobiography in colossal cipher"— all these Emersonian concepts and many more surface in Ellison's composition of an artistic heritage.

The search for that heritage was initiated, Ellison explains, by the works of T. S. Eliot. And certainly the ideas in Eliot's "Tradition and the Individual Talent" are crucial to Ellison's conception of the word *heritage*. Eliot's assertions that a poet needs a "historical sense" and that whatever the individual poet creates "re-arranges" the whole order of the artistic heritage are certainly basic to the Ellison aesthetic. The argument that each individual poet chooses his heritage is clearly visible when Ellison says that "I understand a bit more about myself as Negro because literature has taught me something

---

1. Ralph Ellison, "The World and the Jug."

of my identity as Western man, as political being." [2] Another of Eliot's ideas has perhaps an even greater influence on Ellison—namely, the assertion that the "more perfect the artist, the more completely separate in him will be the man who suffers and the mind which creates." Particularly in any attempt to confront the problem of the black experience in America Ellison's primary concern always seems to be "how much of his life the individual writer is able to transform into art." [3]

While Ellison is certainly influenced by Emerson and Eliot, he is also aware of another kind of literary tradition, and that tradition is the subject of Sterling Brown's "Negro Character as Seen by White Authors." Acknowledging one's heritage as Western man, utilizing the ritualistic and mythic patterns of Western literature, as Ellison certainly does in *Invisible Man*, is admirable except, as Brown's essay suggests, that heritage denies the full human complexity of the black man. Brown's abundantly documented list of seven stereotypes points out that "the Negro has met with as great injustice in American literature as he has in American life." Following the model of Yeats' use of Celtic heritage, Ellison attempted in *Invisible Man* to establish the symbolic interrelationship of the ritualistic and mythic patterns of his black heritage and those larger patterns that are his heritage as Western man. But part of that black-white heritage in America—indeed what Ellison has called the American joke—is the problem of masks, the illusion of identity. The ironic humor of identity and masking is the key issue in *Invisible Man* and Brown's categories provides an indispensable guide to that central joke.

One of the problems suggested by Sterling Brown's discussion of stereotypes is that black authors are not immune from repeating the distortions initiated by white writers. In fact, the history of black American literature has been dominated by debates over the problem of how best to avoid stereotyping and render the true black experience. It is this issue that white critic Irving Howe speaks to in "Black Boys and Native Sons." Howe juxtaposes Baldwin (and by extension Ellison) with Richard Wright, suggesting that in their attempts to transcend the limitations of black protest writing Ellison and Baldwin have avoided the true black experience, while Wright,

2. *Ibid.*
3. *Ibid.*

despite his weaknesses as a writer, has been true to that experience because of his uncompromising militancy.

The issues raised by Howe's essay are immensely complicated. In the first place he is suggesting that there is only one kind of black experience and that if black artists are to be true to their experience they must write about that one experience. Such suggestions are, of course, simply a more sophisticated kind of stereotyping. There are millions of individual black experiences. But because there is a shared black *condition*—the problem of living in white America—Howe's criticism *seems* to have some merit. A collateral issue raised by Howe's essay deals with the relationship between art and life, the artist and the citizen, "the man who suffers and the mind which creates." Howe suggests that distinctions between the social experience and the literary experience are at best academic. Affirmations of individual freedom and the possibilities of self-fulfillment, themes crucial to Ellison's novel, may not be made, Howe argues, unilaterally. Inevitably the self must act in a world of social realities.

It is to all of these traditions, racial, cultural, national, and literary that Ellison speaks in "The World and the Jug." The occasion for Ellison's essay is Howe's accusation, but in the process of countering Howe and defending himself Ellison reassesses the issues of what it means to be black, to be an American, and to be an artist. This exchange is destined to become a classic in the annals of American literature.

THE POET
Ralph Waldo Emerson

The Poet

*A moody child and wildly wise
Pursued the game with joyful eyes,
Which chose, like meteors, their way,
And rived the dark with private ray:
They overleapt the horizon's edge,
Searched with Apollo's privilege;
Through man, and woman, and sea, and star
Saw the dance of nature forward far;
Through worlds, and races, and terms, and times
Saw musical order, and pairing rhymes.*

*Olympian bards who sung
Divine ideas below,
Which always find us young.
And always keep us so.*

Those who are esteemed umpires of taste are often persons who have acquired some knowledge of admired pictures or sculptures, and have an inclination for whatever is elegant; but if you inquire whether they are beautiful souls, and whether their own acts are like fair pictures, you learn that they are selfish and sensual. Their cultivation is local, as if you should rub a log of dry wood in one spot to produce fire, all the rest remaining cold. Their knowledge of the fine arts is some study of rules and particulars, or some limited judgment of color or form, which is exercised for amusement or for show. It is a proof of the shallowness of the doctrine of beauty as it lies in the minds of our amateurs, that men seem to have lost the perception of the instant dependence of form upon soul. There is no doctrine of forms in our philosophy. We were put into our bodies, as fire is put into a pan to be carried about; but there is no accurate adjust-

SOURCE: Ralph Waldo Emerson, "The Poet," *The Complete Works of Ralph Waldo Emerson*, III, ed. Edward Waldo Emerson (Boston: Houghton Mifflin Company, 1903-4), pp. 3-42.

ment between the spirit and the organ, much less is the latter the germination of the former. So in regard to other forms, the intellectual men do not believe in [3] any essential dependence of the material world on thought and volition. Theologians think it a pretty air-castle to talk of the spiritual meaning of a ship or a cloud, of a city or a contract, but they prefer to come again to the solid ground of historical evidence; and even the poets are contented with a civil and conformed manner of living, and to write poems from the fancy, at a safe distance from their own experience. But the highest minds of the world have never ceased to explore the double meaning, or shall I say the quadruple or the centuple or much more manifold meaning, of every sensuous fact; Orpheus, Empedocles, Heraclitus, Plato, Plutarch, Dante, Swedenborg, and the masters of sculpture, picture and poetry. For we are not pans and barrows, nor even porters of the fire and torch-bearers, but children of the fire, made of it, and only the same divinity transmuted and at two or three removes, when we know least about it. And this hidden truth, that the fountains whence all this river of Time and its creatures floweth are intrinsically ideal and beautiful, draws us to the consideration of the nature and functions of the Poet, or the man of Beauty, to the means and materials he uses, and to the general aspect of the art in the present time. [4]

The breadth of the problem is great, for the poet is representative. He stands among partial men for the complete man, and apprises us not of his wealth, but of the common wealth. The young man reveres men of genius, because, to speak truly, they are more himself than he is. They receive of the soul as he also receives, but they more. Nature enhances her beauty, to the eye of loving men, from their belief that the poet is beholding her shows at the same time. He is isolated among his contemporaries by truth and by his art, but with this consolation in his pursuits, that they will draw all men sooner or later. For all men live by truth and stand in need of expression. In love, in art, in avarice, in politics, in labor, in games, we study to utter our painful secret. The man is only half himself, the other half is his expression.

Notwithstanding this necessity to be published, adequate expression is rare. I know not how it is that we need an interpreter, but the great majority of men seem to be minors, who have not yet come into possession of their own, or mutes, who cannot report the conversation they have had with nature. There is no man who does not anticipate a supersensual utility in the sun and stars, earth and water. These [5] stand and wait to render him a peculiar service. But there is some obstruction or some excess of phlegm in our constitution, which does not suffer them to yield the due effect. Too feeble fall the impressions of nature on us to make us artists. Every touch should thrill. Every man should be so much an artist that he could report in conversation what had befallen him. Yet, in our experience, the rays or appulses have sufficient force to arrive at the senses, but not enough to reach the quick and compel the reproduction of themselves in speech. The poet is the person in whom these powers are in balance, the man without impediment, who sees and handles that which others dream of, traverses the whole scale of experience, and is representative of man, in virtue of being the largest power to receive and to impart.

For the Universe has three children, born at one time, which reappear under different names in every system of thought, whether they be called cause, operation and effect; or, more poetically, Jove, Pluto, Neptune; or, theologically, the Father, the Spirit and the Son; but which we will call here the Knower, the Doer and the Sayer. These stand respectively for the love of truth, for the love of good, and for [6] the love of beauty. These three are equal. Each is that which he is, essentially, so that he cannot be surmounted or analyzed, and each of these three has the power of the others latent in him and his own, patent.

The poet is the sayer, the namer, and represents beauty. He is a sovereign, and stands on the centre. For the world is not painted or adorned, but is from the beginning beautiful; and God has not made some beautiful things, but Beauty is the creator of the universe. Therefore the poet is not any permissive potentate, but is emperor in his own right. Criticism is infested with a cant of materialism, which assumes that manual skill and activity is the first merit of all men, and disparages such as say and do not, overlooking the fact that some men, namely poets, are natural sayers, sent into the world to the end of expression, and confounds them with those whose province is action but who quit it to imitate the sayers. But Homer's words are as costly and admirable to Homer as Agamemnon's victories are to Agamemnon. The poet does not wait for the hero or the sage, but, as they act and think primarily, so he writes primarily what will and must be spoken, reckoning the others, though primaries also, yet, [7] in respect to him, secondaries and servants; as sitters or models in the studio of a painter, or as assistants who bring building-materials to an architect.

For poetry was all written before time was, and whenever we are so finely organized that we can penetrate into that region where the air is music, we hear those primal warblings and attempt to write them down, but we lose ever and anon a word or a verse and substitute something of our own, and thus miswrite the poem. The men of more delicate ear write down these cadences more faithfully, and these transcripts, though imperfect, become the songs of the nations. For nature is as truly beautiful as it is good, or as it is reasonable, and must as much appear as it must be done, or be known. Words and deeds are quite indifferent modes of the divine energy. Words are also actions, and actions are a kind of words.

The sign and credentials of the poet are that he announces that which no man foretold. He is the true and only doctor; he knows and tells; he is the only teller of news, for he was present and privy to the appearance which he describes. He is a beholder of ideas and an utterer of the necessary and causal. For we do not speak now [8] of men of poetical talents, or of industry and skill in metre, but of the true poet. I took part in a conversation the other day concerning a recent writer of lyrics, a man of subtle mind, whose head appeared to be a music-box of delicate tunes and rhythms, and whose skill and command of language we could not sufficiently praise. But when the question arose whether he was not only a lyrist but a poet, we were obliged to confess that he is plainly a contemporary, not an eternal man. He does not stand out of our low limitations, like a Chimborazo under the line, running up from a torrid base through all the climates of the globe, with belts of the herbage of every latitude on its high and mottled sides; but this genius is the landscape-garden of a modern house, adorned with fountains and statues, with well-bred men and women standing and sitting in the walks and terraces. We hear, through all the varied music, the groundtone of conventional life. Our poets are men of talents who sing, and not the children of music. The argument is secondary, the finish of the verses is primary.

For it is not metres, but a metre-making argument that makes a poem,—a thought so passionate and alive that like the spirit of a plant [9] or an animal it has an architecture of its own, and adorns nature with a new thing. The thought and the form are equal in the order of time, but in the order of genesis the thought is prior to the form. The poet has a new thought; he has a whole new experience to unfold; he will tell us how it was with him, and all men will be the richer in his fortune. For the experience of each new age requires a new confession, and the world seems always waiting for its poet. I remember when I was young how much I was moved one morning by tidings that genius had appeared in a youth who sat near me at table. He had left his work and gone rambling none knew whither, and had written hundreds of lines, but could not tell whether that which was in him was therein told; he could tell nothing but that all was changed, —man, beast, heaven, earth and sea. How gladly we listened! how credulous! Society seemed to be compromised. We sat in the aurora of a sunrise which was to put out all the stars. Boston seemed to be at twice the distance it had the night before, or was much farther than that. Rome,—what was Rome? Plutarch and Shakspeare were in the yellow leaf, and Homer no more should be heard of. It is much to know that poetry has been written this [10] very day, under this very roof, by your side. What! that wonderful spirit has not expired! These stony moments are still sparkling and animated! I had fancied that the oracles were all silent, and nature had spent her fires; and behold! all night, from every pore, these fine auroras have been streaming. Every one has some interest in the advent of the poet, and no one knows how much it may concern him. We know that the secret of the world is profound, but who or what shall be our interpreter, we know not. A mountain ramble, a new style of face, a new person, may put the key into our hands. Of course the value of genius to us is in the veracity of its report. Talent may frolic and juggle; genius realizes and adds. Mankind in good earnest have availed so far in understanding themselves and their work, that the foremost watchman on the peak announces his news. It is the truest word ever spoken, and the phrase will be the fittest, most musical, and the unerring voice of the world for that time.

All that we call sacred history attests that the birth of a poet is the principal event in chronology. Man, never so often deceived, still watches for the arrival of a brother who can hold him steady to a truth until he has made it his own. [11] With what joy I begin to read a poem which I confide in as an inspiration! And now my chains are to be broken; I shall mount above these clouds and opaque airs in which I live,—opaque, though they seem transparent,—and from the heaven of truth I shall see and comprehend my relations. That will reconcile me to life and renovate nature, to see trifles animated by a tendency, and to know what I am doing. Life will no more be a noise; now I shall see men and women, and know the signs by which they may be discerned from fools and satans. This day shall be better than my birthday: then I became an animal; now I am invited into the science of the real. Such is the hope, but the fruition is postponed. Oftener it falls that this winged man, who will carry me into the heaven, whirls me into mists, then leaps and frisks about with me as it were from cloud to cloud, still affirming that he is bound heavenward; and I, being myself a novice, am slow in perceiving that he does not know the way into the heavens, and is merely bent that I should admire his skill to rise like a fowl or a flying fish, a little way from the ground or the water; but the all-piercing, all-feeding and ocular air of heaven that man shall never inhabit. I tumble down [12] again soon into my old nooks, and lead the life of exaggerations as before, and have lost my faith in the possibility of any guide who can lead me thither where I would be.

But, leaving these victims of vanity, let us, with new hope, observe how nature, by worthier impulses, has insured the poet's fidelity to his office of announcement and affirming, namely by the beauty of things, which becomes a new and higher beauty when expressed. Nature offers all her creatures to him as a picture-language. Being used as a type, a second wonderful value appears in the object, far better than its old value; as the carpenter's stretched cord, if you hold your ear close enough, is musical in the breeze. "Things more excellent than every image," says Jamblichus, "are expressed through images." Things admit of being used as symbols because nature is a symbol, in the whole, and in every part. Every line we can draw in the sand has expression; and there is no body without its spirit or genius. All form is an effect of character; all condition, of the quality of the life; all harmony, of health; and for this reason a perception of beauty should be sympathetic, or proper only to the good. The beautiful rests on the foundations of the necessary. [13] The soul makes the body, as the wise Spenser teaches:—

> So every spirit, as it is more pure,
> And hath in it the more of heavenly light,
> So it the fairer body doth procure

> To habit in, and it more fairly dight,
> With cheerful grace and amiable sight.
> For, of the soul, the body form doth take,
> For soul is form, and doth the body make.

Here we find ourselves suddenly not in a critical speculation but in a holy place, and should go very warily and reverently. We stand before the secret of the world, there where Being passes into Appearance and Unity into Variety.

The Universe is the externization of the soul. Wherever the life is, that bursts into appearance around it. Our science is sensual, and therefore superficial. The earth and the heavenly bodies, physics and chemistry, we sensually treat, as if they were self-existent; but these are the retinue of that Being we have. "The mighty heaven," said Proclus, "exhibits, in its transfigurations, clear images of the splendor of intellectual perceptions; being moved in conjunction with the unapparent periods of intellectual natures." Therefore science always goes abreast with the just elevation of the man, keeping step with [14] religion and metaphysics; or the state of science is an index of our self-knowledge. Since every thing in nature answers to a moral power, if any phenomenon remains brute and dark it is because the corresponding faculty in the observer is not yet active.

No wonder then, if these waters be so deep, that we hover over them with a religious regard. The beauty of the fable proves the importance of the sense; to the poet, and to all others; or, if you please, every man is so far a poet as to be susceptible of these enchantments of nature; for all men have the thoughts whereof the universe is the celebration. I find that the fascination resides in the symbol. Who loves nature? Who does not? Is it only poets, and men of leisure and cultivation, who live with her? No; but also hunters, farmers, grooms and butchers, though they express their affection in their choice of life and not in their choice of words. The writer wonders what the coachman or the hunter values in riding, in horses and dogs. It is not superficial qualities. When you talk with him he holds these at as slight a rate as you. His worship is sympathetic; he has no definitions, but he is commanded in nature by the living power which he feels to be there present. [15] No imitation or playing of these things would content him; he loves the earnest of the north wind, of rain, of stone and wood and iron. A beauty not explicable is dearer than a beauty which we can see to the end of. It is nature the symbol, nature certifying the supernatural, body overflowed by life which he worships with coarse but sincere rites.

The inwardness and mystery of this attachment drive men of every class to the use of emblems. The schools of poets and philosophers are not more intoxicated with their symbols than the populace with theirs. In our political parties, compute the power of badges and emblems. See the great ball which they roll from Baltimore to Bunker Hill! In the political processions, Lowell goes in a loom, and Lynn in a shoe, and Salem in a ship. Witness the cider-barrel, the log-cabin, the hickory-stick, the palmetto, and all the cognizances of party. See the power of national emblems. Some stars, lilies, leopards, a crescent, a lion, an eagle, or other figure which came into credit God knows how, on an old rag of bunting, blowing in the wind on a fort at the ends of the earth, shall make the blood tingle under the rudest or the most conventional exterior. The people fancy [16] they hate poetry, and they are all poets and mystics!

Beyond this universality of the symbolic language, we are apprised of the divineness of this superior use of things, whereby the world is a temple whose walls are covered with emblems, pictures and commandments of the Deity,—in this, that there is no fact in nature which does not carry the whole sense of nature; and the distinctions which we make in events and in affairs, of low and high, honest and base, disappear when nature is used as a symbol. Thought makes everything fit for use. The vocabulary of an omniscient man would embrace words and images excluded from polite conversation. What would be base, or even obscene, to the obscene, becomes illustrious, spoken in a new connection of thought. The piety of the Hebrew prophets purges their grossness. The circumcision is an example of the power of poetry to raise the low and offensive. Small and mean things serve as well as great symbols. The meaner the type by which a law is expressed, the more pungent it is, and the more lasting in the memories of men; just as we choose the smallest box or case in which any needful utensil can be carried. Bare lists of words are found [17] suggestive to an imaginative and excited mind; as it is related of Lord Chatham that he was accustomed to read in Bailey's Dictionary when he was preparing to speak in Parliament. The poorest experience is rich enough for all the purposes of expressing thought. Why covet a knowledge of new facts? Day and night, house and garden, a few books, a few actions, serve us as well as would all trades and all spectacles. We are far from having exhausted the significance of the few symbols we use. We can come to use them yet with a terrible simplicity. It does not need that a poem should be long. Every word was once a poem. Every new relation is a new word. Also we use defects and deformities to a sacred purpose, so expressing our sense that the evils of the world are such only to the evil eye. In the old mythology, mythologists observe, defects are ascribed to divine natures, as lameness to Vulcan, blindness to Cupid, and the like,—to signify exuberances.

For as it is dislocation and detachment from the life of God that makes things ugly, the poet, who re-attaches things to nature and the Whole,—re-attaching even artificial things and violation of nature, to nature, by a deeper insight,—disposes very easily of the most disagreeable [18] facts. Readers of poetry see the factory-village and the railway, and fancy that the poetry of the landscape is broken up by these; for these works of art are not yet consecrated in their reading; but the poet sees them fall within the great Order not less than the beehive or the spider's geometrical web. Nature adopts them very fast into her vital circles, and the gliding train of cars she loves like her own. Besides, in a centred mind, it signifies nothing how many mechanical inventions you exhibit. Though you add millions, and never so surprising, the fact of mechanics has not gained a grain's weight. The spiritual fact remains unalterable, by many or by few particulars; as no mountain is of any appreciable height to break the curve of the sphere. A shrewd country-boy goes to the city for the first time, and the complacent citizen is not satisfied with his little wonder. It is not that he does not see all the fine houses and know that he never saw such before, but he disposes of them as easily as the poet finds place for the railway. The chief value of the new fact is to enhance the great and constant fact of Life, which can dwarf any and every circumstance, and to which the belt of wampum and the commerce of America are alike. [19]

The world being thus put under the mind for verb and noun, the poet is he who can articulate it. For though life is great, and fascinates and absorbs; and though all men are intelligent of the symbols through which it is named; yet they cannot originally use them. We are symbols and inhabit symbols; workmen, work, and tools, words and things, birth and death, all are emblems; but we sympathize with the symbols, and being infatuated with the economical uses of things, we do not know that they are thoughts. The poet, by an ulterior intellectual perception, gives them a power which makes their old use forgotten, and puts eyes and a tongue into every dumb and inanimate object. He perceives the independence of the thought on the symbol, the stability of the thought, the accidency and fugacity of the symbol. As the eyes of Lyncæus were said to see through the earth, so the poet turns the world to glass, and shows us all things in their right series and procession. For through that better perception he stands one step nearer to things, and sees the flowing or metamorphosis; perceives that thought is multiform; that within the form of every creature is a force impelling it to ascend into a higher form; and following with his eyes the life, uses the forms [20] which express that life, and so his speech flows with the flowing of nature. All the facts of the animal economy, sex, nutriment, gestation, birth, growth, are symbols of the passage of the world into the soul of man, to suffer there a change and reappear a new and higher fact. He uses forms according to the life, and not according to the form. This is true science. The poet alone knows astronomy, chemistry, vegetation and animation, for he does not stop at these facts, but employs them as signs. He knows why the plain or meadow of space was strown with these flowers we call suns and moons and stars; why the great deep is adorned with animals, with men, and gods; for in every word he speaks he rides on them as the horses of thought.

By virtue of this science the poet is the Namer or Language-maker, naming things sometimes after their appearance, sometimes after their essence, and giving to every one its own name and not another's, thereby rejoicing the intellect, which delights in detachment or boundary. The poets made all the words, and therefore language is the archives of history, and, if we must say it, a sort of tomb of the muses. For though the origin of most of our words is forgotten, each [21] word was at first a stroke of genius, and obtained currency because for the moment it symbolized the world to the first speaker and to the hearer. The etymologist finds the deadest word to have been once a brilliant picture. Language is fossil poetry. As the limestone of the continent consists of infinite masses of the shells of animalcules, so language is made up of images or tropes, which now, in their secondary use, have long ceased to remind us of their poetic origin. But the poet names the thing because he sees it, or comes one step nearer to it than any other. This expression or naming is not art, but a second nature, grown out of the first, as a leaf out of a tree. What we call nature is a certain self-regulated motion or change; and nature does all things by her own hands, and does not leave another to baptize her but baptizes herself; and this through the metamorphosis again. I remember that a certain poet described it to me thus:—

> Genius is the activity which repairs the decays of things, whether wholly or partly of a material and finite kind. Nature, through all her kingdoms, insures herself. Nobody cares for planting the poor fungus; so she shakes down from [22] the gills of one agaric countless spores, any one of which, being preserved, transmits new billions of spores to-morrow or next day. The new agaric of this hour has a chance which the old one had not. This atom of seed is thrown into a new place, not subject to the accidents which destroyed its parent two rods off. She makes a man; and having brought him to ripe age, she will no longer run the risk of losing this wonder at a blow, but she detaches from him a new self, that the kind may be safe from accidents to which the individual is exposed. So when the soul of the poet has come to ripeness of thought, she detaches and sends away from it its poems or songs,—a fearless, sleepless, deathless progeny, which is not exposed to the accidents of the weary kingdom of time; a fearless, vivacious offspring, clad with wings (such was the virtue of the soul out of which they came) which carry them fast and far, and infix them irrecoverably into the hearts of men. These wings are the beauty of the poet's soul. The songs, thus flying immortal from their mortal parent, are pursued by clamorous flights of censures, which swarm in far greater numbers and threaten to devour them; but these last are not winged. At the end of a very short leap [23] they fall plump down and rot, having received from the souls out of which they came no beautiful wings. But the melodies of the poet ascend and leap and pierce into the deeps of infinite time.

So far the bard taught me, using his freer speech. But nature has a higher end, in the production of new individuals, than security, namely *ascension,* or the passage of the soul into higher forms. I knew in my younger days the sculptor who made the statue of the youth which stands in the public garden. He was, as I remember, unable to tell directly what made him happy or unhappy, but by wonderful indirections he could tell. He rose one day, according to his habit, before the dawn, and saw the morning break, grand as the eternity out of which it came, and for many days after, he strove to express this tranquillity, and lo! his chisel had fashioned out of marble the form of a beautiful youth, Phosphorus, whose aspect is such that it is said all persons who look on it become silent. The poet also resigns himself to his mood, and that thought which agitated him is expressed, but *alter idem,* in a manner totally new. The expression is organic, or the new type which things themselves take when liberated. As, in the [24] sun, objects paint their images on the retina of the eye, so they, sharing the aspiration of the whole universe, tend to paint a far more delicate copy of their essence in his mind. Like the metamorphosis of things into higher organic forms is their change into melodies. Over everything stands its dæmon or soul, and, as the form of the thing is reflected by the eye, so the soul of the thing is reflected by a melody. The sea, the mountain-ridge, Niagara, and every flower-bed, pre-exist, or super-exist, in pre-cantations, which sail like odors in the air, and when any man goes by with an ear sufficiently fine, he overhears them and endeavors to write down the notes without diluting or depraving them. And herein is the legitimation of criticism, in the mind's faith that the poems are a corrupt version of some text in nature with which they ought to be made to tally. A rhyme in one of our sonnets should not be less pleasing than the iterated nodes of a seashell, or the resembling difference of a group of flowers. The pairing of the birds is an idyl, not tedious as our idyls are; a tempest is a rough ode, without falsehood or rant; a summer, with its harvest sown, reaped and stored, is an epic song, subordinating how many admirably executed [25] parts. Why should not the symmetry and truth that modulate these, glide into our spirits, and we participate the invention of nature?

This insight, which expresses itself by what is called Imagination, is a very high sort of seeing, which does not come by study, but by the intellect being where and what it sees; by sharing the path or circuit of things through forms, and so making them translucid to others. The path of things is silent. Will they suffer a speaker to go with them? A spy they will not suffer; a lover, a poet, is the transcendency of their own nature,—him they will suffer. The condition of true naming, on the poet's part, is his resigning himself to the divine *aura* which breathes through forms, and accompanying that.

It is a secret which every intellectual man quickly learns, that beyond the energy of his possessed and conscious intellect he is capable of a new energy (as of an intellect doubled on itself), by abandonment to the nature of things; that beside his privacy of power as an individual man, there is a great public power on which he can draw, by unlocking, at all risks, his human doors, and suffering the ethereal tides to roll and circulate through him; then he is caught up into the life of the Universe, his speech is thunder, [26] his thought is law, and his words are universally intelligible as the plants and animals. The poet knows that he speaks adequately then only when he speaks somewhat wildly, or "with the flower of the mind"; not with the intellect used as an organ, but with the intellect released from all service and suffered to take its direction from its celestial life; or as the ancients were wont to express themselves, not with intellect alone but with the intellect inebriated by nectar. As the traveller who has lost his way throws his reins on his horse's neck and trusts to the instinct of the animal to find his road, so must we do with the divine animal who carries us through this world. For if in any manner we can stimulate this instinct, new passages are opened for us into nature; the mind flows into and through things hardest and highest, and the metamorphosis is possible.

This is the reason why bards love wine, mead, narcotics, coffee, tea, opium, the fumes of sandalwood and tobacco, or whatever other procurers of animal exhilaration. All men avail themselves of such means as they can, to add this extraordinary power to their normal powers; and to this end they prize conversation, music, pictures, sculpture, dancing, theatres, travelling, war, mobs, [27] fires, gaming, politics, or love, or science, or animal intoxication,—which are several coarser or finer *quasi*-mechanical substitutes for the true nectar, which is the ravishment of the intellect by coming nearer to the fact. These are auxiliaries to the centrifugal tendency of a man, to his passage out into free space, and they help him to escape the custody of that body in which he is pent up, and of that jail-yard of individual relations in which he is enclosed. Hence a great number of such as were professionally expressers of Beauty, as painters, poets, musicians and actors, have been more than others wont to lead a life of pleasure and indulgence; all but the few who received the true nectar; and, as it was a spurious mode of attaining freedom, as it was an emancipation not into the heavens but into the freedom of baser places, they were punished for that advantage they won, by a dissipation and deterioration. But never can any advantage be taken of nature by a trick. The spirit of the world, the great calm presence of the Creator, comes not forth to the sorceries of opium or of wine. The sublime vision comes to the pure and simple soul in a clean and chaste body. That is not an inspiration, which we owe to narcotics, but some counterfeit excitement and fury. [28] Milton says that the lyric poet may drink wine and live generously, but the epic poet, he who shall sing of the gods and their descent unto men, must drink water out of a wooden bowl. For poetry is not "Devil's wine," but God's wine. It is with this as it is with toys. We fill the hands and nurseries of our children with all manner of dolls, drums and horses; withdrawing their eyes from the plain face and sufficing objects of nature, the sun and moon, the animals, the water and stones, which should be their toys. So the poet's habit of living should be set on a key so low that the common influences should delight him. His cheerfulness should be the gift of the sunlight; the air should suffice for his inspiration, and he should be tipsy with water. That spirit which suffices quiet hearts, which seems to come forth to such from every dry knoll of sere grass, from every pine stump and half-imbedded stone on which the dull March sun shines, comes forth to the poor and hungry, and such as are of simple taste. If thou fill thy brain with Boston and New York, with fashion and covetousness, and wilt stimulate thy jaded senses with wine and French coffee, thou shalt find no radiance of wisdom in the lonely waste of the pine woods. [29]

If the imagination intoxicates the poet, it is not inactive in other men. The metamorphosis excites in the beholder an emotion of joy. The use of symbols has a certain power of emancipation and exhilaration for all men. We seem to be touched by a wand which makes us dance and run about happily, like children. We are like persons who come out of a cave or cellar into the open air. This is the effect on us of tropes, fables, oracles and all poetic forms. Poets are thus liberating gods. Men have really got a new sense, and found within their world another world, or nest of worlds; for, the metamorphosis once seen, we divine that it does not stop. I will not now consider how much this makes the charm of algebra and the mathematics, which also have their tropes, but it is felt in every definition; as when Aristotle defines *space* to be an immovable vessel in which things are contained;—or when Plato defines a *line* to be a flowing point; or *figure* to be a bound of solid; and many the like. What a joyful sense of freedom we have when Vitruvius announces the old opinion of artists that no architect can build any house well who does not know something of anatomy. When Socrates, in Charmides, tells us that the soul is cured of its maladies by certain [30] incantations, and that these incantations are beautiful reasons, from which temperance is generated in souls; when Plato calls the world an animal, and Timæus affirms that the plants also are animals; or affirms a man to be a heavenly tree, growing with his root, which is his head, upward; and, as George Chapman, following him, writes,

> So in our tree of man, whose nervie root
> Springs in his top; . . .

when Orpheus speaks of hoariness as "that white flower which marks extreme old age"; when Proclus calls the universe the statue of the intellect; when Chaucer, in his praise of "Gentilesse," compares good blood in mean condition to fire, which, though carried to the darkest house betwixt this and the mount of Caucasus, will yet hold its natural office and burn as bright as if twenty thousand men did it behold; when John saw, in the Apocalypse, the ruin of the world through evil, and the stars fall from heaven as the fig tree casteth her untimely fruit; when Aesop reports the whole catalogue of common daily relations through the masquerade of birds and beasts;—we take the cheerful hint of the immortality of our essence and its versatile habit and escapes, as when the gypsies say of themselves "it is in vain to hang them, they cannot die." [31]

The poets are thus liberating gods. The ancient British bards had for the title of their order, "Those who are free throughout the world." They are free, and they make free. An imaginative book renders us much more service at first, by stimulating us through its tropes, than afterward when we arrive at the precise sense of the author. I think nothing is of any value in books excepting the transcendental and extraordinary. If a man is inflamed and carried away by his thought, to that degree that he forgets the authors and the public and heeds only this one dream which holds him like an insanity, let me read his paper, and you may have all the arguments and histories and criticism. All the value which attaches to Pythagoras, Paracelsus, Cornelius Agrippa, Cardan, Kepler, Swedenborg, Schelling, Oken, or any other who introduces questionable facts into his cosmogony, as angels, devils, magic, astrology, palmistry, mesmerism, and so on, is the certificate we have of departure from routine, and that here is a new witness. That also is the best success in conversation, the magic of liberty, which puts the world like a ball in our hands. How cheap even the liberty then seems; how mean to study, when an emotion communicates to the [32] intellect the power to sap and upheave nature; how great the perspective! nations, times, systems, enter and disappear like threads in tapestry of large figure and many colors; dream delivers us to dream, and while the drunkenness lasts we will sell our bed, our philosophy, our religion, in our opulence.

There is good reason why we should prize this liberation. The fate of the poor shepherd, who, blinded and lost in the snow-storm, perishes in a drift within a few feet of his cottage door, is an emblem of the state of man. On the brink of the waters of life and truth, we are miserably dying. The inaccessibleness of every thought but that we are in, is wonderful. What if you come near to it; you are as remote when you are nearest as when you are farthest. Every thought is also a prison; every heaven is also a prison. Therefore we love the poet, the inventor, who in any form, whether in an ode or in an action or in looks and behavior, has yielded us a new thought. He unlocks our chains and admits us to a new scene.

This emancipation is dear to all men, and the power to impart it, as it must come from greater depth and scope of thought, is a measure of intellect. Therefore all books of the imagination [33] endure, all which ascend to that truth that the writer sees nature beneath him, and uses it as his exponent. Every verse or sentence possessing this virtue will take care of its own immortality. The religions of the world are the ejaculations of a few imaginative men.

But the quality of the imagination is to flow, and not to freeze. The poet did not stop at the color or the form, but read their meaning; neither may he rest in this meaning, but he makes the same objects exponents of his new thought. Here is the difference betwixt the poet and the mystic, that the last nails a symbol to one sense, which was a true sense for a moment, but soon becomes old and false. For all symbols are fluxional; all language is vehicular and transitive, and is good, as ferries and horses are, for conveyance, not as farms and houses are, for homestead. Mysticism consists in the mistake of an accidental and individual symbol for an universal one. The morning-redness happens to be the favorite meteor to the eyes of Jacob Behmen, and comes to stand to him for truth and faith; and, he believes, should stand for the same realities to every reader. But the first reader prefers as naturally the symbol of a mother and child, or a gardener [34] and his bulb, or a jeweller polishing a gem. Either of these, or of a myriad more, are equally good to the person to whom they are significant. Only they must be held lightly, and be very willingly translated into the equivalent terms which others use. And the mystic must be steadily told,—All that you say is just as true without the tedious use of that symbol as with it. Let us have a little algebra, instead of this trite rhetoric,—universal signs, instead of these village symbols,—and we shall both be gainers. The history of hierarchies seems to show that all religious error consisted in making the symbol too stark and solid, and was at last nothing but an excess of the organ of language.

Swedenborg, of all men in the recent ages, stands eminently for the translator of nature into thought. I do not know the man in history to whom things stood so uniformly for words. Before him the metamorphosis continually plays. Everything on which his eye rests, obeys the impulses of moral nature. The figs become grapes whilst he eats them. When some of his angels affirmed a truth, the laurel twig which they held blossomed in their hands. The noise which at a distance appeared like gnashing and thumping, on coming nearer was found to be [35] the voice of disputants. The men in one of his visions, seen in heavenly light, appeared like dragons, and seemed in darkness; but to each other they appeared as men, and when the light from heaven shone into their cabin, they complained of the darkness, and were compelled to shut the window that they might see.

There was this perception in him which makes the poet or seer an object of awe and terror, namely that the same man or society of men may wear one aspect to themselves and their companions, and a different aspect to higher intelligences. Certain priests, whom he describes as conversing very learnedly together, appeared to the children who were at some distance, like dead horses; and many the like misappearances. And instantly the mind inquires whether these fishes under the bridge, yonder oxen in the pasture, those dogs in the yard, are immutably fishes, oxen and dogs, or only so appear to me, and perchance to themselves appear upright men; and whether I appear as a man to all eyes. The Brahmins and Pythagoras propounded the same question, and if any poet has witnessed the transformation he doubtless found it in harmony with various experiences. We have all seen changes as considerable in wheat and caterpillars. [36] He is the poet and shall draw us with love and terror, who sees through the flowing vest the firm nature, and can declare it.

I look in vain for the poet whom I describe. We do not with sufficient plainness or sufficient profoundness address ourselves to life, nor dare we chaunt our own times and social circumstance. If we filled the day with bravery, we should not shrink from celebrating it. Time and nature yield us many gifts, but not yet the timely man, the new religion, the reconciler, whom all things await. Dante's praise is that he dared to write his autobiography in colossal cipher, or into universality. We have yet had no genius in America, with tyrannous eye, which knew the value of our incomparable materials, and saw, in the barbarism and materialism of the times, another carnival of the same gods whose picture he so much admires in Homer; then in the Middle Age; then in Calvinism. Banks and tariffs, the newspaper and caucus, Methodism and Unitarianism, are flat and dull to dull people, but rest on the same foundations of wonder as the town of Troy and the temple of Delphi, and are as swiftly passing away. Our log-rolling, our stumps and their politics, our fisheries, our Negroes and Indians, our boats and our repudiations, the wrath [37] of rogues and the pusillanimity of honest men, the northern trade, the southern planting, the western clearing, Oregon and Texas, are yet unsung. Yet America is a poem in our eyes; its ample geography dazzles the imagination, and it will not wait long for metres. If I have not found that excellent combination of gifts in my countrymen which I seek, neither could I aid myself to fix the idea of the poet by reading now and then in Chalmers's collection of five centuries of English poets. These are wits more than poets, though there have been poets among them.

But when we adhere to the ideal of the poet, we have our difficulties even with Milton and Homer. Milton is too literary, and Homer too literal and historical.

But I am not wise enough for a national criticism, and must use the old largeness a little longer, to discharge my errand from the muse to the poet concerning his art.

Art is the path of the creator to his work. The paths or methods are ideal and eternal, though few men ever see them; not the artist himself for years, or for a lifetime, unless he come into the conditions. The painter, the sculptor, the composer, the epic rhapsodist, the orator, all partake one desire, namely to express [38] themselves symmetrically and abundantly, not dwarfishly and fragmentarily. They found or put themselves in certain conditions, as, the painter and sculptor before some impressive human figures; the orator into the assembly of the people; and the others in such scenes as each has found exciting to his intellect; and each presently feels the new desire. He hears a voice, he sees a beckoning. Then he is apprised, with wonder, what herds of dæmons hem him in. He can no more rest; he says, with the old painter, "By God it is in me and must go forth of me." He pursues a beauty, half seen, which flies before him. The poet pours out verses in every solitude. Most of the things he says are conventional, no doubt; but by and by he says something which is original and beautiful. That charms him. He would say nothing else but such things. In our way of talking we say "That is yours, this is mine"; but the poet knows well that is not his; that it is as strange and beautiful to him as to you; he would fain hear the like eloquence at length. Once having tasted this immortal ichor, he cannot have enough of it, and as an admirable creative power exists in these intellections, it is of the last importance that these things get spoken. What [39] a little of all we know is said! What drops of all the sea of our science are baled up! and by what accident it is that these are exposed, when so many secrets sleep in nature! Hence the necessity of speech and song; hence these throbs and heart-beatings in the orator, at the door of the assembly, to the end namely that thought may be ejaculated as Logos, or Word.

Doubt not, O poet, but persist. Say "It is in me, and shall out." Stand there, balked and dumb, stuttering and stammering, hissed and hooted, stand and strive, until at last rage draw out of thee that *dream*-power which every night shows thee is thine own; a power transcending all limit and privacy, and by virtue of which a man is the conductor of the whole river of electricity. Nothing walks, or creeps, or grows, or exists, which must not in turn arise and walk before him as exponent of his meaning. Comes he to that power, his genius is no longer exhaustible. All the creatures by pairs and by tribes pour into his mind as into a Noah's ark, to come forth again to people a new world. This is like the stock of air for our respiration or for the combustion of our fireplace; not a measure of gallons, but the entire atmosphere if wanted. And therefore the rich poets, as [40] Homer, Chaucer, Shakspeare, and Raphael, have obviously no limits to their works except the limits of their lifetime, and resemble a mirror carried through the street, ready to render an image of every created thing.

O poet! a new nobility is conferred in groves and pastures, and not in castles or by the sword-blade any longer. The conditions are hard, but equal. Thou shalt leave the world, and know the muse only. Thou shalt not know any longer the times, customs, graces, politics, or opinions of men, but shalt take all from the muse. For the time of towns is tolled from the world by funereal chimes, but in nature the universal hours are counted by succeeding tribes of animals and plants, and by growth of joy on joy. God wills also that thou abdicate a manifold and duplex life, and that thou be content that others speak for thee. Others shall be thy gentlemen and shall represent all courtesy and worldly life for thee; others shall do the great and resounding actions also. Thou shalt lie close hid with nature, and canst not be afforded to the Capitol or the Exchange. The world is full of renunciations and apprenticeships, and this is thine; thou must pass for a fool and a churl for a long season. This is the screen and sheath in [41] which Pan has protected his well-beloved flower, and thou shalt be known only to thine own, and they shall console thee with tenderest love. And thou shalt not be able to rehearse the names of thy friends in thy verse, for an old shame before the holy ideal. And this is the reward; that the ideal shall be real to thee, and the impressions of the actual world shall fall like summer rain, copious, but not troublesome to thy invulnerable essence. Thou shalt have the whole land for thy park and manor, the sea for thy bath and navigation, without tax and without envy; the woods and the rivers thou shalt own, and thou shalt possess that wherein others are only tenants and boarders. Thou true land-lord! sea-lord! air-lord! Wherever snow falls or water flows or birds fly, wherever day and night meet in twilight, wherever the blue heaven is hung by clouds or sown with stars, wherever are forms with transparent boundaries, wherever are outlets into celestial space, wherever is danger, and awe, and love,—there is Beauty, plenteous as rain, shed for thee, and though thou shouldst walk the world over, thou shalt not be able to find a condition inopportune or ignoble. [42]

TRADITION AND THE INDIVIDUAL TALENT
T. S. Eliot

In English writing we seldom speak of tradition, though we occasionally apply its name in deploring its absence. We cannot refer to "the tradition" or to "a tradition"; at most, we employ the adjective in saying that the poetry of So-and-so is "traditional" or even "too traditional." Seldom, perhaps, does the word appear except in a phrase of censure. If otherwise, it is vaguely approbative, with the implication, as to the work approved, of some pleasing archaeological reconstruction. You can hardly make the word agreeable to English ears without this comfortable reference to the reassuring science of archaeology.

Certainly the word is not likely to appear in our appreciations of living or dead writers. Every nation, every race, has not only its own creative, but its own critical turn of mind; and is even more oblivious of the shortcomings and limitations of its critical habits than of those of its creative genius. We know, or think we know, from the enormous mass of critical writing that has appeared in the French language the critical method or habit of the French; we only conclude (we are such unconscious people) that the French are "more critical" than we, and sometimes even plume ourselves a little with the fact, as if the French were the less spontaneous. Perhaps they are; but we might remind ourselves that criticism is as inevitable as breathing, and that we should be none the worse for articulating what passes in our minds when we read a book and feel an emotion about it, for criticizing our own minds in their work of criticism. One of the facts that might come to light in this process is our tendency to [3] insist, when we praise a poet, upon those aspects of his work in which he least resembles any one else. In these aspects or parts of his work we pretend to find what is individual, what is the peculiar essence of the man. We dwell with satisfaction upon the poet's difference from his predecessors, especially his immediate predecessors; we endeavour to find something that can be

SOURCE: T. S. Eliot, "Tradition and the Individual Talent," *Selected Essays*, New Edition. Copyright, 1932, 1936, 1950, by Harcourt Brace Jovanovich, Inc.; copyright 1960, 1964, by T. S. Eliot. Pp. 3–11 (1932 edition). Reprinted by permission of Harcourt Brace Jovanovich and Faber and Faber Ltd.

isolated in order to be enjoyed. Whereas if we approach a poet without this prejudice we shall often find that not only the best, but the most individual parts of his work may be those in which the dead poets, his ancestors, assert their immortality most vigorously. And I do not mean the impressionable period of adolescence, but the period of full maturity.

Yet if the only form of tradition, of handing down, consisted in following the ways of the immediate generation before us in a blind or timid adherence to its successes, "tradition" should positively be discouraged. We have seen many such simple currents soon lost in the sand; and novelty is better than repetition. Tradition is a matter of much wider significance. It cannot be inherited, and if you want it you must obtain it by great labour. It involves, in the first place, the historical sense, which we may call nearly indispensable to any one who would continue to be a poet beyond his twenty-fifth year; and the historical sense involves a perception, not only of the pastness of the past, but of its presence; the historical sense compels a man to write not merely with his own generation in his bones, but with a feeling that the whole of the literature of Europe from Homer and within it the whole of the literature of his own country has a simultaneous existence and composes a simultaneous order. This historical sense, which is a sense of the timeless as well as of the temporal and of the timeless and of the temporal together, is what makes a writer traditional. And it is at the same time what makes a writer most acutely conscious of his place in time, of his own contemporaneity.

No poet, no artist of any art, has his complete meaning alone. His significance, his appreciation is the appreciation of his relation to the dead poets and artists. You cannot value him alone; you must set him, for contrast and comparison, among the dead. I mean this as a principle of aesthetic, not merely historical, [4] criticism. The necessity that he shall conform, that he shall cohere, is not onesided; what happens when a new work of art is created is something that happens simultaneously to all the works of art which preceded it. The existing monuments form an ideal order among themselves, which is modified by the introduction of the new (the really new) work of art among them. The existing order is complete before the new work arrives; for order to persist after the supervention of novelty, the *whole* existing order must be, if ever so slightly, altered; and so the relations, proportions, values of each work of art toward the whole are readjusted; and this is conformity between the old and the new. Whoever has approved this idea of order, of the form of European, of English literature will not find it preposterous that the past should be altered by the present as much as the present is directed by the past. And the poet who is aware of this will be aware of great difficulties and responsibilities.

In a peculiar sense he will be aware also that he must inevitably be judged by the standards of the past. I say judged, not amputated, by them; not judged to be as good as, or worse or better than, the dead; and certainly not judged by the canons of dead critics. It is a judgment, a comparison, in which two things are measured by each other. To conform merely would be for the new work not really to conform at all; it would not be new, and would therefore not be a work of art. And we do not quite say that the new is more valuable because it fits in; but its fitting in is a test of its value—a test, it is true, which can only be slowly and cautiously applied, for we are none of us infallible judges of conformity. We say: it appears to conform, and is perhaps individual, or it appears individual, and may conform; but we are hardly likely to find that it is one and not the other.

To proceed to a more intelligible exposition of the relation of the poet to the past: he can neither take the past as a lump, an indiscriminate bolus, nor can he form himself wholly on one or two private admirations, nor can he form himself wholly upon one preferred period. The first course is inadmissible, the second is an important experience of youth, and the third is a pleasant and highly desirable supplement. The poet must be very conscious of the main current, which does not at all flow invariably [5] through the most distinguished reputations. He must be quite aware of the obvious fact that art never improves, but that the material of art is never quite the same. He must be aware that the mind of Europe—the mind of his own country—a mind which he learns in time to be much more important than his own private mind—is a mind which changes, and that this change is a development which abandons nothing *en route,* which does not superannuate either Shakespeare, or Homer, or the rock drawing of the Magdalenian draughtsmen. That this development, refinement perhaps, complication certainly, is not, from the point of view of the artist, any improvement. Perhaps not even an improvement from the point of view of the psychologist or not to the extent which we imagine; perhaps only in the end based upon a complication in economics and machinery. But the difference between the present and the past is that the conscious present is an awareness of the past in a way and to an extent which the past's awareness of itself cannot show.

Some one said: "The dead writers are remote from us because we *know* so much more than they did." Precisely, and they are that which we know.

I am alive to a usual objection to what is clearly part of my programme for the *métier* of poetry. The objection is that the doctrine requires a ridiculous amount of erudition (pedantry), a claim which can be rejected by appeal to the lives of poets in any pantheon. It will even be affirmed that much learning deadens or perverts poetic sensibility. While, however, we persist in believing that a poet ought to know as much as will not encroach upon his necessary receptivity and necessary laziness, it is not desirable to confine knowledge to whatever can be put into a useful shape for examinations, drawing-rooms, or the still more pretentious modes of publicity. Some can absorb knowledge, the more tardy must sweat for it. Shakespeare acquired more essential history from Plutarch than most men could from the whole British Museum. What is to be insisted upon is that the poet must develop or procure the consciousness of the past and that he should continue to develop this consciousness throughout his career.

What happens is a continual surrender of himself as he is at [6] the moment to something which is more valuable. The progress of an artist is a continual self-sacrifice, a continual extinction of personality.

There remains to define this process of depersonalization and its relation to the sense of tradition. It is in this depersonalization that art may be said to approach the condition of science. I, therefore, invite you to consider, as a suggestive analogy, the action which takes place when a bit of finely filiated platinum is introduced into a chamber containing oxygen and sulphur dioxide.

II

Honest criticism and sensitive appreciation are directed not upon the poet but upon the poetry. If we attend to the confused cries of the newspaper critics and the *susurrus* of popular repetition that follows, we shall hear the names of poets in great numbers; if we seek not Blue-book knowledge but the enjoyment of poetry, and ask for a poem, we shall seldom find it. I have tried to point out the importance of the relation of the poem to other poems by other authors, and suggested the conception of poetry as a living whole of all the poetry that has ever been written. The other aspect of this Impersonal theory of poetry is the relation of the poem to its author. And I hinted, by an analogy, that the mind of the mature poet differs from that of the immature one not precisely in any valuation of "personality," not being necessarily more interesting, or having "more to say," but rather by being a more finely perfected medium in which special, or very varied, feelings are at liberty to enter into new combinations.

The analogy was that of the catalyst. When the two gases previously mentioned are mixed in the presence of a filament of platinum, they form sulphurous acid. This combination takes place only if the platinum is present; nevertheless the newly formed acid contains no trace of platinum, and the platinum itself is apparently unaffected; has remained inert, neutral, and unchanged. The mind of the poet is the shred of platinum. It may partly or exclusively operate upon the experience of the man himself; but, the more perfect the artist, the more completely [7] separate in him will be the man who suffers and the mind which creates; the more perfectly will the mind digest and transmute the passions which are its material.

The experience, you will notice, the elements which enter the presence of the transforming catalyst, are of two kinds: emotions and feelings. The effect of a work of art upon the person who enjoys it is an experience different in kind from any experience not of art. It may be formed out of one emotion, or may be a combination of several; and various feelings, inhering for the writer in particular words or phrases or images, may be added to compose the final result. Or great poetry may be made without the direct use of any emotion whatever: composed out of feelings solely. Canto XV of the *Inferno* (Brunetto Latini) is a working up of the emotion evident in the situation; but the effect, though single as that of any work of art, is obtained by considerable complexity of detail. The last quatrain gives an image, a feeling attaching to an image, which "came," which did not develop simply out of what precedes, but which was probably in suspension in the poet's mind until the proper combination arrived for it to add itself to. The poet's mind is in fact a receptacle for seizing and storing up numberless feelings, phrases, images, which remain there until all the particles which can unite to form a new compound are present together.

If you compare several representative passages of the greatest poetry you see how great is the variety of types of combination, and also how completely any semi-ethical criterion of "sublimity" misses the mark. For it is not the "greatness," the intensity, of the emotions, the components, but the intensity of the artistic process, the pressure, so to speak, under which the fusion takes place, that counts. The episode of Paolo and Francesca employs a definite emotion, but the intensity of the poetry is something quite different from whatever intensity in the supposed experience it may give the impression of. It is no more intense, furthermore, than Canto XXVI, the voyage of Ulysses, which has not the direct dependence upon an emotion. Great variety is possible in the process of transmutation of emotion: the murder of Agamemnon, or the agony of Othello, gives an artistic effect apparently closer to a possible original than the scenes from Dante. [8] In the *Agamemnon*, the artistic emotion approximates to the emotion of an actual spectator; in *Othello* to the emotion of the protagonist himself. But the difference between art and the event is always absolute; the combination which is the murder of Agamemnon is probably as complex as that which is the voyage of Ulysses. In either case there has been a fusion of elements. The ode of Keats contains a number of feelings which have nothing particular to do with the nightingale, but which the nightingale, partly, perhaps, because of its attractive name, and partly because of its reputation, served to bring together.

The point of view which I am struggling to attack is perhaps related to the metaphysical theory of the substantial unity of the soul: for my meaning is, that the poet has, not a "personality" to express, but a particular medium, which is only a medium and not a personality, in which impressions and experiences combine in peculiar and unexpected ways. Impressions and experiences which are important for the man may take no place in the poetry, and those which become important in the poetry may play quite a negligible part in the man, the personality.

I will quote a passage which is unfamiliar enough to be regarded with fresh attention in the light—or darkness—of these observations:

> And now methinks I could e'en chide myself
> For doating on her beauty, though her death
> Shall be revenged after no common action.
> Does the silkworm expend her yellow labours
> For thee? For thee does she undo herself?
> Are lordships sold to maintain ladyships
> For the poor benefit of a bewildering minute?
> Why does yon fellow falsify highways,
> And put his life between the judge's lips,
> To refine such a thing—keeps horse and men
> To beat their valours for her? . . .

In this passage (as is evident if it is taken in its context) there is a combination of positive and negative emotions: an intensely strong attraction toward beauty and an equally intense fascination by the ugliness which is contrasted with it and which destroys [9] it. This balance of contrasted emotion is in the dramatic situation to which the speech is pertinent, but that situation alone is inadequate to it. This is, so to speak, the structural emotion, provided by the drama. But the whole effect, the dominant tone, is due to the fact that a number of floating feelings, having an affinity to this emotion by no means superficially evident, have combined with it to give us a new art emotion.

It is not in his personal emotions, the emotions provoked by particular events in his life, that the poet is in any way remarkable or interesting. His particular emotions may be simple, or crude, or flat. The emotion in his poetry will be a very complex thing, but not with the complexity of the emotions of people who have very complex or unusual emotions in life. One error, in fact, of eccentricity in poetry is to seek for new human emotions to express; and in this search for novelty in the wrong place it discovers the perverse. The business of the poet is not to find new emotions, but to use the ordinary ones and, in working them up into poetry, to express feelings which are not in actual emotions at all. And emotions which he has never experienced will serve his turn as well as those familiar to him. Consequently, we must believe that "emotion recollected in tranquillity" is an inexact formula. For it is neither emotion, nor recollection, nor, without distortion of meaning, tranquillity. It is a concentration, and a new thing resulting from the concentration, of a very great number of experiences which to the practical and active person would not seem to be experiences at all; it is a concentration which does not happen consciously or of deliberation. These experiences are not "recollected," and they finally unite in an atmosphere which is "tranquil" only in that it is a passive attending upon the event. Of course this is not quite the whole story. There is a great deal, in the writing of poetry, which must be conscious and deliberate. In fact, the bad poet is usually unconscious where he ought to be conscious, and conscious where he ought to be unconscious. Both errors tend to make him "personal." Poetry is not a turning loose of emotion, but an escape from emotion; it is not the expression of personality, but an escape from personality. But, of course, only [10] those who have personality and emotions know what it means to want to escape from these things.

III

ὁ δὲ νοῦς ἴσως θειότερόν τι χαὶ ἀπαθές ἐστιν.

This essay proposes to halt at the frontier of metaphysics or mysticism, and confine itself to such practical conclusions as can be applied by the responsible person interested in poetry. To divert interest from the poet to the poetry is a laudable aim: for it would conduce to a juster estimation of actual poetry, good and bad. There are many people who appreciate the expression of sincere emotion in verse, and there is a smaller number of people who can appreciate technical excellence. But very few know when there is an expression of *significant* emotion, emotion which has its life in the poem and not in the history of the poet. The emotion of art is impersonal. And the poet cannot reach this impersonality without surrendering himself wholly to the work to be done. And he is not likely to know what is to be done unless he lives in what is not merely the present, but the present moment of the past, unless he is conscious, not of what is dead, but of what is already living. [11]

NEGRO CHARACTER AS SEEN BY WHITE AUTHORS
Sterling A. Brown

Introduction

There are three types of Negroes, says Roark Bradford, in his sprightly manner: "the nigger, the 'colored person,' and the Negro—upper case N." In his foreword to *Ol' Man Adam an' His Chillun*, the source from which Marc Connelly drew the *Green Pastures*, and a book causing the author to be considered, in some circles, a valid interpreter of *the* Negro, Roark Bradford defines *the* Negro's character and potentialities. The Negro, he says, is the race leader, not too militant, concerned more with economic independence than with civil equality. The colored person, "frequently of mixed blood, loathes the blacks and despises the whites. . . . Generally he inherits the weaknesses of both races and seldom inherits the strength of either. He has the black man's emotions and the white man's inhibitions." [1] Together with the "poor white trash" it is the "colored persons" who perpetuate racial hatreds and incite race riots and lynchings. "The nigger" interests Mr. Bradford more than the rest. He is indolent, entirely irresponsible, shiftless, the bugaboo of Anglo-Saxon ideals, a poor fighter and a poor hater, primitively emotional and uproariously funny.

Such are the "original" contributions of Mr. Bradford, who states modestly that, in spite of the Negro's penchant to lying:

> I believe I know them pretty well. I was born on a plantation that was worked by them; I was nursed by one as an infant and I played with one when I was growing up. I have watched them at work in the fields, in the levee camps, and on the river. I have watched them at home, in church, at their picnics and their funerals.[2]

SOURCE: Sterling A. Brown, "Negro Character as Seen by White Authors," *Journal of Negro Education*, II (April, 1933), 179–203. Reprinted by permission of the publisher.

1. Roark Bradford, *Ol' Man Adam an' His Chillun*, New York: Harper and Bros., 1928, p. xi.
2. *Ibid.*, p. ix.

All of this, he believes, gives him license to step forth as their interpreter and repeat stereotypes time-hallowed in the South. It doesn't. Mr. Bradford's stories remain highly amusing; his generalizations about *the* Negro remain a far better analysis of a white man than of *the* Negro. We see that, even in pontifical moments, one white Southerner cannot escape being influenced by current folk-beliefs.

Mr. Bradford's views have been restated at some length to show how obviously dangerous it is to rely upon literary artists when they advance themselves as sociologists and ethnologists. Mr. Bradford's easy pigeonholing of an entire race into three small compartments is a familiar phenomenon in American literature, where the Indian, the Mexican, the Irishman, and the Jew have been similarly treated. Authors are too anxious to have it said, "Here is *the* Negro," rather than here are a few Negroes whom I have seen. If one wishes to learn of Negro individuals observed from very specialized points of view, American literature can help him out. Some books will shed a great deal of light upon Negro experience. But if one wishes to learn of *the* Negro, it would be best to study *the* Negro himself; a study that might result in the discovery that *the* Negro is more difficult to find than the countless human beings called Negroes.

The Negro has met with as great injustice in American literature as he has in American life. The majority of books about Negroes merely stereotype Negro character. It is the purpose of this paper to point out the prevalence and history of these stereotypes. Those considered important enough for separate classification, although overlappings *do* occur, are seven in number: (1) The Contented Slave, (2) The Wretched Freeman, (3) The Comic Negro, (4) The Brute Negro, (5) The Tragic Mulatto, (6) The Local Color Negro, and (7) The Exotic Primitive.

A detailed evaluation of each of these is impracticable because of limitations of space. It can be said, however, that all of these stereotypes are marked either by exaggeration or omissions; that they all agree in stressing the Negro's divergence from an Anglo-Saxon norm to the flattery of the latter; they could all be used, as they probably are, as justification of racial proscription; they all illustrate dangerous specious generalizing from a few particulars recorded by a single observer from a restricted point of view—which is itself generally dictated by the desire to perpetuate a stereotype. All of these stereotypes are abundantly to be found in American literature, and are generally accepted as contributions to true racial understanding. Thus one critic, setting out imposingly to discuss "the Negro character" in American literature, can still say, unabashedly, that *"The whole range of the Negro character is revealed thoroughly,"* [3] in one twenty-six-line sketch by Joel Chandler Harris of Br'er Fox and Br'er Mud Turtle.

The writer of this essay does not consider everything a stereotype that shows up the weaknesses of Negro character; sometimes the stereotype makes the Negro appear too virtuous. Nor does he believe the stereotypes of contented slaves and buffoons are to be successfully balanced by pictures of Negroes who are unbelievably intellectual, noble, self-sacrificial, and faultless. Any stereotyping is fatal to great, or even to convincing literature. Furthermore, he believes that he has considered to be stereotypes only those patterns whose frequent and tedious recurrence can be demonstrably proved by even a cursory acquaintance with the literature of the subject.

The Contented Slave

"Massa make de darkies lub him
'Case he was so kind. . . ."
STEPHEN FOSTER

The first lukewarm stirrings of abolitionary sentiment in the South were chilled with Eli Whitney's invention of the cotton gin at the close of the 18th century. Up until this time the *raison d'être of* slavery had not been so powerful. But now there was a way open to quick wealth; Cotton was crowned King, and a huge army of black servitors was necessary to keep him upon the throne; considerations of abstract justice had to give way before economic expediency. [180] A complete rationale of slavery was evolved.

One of the most influential of the authorities defending slavery was President Dew of William and Mary College, who stated, in 1832,

> . . . slavery had been the condition of all ancient culture, that Christianity approved servitude, and that the law of Moses had

---

3. John Herbert Nelson, *The Negro Character in American Literature*, Lawrence, Kansas: The Department of Journalism Press, 1926, p. 118.

> both assumed and positively established slavery. . . . It is the order of nature and of God that the being of superior faculties and knowledge, and therefore of superior power, should control and dispose of those who are inferior. It is as much in the order of nature that men should enslave each other as that other animals should prey upon each other.[4]

The pamphlet of this young teacher was extensively circulated, and was substantiated by Chancellor Harper of the University of South Carolina in 1838:

> Man is born to subjection. . . . The proclivity of the natural man is to domineer or to be subservient. . . . If there are sordid, servile, and laborious offices to be performed, is it not better that there should be sordid, servile, and laborious beings to perform them?[5]

The economic argument had frequent proponents; an ex-governor of Virginia showed that, although Virginia was denied the tremendous prosperity accruing from cotton raising, it was still granted the opportunity to profit from selling Negroes to the far South. Sociologists and anthropologists hastened forward with proof of the Negro's three-fold inferiority: physically (except for his adaptability to cotton fields and rice swamps), mentally, and morally. Theologians advanced the invulnerable arguments from the Bible; in one of the "Bible Defences of Slavery" we read: "The curse of Noah upon *Ham*, had a *general* and *interminable* application to the whole Hamite race, in placing them under a *peculiar* liability of being enslaved by the races of the two other brothers."[6]

The expressions of these dominant ideas in the fiction and poetry of the period did not lag far behind. In fact, one influential novel was among the leaders of the van, for in 1832, the year in which Professor Dew stated the argument that was to elevate him to the

---

4. William E. Dodd, *The Cotton Kingdom*, Chapter III, Philosophy of the Cotton Planter, p. 53.
5. *Ibid.*, p. 57.
6. Josiah Priest, *Bible Defence of Slavery*. Glasgow, Ky.: W. S. Brown, 1851, p. 52.

presidency of William and Mary College, John P. Kennedy published a work that was to make him one of the most widely read and praised authors of the Southland. His ideas of the character of the Negro and of slavery are in fundamental agreement with those of Dew and Harper. According to F. P. Gaines, in *The Southern Plantation*, Kennedy's *Swallow Barn* has the historical significance of starting the plantation tradition, a tradition hoary and mildewed in our own day, but by no means moribund.

Swallow Barn is an idyllic picture of slavery on a tidewater plantation. The narrator, imagined to be from the North (Kennedy himself was from Tidewater, Maryland), comes to Virginia, expecting to see a drastic state of affairs. Instead, he finds a kindly patriarchy and grateful, happy slaves. After vignettes of the Negro's laziness, mirth, vanity, improvidence, done with some charm and, for a Southern audience, considerable persuasiveness, the "Northern" narrator concludes:

> I am quite sure they never could become a happier people than I find them here. . . . [181] No tribe of people has ever passed from barbarism to civilization whose . . . progress has been more secure from harm, more genial to their character, or better supplied with mild and beneficent guardianship, adapted to the actual state of their intellectual feebleness, than the Negroes of *Swallow Barn*. And, from what I can gather, it is pretty much the same on the other estates in this region.[7]

Shortly after the publication of *Swallow Barn*, Edgar Allan Poe wrote:

> . . . we must take into consideration the peculiar character (I may say the peculiar nature) of the Negro. . . . [Some believe that Negroes] are, like ourselves, the sons of Adam and must, therefore, have like passions and wants and feelings and tempers in all respects. This we deny and appeal to the knowledge of all who know. . . . We shall take leave to speak as of things *in esse*, in a degree of loyal devotion on the part of the slave to which the white man's heart is a stranger, and of the

---

7. John P. Kennedy, *Swallow Barn*, p. 453.

master's reciprocal feeling of parental attachment to his humble dependent. . . . That these sentiments in the breast of the Negro and his master are stronger than they would be under like circumstances between individuals of the white race, we believe.[8]

In *The Gold-Bug*, Poe shows this reciprocal relationship between Jupiter, a slave, and his master. Southern fiction of the thirties and forties supported the thesis of Kennedy and Poe without being so explicit. The mutual affection of the races, the slave's happiness with his status, and his refusal to accept freedom appear here and there, but the books were dedicated less to the defense of the peculiar institution than to entertainment. William Gilmore Simms, for instance, includes in *The Yemassee*, a novel published in the same year as *Swallow Barn*, the typical pro-slavery situation of a slave's refusing freedom: "I d—n to h—ll, maussa, ef I guine to be free!" roared the *adhesive* black, in a tone of unrestrainable determination.[9] But the burden of this book is not pro-slavery; Hector earns his freedom by the unslavish qualities of physical prowess, foresight, and courage in battle.

In 1853, Simms, in joining forces with Dew and Harper in the *Pro-Slavery Argument*, writes: "Slavery has elevated the Negro from savagery. The black man's finer traits of fidelity and docility were encouraged in his servile position. . . ."[10] Simms turned from cursory references to slavery to ardent pro-slavery defense, in company with other novelists of the South, for a perfectly definite reason. The abolitionary attacks made by men like Garrison had taken the form of pamphlets, and these had been answered in kind. The publication of *Uncle Tom's Cabin* in 1851, however, showed that the abolitionists had converted the novel into a powerful weapon. Pro-slavery authors were quick to take up this weapon, although their wielding of it was without the power of Harriet Beecher Stowe. *Swallow Barn* was reissued in 1851, and "besides the numerous controversial pam-

---

8. Edgar Allan Poe, *Literary Criticism*, Vol. 1, "Slavery in the United States," p. 271.
9. William Gilmore Simms, *The Yemassee*. Richmond: B. F. Johnson Publishing Co., 1911, p. 423. The italics are mine but not the omissions.
10. Jeanette Reid Tandy, "Pro-Slavery Propaganda in American Fiction of the Fifties," *South Atlantic Quarterly*, Vol. XXI, No. 1, p. 41.

phlets and articles in periodicals there were no fewer than fourteen pro-slavery novels and one long poem published in the three years (1852–54) following the appearance of *Uncle Tom's Cabin*."[11]

These novels are all cut out of the same cloth. Like *Swallow Barn*, they omit the economic basis of slavery, [182] and minimize "the sordid, servile and laborious offices" which Chancellor Harper had considered the due of "sordid, servile, and laborious beings." The pro-slavery authors use the first adjective only in considering free Negroes, or those who, by some quirk of nature, are disobedient; admit the second completely; and deny the third. Slavery to all of them is a beneficent guardianship, the natural and inevitable state for a childish people.

There is very little reference to Negroes working in the fields; even then they are assigned to easy tasks which they lazily perform to the tune of slave melodies. They are generally described as "leaving the fields." They are allowed to have, for additional provisions and huckstering, their own garden-plots, which they attend in their abundant leisure. Their holidays are described at full length: the corn huskings, barbecuing, Yuletide parties, and hunting the possum by the light of a kindly moon.

In *Life at the South, or Uncle Tom's Cabin As It Is* (1852), Uncle Tom, out of hurt vanity, but not for any more grievous cause, runs away. His wife, Aunt Dinah, although loving Tom, realizes that her greater loyalty is due to her master, and not to her errant spouse, and refuses to escape with him. Tom, after experiencing the harshness of the unfeeling North, begs to return to slavery. In *The Planter's Northern Bride*, the bride, having come to the slave South with misgivings, is quickly converted to an enthusiast for slavery, since it presents "an aspect so tender and affectionate." One fears that the bride is not unpartisan, however, since her appearance on the plantation elicited wild cries of worship, and her beloved husband is a great ethnologist, proving that the Negro's peculiar skull and skin were decreed by the divine fiat so that he could pick cotton. In *The Yankee Slave Dealer*, the meddling abolitionist cannot persuade any slaves to run off with him except a half-witted rogue. One slave recited to him *verbatim* a miniature *Bible Defence of Slavery*, citing the book of the Bible, the chapter, and the verse. In *The Hireling and The Slave*,

11. *Ibid.*, p. 41.

William J. Grayson, "poet laureate" of South Carolina, contrasts the lot of the industrial worker of the North with that of the slave. Gems of this widely read poetical disquisition follow:

> And yet the life, so unassailed by care,
> So blessed with moderate work, with ample fare,
> With all the good the starving pauper needs,
> The happier slave on each plantation leads . . . . (p. 50)
> And Christian slaves may challenge as their own,
> The blessings claimed in fabled states alone . . . . (p. 50)

This pattern of the joyous contentment of the slave in a paradisaical bondage persisted and was strongly reenforced in Reconstruction days. If it was no longer needed for the defense of a tottering institution, it was needed for reasons nearly as exigent. Ancestor worshippers, the sons of a fighting generation, remembering bitterly the deaths or sufferings of their fathers, became elegists of a lost cause and cast a golden glow over the plantation past; unreconstructed "fire-eaters," determined to resurrect slavery as far as they were able, needed as a cardinal principle the belief that Negroes were happy as slaves, and hopelessly unequipped for freedom. Both [183] types were persuasive, the first because the romantic idealizing of the past will always be seductive to a certain large group of readers, and the second because the sincere unremitting harping upon one argument will finally make it seem plausible. We find, therefore, that whereas *Uncle Tom's Cabin* had triumphed in the antebellum controversy, the pro-slavery works of Page, Russell, and Harris swept the field in Reconstruction days. It is from these last skillful authors, undeniably acquainted with Negro folk-life, and affectionate toward certain aspects of it, that the American reading public as a whole has accepted the delusion of the Negro as contented slave, entertaining child, and docile ward.

Mutual affection between the races is a dominant theme. Thus, Irwin Russell, the first American poet to treat Negro life in folk speech, has his ex-slave rhapsodizing about his "Mahsr John." "Washintum an' Franklum . . . wuzn't nar a one . . . come up to Mahsr John":

> Well times is changed. De war it come an' sot de niggers free
> An' now ol' Mahsr John ain't hardly wuf as much as me;

He had to pay his debts, an' so his lan' is mos'ly gone—
An' I declar' I's sorry for my pore ol' Mahsr John.[12]

The volume has many other references to the slave's docility toward, and worship of his master.

Irwin Russell implies throughout that the Southern white best understands how to treat the Negro. Perhaps this is one reason for Joel Chandler Harris' praise:

> But the most wonderful thing about the dialect poetry of Irwin Russell is his accurate conception of the negro character. . . .
> I do not know where could be found today a happier or a more perfect representation of negro character.

On reading Russell's few poems, one is struck by the limited gamut of characteristics allowed to Negroes. Inclined to the peccadilloes of cheating, lying easily; a good teller of comic stories, a child of mirth, his greatest hardship that of being kicked about by refractory mules, and his deepest emotion, compassion for his master's lost estate—surely this is hardly a "perfect" representation of even Negro folk character?

Thomas Nelson Page followed Russell's lead in poetry. In the poems of *Befo' De War*, Page puts into the mouths of his Negroes yearnings for the old days and expressions of the greatest love for old marster. One old slave welcomes death if it will replace him in old "Marster's service." Old Jack entrusts his life-earnings to his son to give to young "Marster," since the latter can't work and needs them more.[13]

In most of Page's widely influential stories, there is the stock situation of the lifelong devotion of master and body-servant. In *Marse Chan*, old "Marse" is blinded in rescuing a slave from a burning barn. Sam accompanies his young Marse Chan to the war, his devotion overcoming "racial cowardice" to such a degree that he rides to the very cannon's mouth with him, and brings back his master's body. Of slavery, Sam speaks thus:

---

12. Irwin Russell, *Christmas Night in the Quarters*, New York: The Century Co., 1917, pp. 63 ff.
13. Thomas Nelson Page, *Befo' De War*. New York: Chas. Scribner's Sons, 1906, "Little Jack."

> Dem wuz good old times, marster—de bes' Sam ever see! Dey wuz, in fac'! Niggers [184] didn't hed nothin 't all to do—jes' hed to 'ten to de feedin' an' cleanin' de hosses, an' doin' what de marster tell 'em to do; an' when dey wuz sick, dey had things sont 'em out de house, an' de same doctor come to see 'em whar ten' do de white folks when dey wuz po'ly. D'yar warn' no trouble nor nothin.[14]

Over all his fiction there is the reminiscent melancholy of an exiled Adam, banished by a flaming sword—wielded not by Michael but by a Yankee devil, from what was truly an Eden. In *The Negro: The Southerner's Problem,* we read:

> In fact, the ties of pride were such that it was often remarked that the affection of the slaves was stronger toward the whites than toward their own offspring.[15]

And in the same book there is an apostrophe to the "mammy" that is a worthy forerunner of the bids so many orators make for interracial good-will, and of the many remunerative songs that emerge from Tin Pan Alley.

Joel Chandler Harris is better known for his valuable contribution to literature and folk-lore in recording the Uncle Remus stories than for his aid in perpetuation of the "plantation Negro" stereotype. Nevertheless, a merely cursory study of Uncle Remus' character would reveal his close relationship to the "Caesars," "Hectors," "Pompeys," *et al.* of the pro-slavery novel, and to Page's "Uncle Jack" and "Uncle Billy." In Uncle Remus's philosophizing about the old days of slavery there is still the wistful nostalgia. Harris comments, "In Middle Georgia the relations between master and slave were as perfect as they could be under the circumstances." This might mean a great deal, or nothing, but it is obvious from other words of Harris that, fundamentally, slavery was to him a kindly institution, and the Negro was contented. Slavery was:

---

14. Thomas Nelson Page, *In Ole Virginia.* New York: Chas. Scribner's Sons, 1889.
15. Thomas Nelson Page, *The Negro: The Southerner's Problem.* New York: Chas. Scribners' Sons, 1904, p. 174.

... in some of its aspects far more beautiful and inspiring than *any* of the relations between employers and the employed in this day.[16]

George Washington Cable, although more liberal in his views upon the Negro than his Southern contemporaries, gives an example of the self-abnegating servant in *Posson Jone'*. This slave uses his wits to safeguard his master. A goodly proportion of the Negro servants are used to solve the complications of their "white-folks." They are in a long literary tradition—that of the faithful, clever servant—and they probably are just as true to Latin prototypes as to real Negroes. In the works of F. Hopkinson Smith, Harry Stilwell Edwards, and in Maurice Thompson's *Balance of Power*, we have this appearance of a black *deus ex machina*.

To deal adequately with the numerous books of elegiac reminiscence of days "befo' de war" would be beyond the scope and purpose of this essay. The tone of them all is to be found in such sad sentences as these:

> Aunt Phebe, Uncle Tom, Black Mammy, Uncle Gus, Aunt Jonas, Uncle Isom, and all the rest—who shall speak all your virtues or enshrine your simple faith and fidelity? It is as impossible as it is to describe the affection showered upon you by those whom you called "Marster" and "Mistis." [17]

Ambrose Gonzales grieves that "the old black folk are going fast" with the [185] passing of the "strict but kindly discipline of slavery," yearning, in Tennysonian accents, "for the tender grace of a day that is dead." [18]

Although the realism of today is successfully discounting the sentimentalizing of the Old South, there are still many contemporary

---

16. Julia Collier Harris, *Joel Chandler Harris, Editor and Essayist*. Chapel Hill: University of North Carolina Press, 1931, "The Old-Time Darky," p. 129.
17. Essie Collins Matthews, *Aunt Phebe, Uncle Tom and Others*. Columbus, Ohio: The Champlin Press, 1915, p. 13.
18. Ambrose Gonzales, *With Aesop Along the Black Border*. Columbia, S.C.: The State Co., 1924, p. xiv.

manifestations of the tradition. Hergesheimer, arch-romanticist that he is, writes that he would be happy to pay with everything the wasted presence holds for the return of the pastoral civilization based on slavery.[19]

Donald Davidson, a Tennessee poet, has written this:

> Black man, when you and I were young together,
> We knew each other's hearts. Though I am no longer
> A child, and you perhaps unfortunately
> Are no longer a child, we still understand
> Better maybe than others. There is the wall
> Between us, anciently erected. Once
> It might have been crossed, men say. But now I cannot
> Forget that I was master, and you can hardly
> Forget that you were slave. We did not build
> The ancient wall, but there it painfully is.
> Let us not bruise our foreheads on the wall.[20]

Ol' Massa's People, by Orlando Kay Armstrong, is one of the most recent of the books in which ex-slaves speak—as in Page apparently with their master's voice—their praise of slavery. The theme seems inexhaustible; in the February issue of the *Atlantic Monthly* it is restated in nearly the words that have already been quoted. Designed originally to defend slavery, it is now a convenient argument for those wishing to keep "the Negro in his place"—out of great love for him, naturally—believing that he will be happier so.

The Wretched Freeman

"Go tell Marse Linkum, to tek his freedom back."

As a foil to the contented slave, pro-slavery authors set up another puppet—the wretched free Negro. He was necessary for the argu-

19. Joseph Hergesheimer, *Quiet Cities*. New York: Alfred A. Knopf, 1928, pp. 14 ff.
20. Donald Davidson, *The Tall Men*. New York: Houghton Mifflin Co., 1927, p. 39.

ment. Most of the pro-slavery novels paid a good deal of attention to his degradation. Either the novelist interpolated a long disquisition on the disadvantages of his state both to the country and to himself, or had his happy slaves fear contact with him as with a plague.

In *Life at The South, or Uncle Tom's Cabin as It Is,* Uncle Tom experiences harsh treatment from unfeeling Northern employers, sees Negroes frozen to death in snow storms, and all in all learns that the North and freedom is no stopping place for him. In *The Yankee Slave Dealer,* the slaves are insistent upon the poor lot of free Negroes. In *The Planter's Northern Bride,* Crissy runs away from freedom in order to be happy again in servitude. Grayson in *The Hireling and Slave* prophesies thus:

> Such, too, the fate the Negro must deplore
> If slavery guards his subject race no more,
> If by weak friends or vicious counsels led
> To change his blessings for the hireling's bread. . . .
> There in the North in suburban dens and human sties,
> In foul excesses sung, the Negro lies;
> A moral pestilence to taint and stain.
> His life a curse, his death a social gain,
> Debased, despised, the Northern pariah knows
> He shares no good that liberty bestows;
> Spurned from her gifts, with each successive year,
> In drunken want his numbers disappear.[21] [186]

There was a carry-over of these ideas in the Reconstruction. Harris, in one of his most moving stories, *Free Joe,* showed the tragedy of a free Negro in a slave-holding South, where he was considered a bad model by slave-owners, an economic rival by poor whites, and something to be avoided by the slaves. The story might be considered as a condemnation of a system, but in all probability was taken to be another proof of the Negro's incapacity for freedom. Although Harris wrote generously of Negro advancement since emancipation, there is little doubt that the implications of many passages furthered the stereotype under consideration.

21. William J. Grayson, *The Hireling and the Slave.* Charleston, S.C.: Mc-Carter and Co., 1856, pp. 68 ff.

Page, a bourbon "fire-eater," for all of his yearnings for his old mammy, saw nothing of good for Negroes in emancipation:

> Universally, they [Southerners] will tell you that while the old-time Negroes were industrious, saving, and, when not misled, well-behaved, kindly, respectful, and self-respecting, and while the remnant of them who remain still retain generally these characteristics, the "new issue," for the most part, are lazy, thriftless, intemperate, insolent, dishonest, and without the most rudimentary elements of morality . . . . Universally, they report a general depravity and retrogression of the Negroes at large, in sections in which they are left to themselves, closely resembling a reversion to barbarism.[22]

The notion of the Negro's being doomed to extinction was sounded by a chorus of pseudo-scientists, bringing forth a formidable (?) array of proofs. Lafcadio Hearn yielded to the lure of posing as a prophet:

> As for the black man, he must disappear with the years. Dependent like the ivy, he needs some strong oak-like friend to cling to. His support has been cut from him, and his life must wither in its prostrate helplessness. Will he leave no trace of his past? . . . . Ah, yes! . . . the weird and beautiful melodies born in the hearts of the poor, child-like people to whom freedom was destruction.[23]

Many were the stories ringing changes on the theme: "Go tell Marse Linkum, to tek his freedom back." Thus, in *The Carolina Low Country*, Mr. Sass writes of Old Aleck, who, on being freed, spoke his little piece: "Miss, I don't want no wagis." "God bless you, old Aleck," sighs Mr. Sass.

Modern neo-confederates repeat the stereotype. Allen Tate, co-member with Donald Davidson of the Nashville saviors of the South,

---

22. Thomas Nelson Page, *The Negro: The Southerner's Problem, op. cit.*, p. 80.
23. Lafcadio Hearn, *Letters from the Raven*. New York: A. & C. Boni, 1930, p. 168.

implies in *Jefferson Davis, His Rise and Fall*, that to educate a Negro beyond his station brings him unhappiness. One of the chief points of agreement in the Neo-Confederate *I'll Take My Stand* by Davidson, Tate and ten others is that freedom has proved to be a perilous state for the Negro. Joseph Hergesheimer agrees: "A free Negro is more often wretched than not." [24] "Slavery was gone, the old serene days were gone. Negroes were bad because they were neither slave nor free." [25] And finally, a modern illustration must suffice. Eleanor Mercein Kelly in an elegy for the vanishing South, called *Monkey Motions*, pities "the helplessness of a simple jungle folk, a bandar-log, set down in the life of cities and expected to be men." [26]

It is, all in all, a sad picture that these savants give. What concerns [187] us here, however, is its persistence, a thing inexpressibly more sad.

The Comic Negro

"That Reminds Me of a Story. There Were Once Two Ethiopians, Sambo and Rastus . . . ."
1,001 *After-Dinner Speakers*

The stereotype of the "comic Negro" is about as ancient as the "contented slave." Indeed, they might be considered complementary, since, if the Negro could be shown as perpetually mirthful, his state could not be so wretched. This is, of course, the familiar procedure when conquerors depict a subject people. English authors at the time of Ireland's greatest persecution built up the stereotype of the comic Irishman, who fascinated English audiences, and unfortunately, in a manner known to literary historians, influenced even Irish authors.[27] Thus, we find, in a melodrama about Irish life, an English officer soliloquizing:

24. Joseph Hergesheimer, *op. cit.*, p. 137.
25. *Ibid.*, p. 293.
26. Blanche Colton Williams, *O. Henry Memorial Award Prize Stories of 1927*. Garden City: Doubleday, Doran & Co., p. 207.
27. *Vide:* George Bernard Shaw's *John Bull's Other Island*, Daniel Corkery's *Synge and Anglo-Irish Literature*, Yeats's *Plays and Controversies*, Lady

> I swear, the Irish nature is beyond my comprehension. A strange people!—merry 'mid their misery—laughing through their tears, like the sun shining through the rain. Yet what simple philosophers they! They tread life's path as if 'twere strewn with roses devoid of thorns, and make the most of life with natures of sunshine and song.[28]

Any American not reading the words "Irish nature" could be forgiven for taking the characterization to refer to American Negroes. Natures of sunshine and song, whose wretchedness becomes nothing since theirs is a simple philosophy of mirth! So runs the pattern.

In her excellent book, *American Humor,* Constance Rourke points out the Negro as one of the chief ingredients of the potpourri of American humor. She traces him as far back as the early '20's when Edwin Forrest made up as a Southern plantation Negro to excite the risibilities of Cincinnati. In *The Spy,* Cooper belabors the grotesqueness of Caesar's appearance, although Caesar is not purely and simply the buffoon:

> . . . . But it was in his legs that nature had indulged her most capricious humor. There was an abundance of material injudiciously used. The calves were neither before nor behind, but rather on the outer side of the limb, inclining forward . . . . The leg was placed so near the center (of the foot) as to make it sometimes a matter of dispute whether he was not walking backward.[29]

Kennedy in his *Swallow Barn* not only reveals the Negro as delighted by the master's benevolence, but also as delighting the master by his ludicrous departure from the Anglo-Saxon norm. Kennedy revels in such descriptions as the following:

> His face . . . was principally composed of a pair of protuberant lips, whose luxuriance seemed intended as an indemnity

---

Gregory's *Our Irish Theatre,* for attacks upon the "comic" Irishman stereotype.
28. John Fitzgerald Murphy, *The Shamrock and The Rose.* Boston: Walter H. Baker Co., n. d., p. 25.
29. James Fenimore Cooper, *The Spy.* New York: Scott, Foresman Co., 1927, p. 45.

for a pair of crushed nostrils. . . . Two bony feet occupied shoes, each of the superfices and figure of a hoe. . . . Wrinkled, decrepit old men, with faces shortened as if with drawing strings, noses that seemed to have run all to nostril, and with feet of the configuration of a mattock. . . .[30]

It was in the early '30's, however, that T. D. Rice first jumped "Jim Crow" in the theaters along the Ohio River and set upon the stage the "minstrel Negro." Apparently immortal, this stereotype was to involve in its perpetuation such famous actors as Joseph Jefferson and David Belasco, to make Amos 'n' Andy as essential [188] to American domesticity as a car in every garage, and to mean affluence for a Jewish comedian of whom only one gesture was asked: that he sink upon one knee, extend his white-gloved hands, and cry out "Mammy."

In pro-slavery fiction the authors seemed to agree on the two aspects of the comic Negro—that he was ludicrous to others, and forever laughing himself. Grayson writes in *The Hireling and the Slave*:

> The long, loud laugh, that freemen seldom share,
> Heaven's boon to bosoms unapproached by care;
> And boisterous jest and humor unrefined . . . .[31]

To introduce comic relief, perhaps, in stories that might defeat their own purposes if confined only to the harrowing details of slavery, anti-slavery authors had their comic characters. Topsy is the classic example; it is noteworthy that in contemporary acting versions of "Uncle Tom's Cabin," Topsy and the minstrel show note, if not dominant, are at least of equal importance to the melodrama of Eliza and the bloodhounds.

Reconstruction literature developed the stereotype. Russell's Negroes give side-splitting versions of the Biblical story (foreshadowing Bradford's *Ol' Man Adam An' His Chillun*), or have a fatal fondness for propinquity to a mule's rear end. Page's Negroes punctuate their worship of "ole Marse" with "Kyah-kyahs," generally directed at themselves. The humor of Uncle Remus is nearer to genuine folk-

---

30. Kennedy, *op. cit., passim.*
31. Grayson, *op. cit.,* p. 51.

humor, which—it might be said in passing—is *not* the same as the "comic Negro" humor. Negroes in general, in the Reconstruction stories, are seen as creatures of mirth—who wouldn't suffer from hardship, even if they had to undergo it. Thus a Negro, sentenced to the chain-gang for stealing a pair of breeches, is made the theme of a comic poem.[32] This is illustrative. There may be random jokes in Southern court rooms, but joking about the Negroes' experiences with Southern "justice" and with the chain-gang is rather ghastly—like laughter at the mouth of hell. Creatures of sunshine and of song!

The "comic Negro" came into his own in the present century, and brought his creators into theirs. Octavius Cohen, who looks upon the idea of Negro doctors and lawyers and society belles as the height of the ridiculous, served such clienteles as that of *The Saturday Evening Post* for a long time with the antics of Florian Slappey. His work is amusing at its best, but is pseudo-Negro. Instead of being a handicap, however, that seems a recommendation to his audience. Trusting to most moth-eaten devices of farce, and interlarding a Negro dialect never heard on land or sea—compounded more of Dogberry and Mrs. Malaprop than of Birmingham Negroes,[33] he has proved to the whites that all along they have known the real Negro—"Isn't he funny, [189] now!"—and has shown to Negroes what whites wanted them to resemble. Mrs. Octavius Roy Cohen follows in the wake of her illustrious husband in *Our Darktown Press,* a gleaning of "boners" from Aframerican newspapers. Editorial carelessness is sadly enough familiar in race journals; every item in the book is vouched for, but the total effect is the reenforcing of a stereotype that America loves to believe in.

Arthur E. Akers, with a following in another widely read magazine, is another farceur. He uses the situation of the domestic difficulty, as old as medieval fabliaux and farces—and places it in a Southern Negro community, and has his characters speak an

---

32. Belle Richardson Harrison, *Poetry of the Southern States,* Edited by Clement Wood. Girard, Kansas: Haldeman-Julius Co., 1924, p. 36.

33. "Yeh, an' was he to git one good bite at a cullud man like me, he'd exterminate me so quick I wouldn't even have a chance to notrify my heirs," "I ain't hahdly sawn her right recent," are examples of his inimitable (fortunately so, although Amos an' Andy try it in "I'se regusted," etc.) dialect; "Drastic" "Unit" "Quinine" "Midnight," and "Sons and Daughters of I Will Arise" are examples of his nomenclature.

approximation to Negro dialect—but too slick and "literary" for conviction. Irate shrews and "Milquetoast" husbands, with razors wielded at departing parts of the anatomy, are Akers' stock-in-trade. Hugh Wiley with his Wildcat, inseparable from his goat, Lady Luck, unsavory but a talisman, is another creator of the farce that Negro life is too generally believed to be. E. K. Means, with obvious knowledge of Southern Negro life, is concerned to show in the main its ludicrous side, and Irvin Cobb, with a reputation of after-dinner wit to uphold, is similarly confined.

The case of Roark Bradford is different. An undoubted humorist, in the great line of Twain and the tall tales of the Southwest, he gleans from a rich store of Negro speech and folkways undeniably amusing tales. But as his belief about the Negro (cf. Introduction) might attest, he has a definite attitude to the Negro to uphold. His stories of the easy loves of the levee (frequently found in *Collier's*) concentrate upon the comic aspect of Negro life, although another observer might well see the tragic. In *Ol' Man Adam an' His Chillun* we have farce manufactured out of the Negro's religious beliefs. It seems to the writer that the weakest sections of *Green Pastures* stick closest to Bradford's stories, and that the majesty and reverence that can be found in the play must come from Marc Connelly. In *John Henry*, Bradford has definitely weakened his material by making over a folk-hero into a clown.

Although the situations in which the comic Negro finds himself range from the fantastic as in Cohen, to the possible as in "The Two Black Crows" and in "Amos 'n' Andy," his characteristics are fairly stable. The "comic Negro" is created for the delectation of a white audience, condescending and convinced that any departure from the Anglo-Saxon norm is amusing, and that any attempt to enter the special provinces of whites, such as wearing a dress suit, is doubly so. The "comic Negro" with certain physical attributes exaggerated—with his razor (generally harmless), his love for watermelon and gin, for craps, his haunting of chicken roosts, use of big words he doesn't understand, grandiloquent names and titles, "loud" clothes, bluster, hysterical cowardice, and manufactured word-play—has pranced his way by means of books, vaudeville skits, shows, radio programs, advertisements, and after-dinner speeches, into the folklore of the nation. As Guy B. Johnson urges there is a sort of—

> ... folk attitude of the white man toward the Negro. ... One cannot help noticing [190] that the white man must have his fun out of the Negro, even when writing serious novels about him. This is partly conscious, indeed a necessity, if one is to portray Negro life as it is, for Negroes are human and behave like other human beings. Sometimes it is unconscious, rising out of our old habit of associating the Negro with the comical.[34]

In pointing out the stereotype, one does not deny the rich comedy to be found in Negro life. One is insisting, however, that any picture concentrating upon this to the exclusion of all else is entirely inadequate, that many of the most popular creators of the "comic Negro," "doctor" their material, and are far from accurate in depicting even the small area of Negro experience they select, and that too often they exceed the prerogative of comedy by making copy out of persecution and injustice.

The Brute Negro

> "*All Scientific Investigation of the Subject Proves the Negro to Be An Ape.*"
> CHAS. CARROLL, *The Negro A Beast*

Because the pro-slavery authors were anxious to prove that slavery had been a benefit to the Negro in removing him from savagery to Christianity, the stereotype of the "brute Negro" was relatively insignificant in antebellum days. There were references to vicious criminal Negroes in fiction (vicious and criminal being synonymous to discontented and refractory), but these were considered as exceptional cases of half-wits led astray by abolitionists. *The Bible Defence of Slavery*, however, in which the Rev. Priest in a most unclerical manner waxes wrathful at abolitionists, sets forth with a great array of theological argument and as much ridiculousness, proofs of the Negro's

---

34. Guy B. Johnson, "Folk Values in Recent Literature on the Negro" in *Folk-Say*, edited by B. A. Botkin. Norman, Oklahoma: 1930, p. 371.

extreme lewdness. Sodom and Gomorrah were destroyed because these were strongholds of *Negro* vice. The book of Leviticus proved that *Negroes*

> outraged all order and decency of human society. Lewdness of the most hideous description was the crime of which they were guilty, blended with idolatry in their adoration of the gods, who were carved out of wood, painted and otherwise made, so as to represent the wild passions of lascivious desires. . . . . The baleful fire of unchaste amour rages through the negro's blood more fiercely than in the blood of any other people . . . on which account they are a people who are suspected of being but little acquainted with the virtue of chastity, and of regarding very little the marriage oath. . . .[35]

H. R. Helper, foe of slavery, was no friend of the Negro, writing, in 1867, *Nojoque,* a lurid condemnation of the Negro, setting up black and beastly as exact synonyms. Van Evrie's *White Supremacy and Negro Subordination, or Negroes A Subordinate Race, and (so-called) Slavery Its Normal Condition* gave "anthropological" support to the figment of the "beastly Negro," and *The Negro A Beast* (1900) gave theological support. The title page of this book runs:

> The Reasoner of the Age, the Revelator of the Century! The Bible As It Is! The Negro and his Relation to the Human Family! The Negro a beast, but created with articulate speech, and hands, that he may be of service to his master—the White Man . . . . by Chas. Carroll, who has spent 15 years of his life and $20,000.00 in its compilation. . . . .

Who could ask for anything more?

Authors stressing the mutual affection between the races looked upon the Negro as a docile mastiff. In the Reconstruction this mastiff turned into a mad dog. "Damyanks," carpetbaggers, scalawags, and New England schoolmarms affected him with the [191] rabies. The works of Thomas Nelson Page are good examples of this metamorphosis. When his Negro characters are in their place, loyally serving and

---

35. Josiah Priest, *op. cit.*, Eighth Section, *passim.*

worshipping ole Marse, they are admirable creatures, but in freedom they are beasts, as his novel *Red Rock* attests. *The Negro: The Southerner's Problem* says that the state of the Negro since emancipation is one of minimum progress and maximum regress.

> [This] is borne out by the increase of crime among them, by the increase of superstition, with its black trail of unnamable immorality and vice; by the homicides and murders, and by the outbreak and growth of that brutal crime which has chiefly brought about the frightful crime of lynching which stains the *good name of the South* and has spread northward with the spread of the ravisher. . . . The crime of rape . . . is the fatal product of new conditions. . . . The Negro's passion, always his controlling force, is now, since the new teaching, for the white woman. [Lynching is justifiable] for it has its root deep in the basic passions of humanity; the determination to put an end to the *ravishing of their women by an inferior race,* or by any race, no matter what the consequence. . . . A crusade has been preached against lynching, even as far as England; but none has been attempted against the ravishing and tearing to pieces of white women and children.[36]

The best known author of Ku Klux Klan fiction after Page is Thomas Dixon. Such works as *The Clansman,* and *The Leopard's Spots,* because of their sensationalism and chapter titles (e.g. "The Black Peril," "The Unspoken Terror," "A Thousand Legged Beast," "The Hunt for the Animal"), seemed just made for the mentality of Hollywood, where D. W. Griffith in *The Birth of a Nation* made for Thomas Dixon a dubious sort of immortality, and finally fixed the stereotype in the mass-mind. The stock Negro in Dixon's books, unless the shuffling hat-in-hand servitor, is a gorilla-like imbecile, who "springs like a tiger" and has the "black claws of a beast." In both books there is a terrible rape, and a glorious ride of the Knights on a Holy Crusade to avenge Southern civilization. Dixon enables his white geniuses to discover the identity of the rapist by using "a microscope of sufficient power [to] reveal on the retina of the dead

---

36. Page, *The Negro: The Southerner's Problem, passim* (Italics mine).

eyes the image of this devil as if etched there by fire." . . . The doctor sees "The bestial figure of a negro—his huge black hand plainly defined. . . . It was Gus." Will the wonders of science never cease? But, perhaps, after all, Negroes have been convicted on even flimsier evidence. Fortunately for the self-respect of American authors, this kind of writing is in abeyance today. Perhaps it fell because of the weight of its own absurdity. But it would be unwise to underestimate this stereotype. It is probably of great potency in certain benighted sections where Dixon, if he could be read, would be applauded—and it certainly serves as a convenient self-justification for a mob about to uphold white supremacy by a lynching.

The Tragic Mulatto

*"The gods bestow on me
A life of hate,
The white man's gift to see
A nigger's fate."*
"The Mulatto Addresses his Savior on Christmas Morning"
SEYMOUR GORDDEN LINK

Stereotyping was by no means the monopoly of pro-slavery authors defending their type of commerce, or justifying their ancestors. Anti-slavery authors, too, fell into the easy habit, but with a striking difference. [192] Where pro-slavery authors had predicated a different set of characteristics for the Negroes, a distinctive sub-human nature, and had stereotyped in accordance with such a comforting hypothesis, anti-slavery authors insisted that the Negro had a common humanity with the whites, that in given circumstances a typically human type of response was to be expected, unless certain other powerful influences were present. The stereotyping in abolitionary literature, therefore, is not stereotyping of *character*, but of *situation*. Since the novels were propagandistic, they concentrated upon abuses: floggings, the slave mart, the domestic slave trade, forced concubinage, runaways, slave hunts, and persecuted freemen—all of these were frequently repeated. Stereotyped or not, heightened if you will, the anti-slavery novel has been supported by the verdict of history—whether recorded by Southern or Northern historians. Facts, after all, are abolitionist. Especially the fact that the Colonel's lady and old Aunt Dinah are sisters under the skin.

Anti-slavery authors did at times help to perpetuate certain proslavery stereotypes. Probably the novelists knew that harping upon the gruesome, to the exclusion of all else, would repel readers, who—like their present-day descendants—yearn for happy endings and do not wish their quick consciences to be harrowed. At any rate, comic relief, kindly masters (in contrast to the many brutes), loyal and submissive slaves (to accentuate the wrongs inflicted upon them) were scattered throughout the books. Such tempering of the attacks was turned to pro-slavery uses. Thus, Harris writes:

> It seems to me to be impossible for any unprejudiced person to read Mrs. Stowe's book and fail to see in it a defence of American slavery as she found it in Kentucky. . . . The real moral that Mrs. Stowe's book teaches is that the possibilities of slavery . . . are shocking to the imagination, while the realities, under the best and happiest conditions, possess a romantic beauty and a tenderness all their own. . . . [37]

Anti-slavery fiction did proffer one stereotype, doomed to unfortunate longevity. This is the tragic mulatto. Pro-slavery apologists had almost entirely omitted (with so many other omissions) mention of concubinage. If anti-slavery authors, in accordance with Victorian gentility, were wary of illustrating the practice, they made great use nevertheless of the offspring of illicit unions. Generally the heroes and heroines of their books are near-whites. There are the intransigent, the resentful, the mentally alert, the proofs of the Negro's possibilities. John Herbert Nelson says with some point:

> Abolitionists tried, by making many of their characters almost white, to work on racial feeling as well. This was a curious piece of inconsistency on their part, an indirect admission that a white man in chains was more pitiful to behold than the African simi-

---

37. Julia Collier Harris, *op. cit.*, p. 117.

larly placed. Their most impassioned plea was in behalf of a person little resembling their swarthy protegés, the quadroon or octoroon.[38]

Nelson himself, however, shows similar inconsistency, as he infers that the "true African—essentially gay, happy-go-lucky, rarely ambitious or idealistic, the eternal child of the present moment, able to leave trouble behind—is unsuited for such portrayal. . . . Only the mulattoes and [193] others of mixed blood have, so far, furnished us with material for convincing tragedy." [39]

The tragic mulatto appears in both of Mrs. Stowe's abolitionary novels. In *Uncle Tom's Cabin*, the fugitives Liza and George Harris and the rebellious Cassy are mulattoes. Uncle Tom, the pure black, remains the paragon of Christian submissiveness. In *Dred*, Harry Gordon and his wife are nearly white. Harry is an excellent manager, and a proud, unsubmissive type:

Mr. Jekyl, that humbug don't go down with me! I'm no more of the race of Ham than you are! I'm Colonel Gordon's oldest son —as white as my brother, who you say owns me! Look at my eyes, and my hair, and say if any of the rules about Ham pertain to me.[40]

The implication that there are "rules about Ham" that do pertain to blacks is to be found in other works. Richard Hildreth's *Archy Moore, or The White Slave*, has as its leading character a fearless, educated mulatto, indistinguishable from whites; Boucicault's *The Octoroon* sentimentalizes the hardships of a slave girl; both make the mixed-blood the chief victim of slavery.

Cable, in *The Grandissimes*, shows a Creole mulatto educated beyond his means, and suffering ignominy, but he likewise shows in the character of Bras-Coupé that he does not consider intrepidity and vindictiveness the monopoly of mixed-bloods. In *Old Creole Days*, however, he discusses the beautiful octoroon, whose best for-

---
38. John Herbert Nelson, *op. cit.*, p. 84.
39. *Ibid.*, p. 136.
40. Harriet Beecher Stowe, *Nina Gordon, or Dred*. Boston: Houghton, Mifflin and Co., 1881, p. 142.

tune in life was to become the mistress of some New Orleans dandy. He shows the tragedy of their lives, but undoubtedly contributed to the modern stereotype that the greatest yearning of the girl of mixed life is for a white lover. Harriet Martineau, giving a contemporary portrait of old New Orleans, wrote:

> The quadroon girls . . . are brought up by their mothers to be what they have been; the mistresses of white gentlemen. The boys are some of them sent to France; some placed on land in the back of the State. . . . The women of their own color object to them, "*ils sont si degoutants!*" [41]

Lyle Saxon says that "the free men of color are always in the background; to use the Southern phrase, 'they know their place.'"

The novelists have kept them in the background. Many recent novels show this: *White Girl, The No-Nation Girl, A Study in Bronze, Gulf Stream, Dark Lustre*—all of these show luridly the melodrama of the lovely octoroon girl. Indeed "octoroon" has come to be a feminine noun in popular usage.

The stereotype that demands attention, however, is the notion of mulatto character, whether shown in male or female. This character works itself out with mathematical symmetry. The older theses ran: First, the mulatto inherits the vices of both races and none of the virtues; second, any achievement of a Negro is to be attributed to the white blood in his veins. The logic runs that even inheriting the worst from whites is sufficient for achieving among Negroes. The present theses are based upon these: The mulatto is a victim of a divided inheritance; from his white blood come his intellectual strivings, [194] his unwillingness to be a slave; from his Negro blood come his baser emotional urges, his indolence, his savagery.

Thus, in *The No-Nation Girl*, Evans Wall writes of his tragic heroine, Précieuse:

> Her dual nature had not developed its points of difference. The warring qualities, her double inheritance of Caucasian and black

---

41. Quoted in Lyle Saxon, *Fabulous New Orleans*. New York: The Century Co., 1928, p. 182.

mingled in her blood, had not yet begun to disturb, and torture, and set her apart from either race. . . .

[As a child,] Précieuse had learned to dance as soon as she could toddle about on her shapely little legs; half-savage little steps with strange movements of her body, exotic gestures and movements that had originated among the remote ancestors of her mother's people in some hot African jungle.

. . . the wailing cry of the guitar was as primitive and disturbing as the beat of a tom-tom to dusky savages gathered for an orgy of dancing and passion in some moon-flooded jungle. . . . Self-control reached its limit. The girl's half-heritage of savagery rose in a flood that washed away all trace of her father's people except the supersensitiveness imparted to her taut nerves. She must dance or scream to relieve the rising torrent of response to the wild, monotonous rhythm.

It is not long before the girl is unable to repress, what Wall calls, the lust inherited from her mother's people; the environment of debauchery, violence, and rapine is exchanged for concubinage with a white paragon, which ends, of course, in the inevitable tragedy. The girl "had no right to be born."

Dark Lustre, by Geoffrey Barnes, transfers the main essentials of the foregoing plot to Harlem. Aline, of the darkly lustrous body, thus analyzes herself in accordance with the old clichés: "The black half of me is ashamed of itself for being there, and every now and then crawls back into itself and tries to let the white go ahead and pass. . . ." Says the author: "There was too much of the nigger in her to let her follow a line of reasoning when the black cloud of her emotions settled over it." Half-white equals reason; half-black equals emotion. She too finds her ideal knight in a white man, and death comes again to the tragic octoroon who should never have been born. *White Girl, Gulf Stream, A Study in Bronze* are in substance very similar to these.

Roark Bradford in *This Side of Jordan* gives an unconscious *reductio ad absurdum* of this stereotype.

The blade of a razor flashed through the air. Scrap has concealed it in the folds of her dress. Her Negro blood sent it unerringly between two ribs. Her Indian blood sent it back for an unnecessary second and third slash.

It might be advanced that Esquimaux blood probably would have kept her from being chilled with horror. The strangest items are attributed to different racial strains: In *No-Nation Girl* a woman cries out in childbirth because of her Negro expressiveness; from the back of Précieuse's "ankles down to her heels, the flesh was slightly thicker" —due to her Negro blood; Lessie in Welbourn Kelley's *Inchin' Along* "strongly felt the urge to see people, to talk to people. . . . That was the white in her maybe. Or maybe it was the mixture of white and black."

This kind of writing should be discredited by its patent absurdity. It is generalizing of the wildest sort, without support from scientific authorities. And yet it has set these *idées fixes* in the mob mind: The Negro of unmixed blood is no theme for tragedy; rebellion and vindictiveness are to be expected only from the mulatto; the mulatto is victim of a divided inheritance [195] and therefore miserable; he is a "man without a race" worshipping the whites and despised by them, despising and despised by Negroes, perplexed by his struggle to unite a white intellect with black sensuousness. The fate of the octoroon girl is intensified—the whole desire of her life is to find a white lover, and then go down, accompanied by slow music, to a tragic end. Her fate is so severe that in some works disclosure of "the single drop of midnight" in her veins makes her commit suicide.

The stereotype is very flattering to a race which, for all its self-assurance, seems to stand in great need of flattery. But merely looking at one of its particulars—that white blood means asceticism and Negro blood means unbridled lust—will reveal how flimsy the whole structure is. It is ingenious that mathematical computation of the amount of white blood in a mulatto's veins will explain his character. And it is a widely held belief. But it is nonsense, all the same.

The Local Color Negro

"The defects of local color inhere in the constitution of the cult itself, which, as its name suggests, thought . . . first of the piquant surfaces and then—if at all—of the stubborn deeps of human life."
    CARL VAN DOREN, *Contemporary American Novelists*

Local color stresses the quaint, the odd, the picturesque, the different. It is an attempt to convey the peculiar quality of a locality. Good realistic practice would insist upon the localizing of speech, garb, and customs; great art upon the revelation of the universal beneath these local characteristics. Local color is now in disrepute because of its being contented with merely the peculiarity of dialect and manners. As B. A. Botkin, editor of *Folk-Say*, has stated: "In the past [local consciousness] has been narrowly sectional rather than broadly human, superficially picturesque rather than deeply interpretative, provincial without being indigenous." [42]

The "local color Negro" is important in any study of the Negro character in American literature. But, since the local colorists of the Negro were more concerned with fidelity to speech and custom, with revelation of his difference in song and dance and story, than with revelation of Negro character, they accepted at face valuation the current moulds into which Negro character had been forced. Therefore, local colorists have been and will be considered under other heads. Page and Russell were local colorists in that they paid close attention to Negro speech, but the Negro they portrayed was the same old contented slave. Their study of Negro speech, however, was fruitful and needed—for pro-slavery authors had been as false in recording Negro speech as they were in picturing Negro experience. Kennedy, for instance, forces a confessedly wretched dialect into the mouths of poor Negroes, and W. L. G. Smith has his Shenandoah Negroes speak

---

42. B. A. Botkin, *Folk-Say, A Regional Miscellany*. Norman: The Oklahoma Folk-Lore Society, 1929, p. 12.

Gullah, because his master, Simms, had written of South Carolina Negroes.

Cable, one of the best of the local colorists, in *The Grandissimes,* goes a step beyond the mere local color formula; *Old Creole Days* is local color, but has been considered under the "Tragic Mulatto." The Negroes in [196] Lyle Saxon's old and new New Orleans, E. Larocque Tinker's old New Orleans, R. Emmett Kennedy's Gretna Green, are in the main kinsfolk to the contented slave; in Evans Wall's Mississippi canebrakes are exotic primitives, or tragic mulattoes; on Roark Bradford's levees are primitives; and those on Julia Peterkin's Blue Brook plantation, in Heyward's Catfish Row, and in John Vandercook's Surinam, Liberia, and Haiti, usually surmount, in the writer's opinion, the deficiencies of local color. Stereotyped, or genuinely interpreted, however, they all agree in one respect: they show the peculiar differences of certain Negroes in well-defined localities.

John B. Sale in *The Tree Named John* records with sympathy the dialect, superstititions, folk-ways of Mississippi Negroes. He is meticulous, perhaps to a fault, in his dialectal accuracy; the milieu is correspondingly convincing. His Negroes do carry on the pattern of mutual affection between the races—and yet they are far nearer flesh and blood than those of Page. Samuel Stoney and Gertrude Shelby, in *Black Genesis,* give the peculiarities of the Gullah Negro's cosmogony. Care is paid to fidelity in recording the dialect, but the authors' comments reveal a certain condescension toward quaintness which is the usual bane of local colorists. In *Po' Buckra* the authors reveal the localized tragedy of the "brass-ankle"—the Croatan-Negro-near-white caste. Much of the "tragic mulatto" theme is in this book, as well as the purely local color interest. Ambrose Gonzales in his Gullah renditions of Aesop, and in his tales of the "black border," reveals for the curious the intricacies of a little known Negro dialect, following the lead of Harris, and C. C. Jones, who recorded the Br'er Rabbit tales in the dialect of the Georgia coast.

Although most of these authors who dwell upon quaint and picturesque divergencies are discussed under other headings, it will not do to underestimate this local color Negro. The showing of Negro peculiarities in speech, superstitions, and customs has been popular for many years, and is likely to be for a long while yet. It undoubtedly has its artistic uses; but being an end in itself is surely not the chief of them.

The Exotic Primitive

"Then I saw the Congo, cutting through the black. . . ."
VACHEL LINDSAY

This stereotype grew up with America's post-war revolt against Puritanism and Babbittry. Literary critics urged a return to spontaneity, to unrestrained emotions; American literature had been too long conventional, drab, without music and color. Human nature had been viewed with too great a reticence. Sex, which the Victorians had considered unmentionable, was pronounced by the school of Freud to have an overwhelming importance in motivating our conduct. So the pendulum swung from the extreme of Victorian prudishness to that of modern expressiveness.

To authors searching "for life in the raw," Negro life and character seemed to beg for exploitation. There was the Negro's savage inheritance, as they conceived it: hot jungle nights, the tom-tom calling to esoteric orgies. There were the frankness and violence to be found in any underprivileged group, or on any frontier. [197] There were the traditional beliefs of the Negro being a creature of his appetites, and although pro-slavery fiction had usually (because of Victorianism) limited these to his yearnings for hog meat and greens, 'possum and yams, and for whiskey on holidays, Reconstruction fiction had stressed his lustfulness. He seemed to be cut out for the hands of certain authors. They promptly rushed to Harlem for color. In Harlem dives and cabarets they found what they believed to be *the* Negro, *au naturel*.

The figure who emerges from their pages is a Negro synchronized to a savage rhythm, living a life of ecstasy, superinduced by jazz (repetition of the tom-tom, awakening vestigial memories of Africa) and gin, that lifted him over antebellum slavery, and contemporary economic slavery, and placed him in the comforting fastnesses of their "mother-land." A kinship exists between this stereotype and that of the contented slave; one is merely a "jazzed-up" version of the other, with cabarets supplanting cabins, and Harlemized "blues," instead of the spirituals and slave reels. Few were the observers who saw in the Negroes' abandon a release from the troubles of this world similar to that afforded in slavery by their singing. Many there were, however, who urged that the Harlem Negro's state was that of an inexhaustible *joie de vivre*.

Carl Van Vechten was one of the pioneers of the hegira from downtown to Harlem; he was one of the early discoverers of the cabaret; and his novel, *Nigger Heaven,* is to the exotic pattern what *Swallow Barn* was to the contented slave. All of the possibilities of the development of the type are inherent in the book. In the prologue, we have the portrait of the "creeper," Don Juan of Seventh Avenue, whose amatory prowess causes him to be sought by women unknown to him. We feel that his prologue sets the tone of the work: we are going to see the Harlem of gin mills and cabarets, of kept men and loose ladies, of all-day sleepers and all-night roisterers. Van Vechten, who was already famed as a sophisticated romantic novelist, writes graphically of this Harlem. His style invited emulation from young men desiring to be men-about-town first and then novelists, just as Kennedy invited emulation from young Southerners desiring to defend slavery first. Van Vechten's novel does more than present the local color of Harlem; there is as well the character study of a young Negro intellectual who cannot withstand the dissipations of the "greatest Negro city." But the Bohemian life in Harlem is the main thing, even in this youngster's life. According to the publisher's blurb, "Herein is caught the fascination and tortured ecstasies of Harlem. . . . The author tells the story of modern Negro life." The blurb claims too much. There is another, there are many other Harlems. And *the* story of modern Negro life will never be found in one volume, or in a thousand.

Lasca Sartoris, exquisite, gorgeous, golden-brown Messalina of Seventh Avenue, is one of the chief characters of the book. On seeing her one of the characters comments: "Whew! She'll make a dent in Harlem." She does. She causes the young hero, Byron, in a drunken rage, to empty his gun in the body of one of her lovers, although [198] the man was already dead, and a policeman was approaching.

Van Vechten has a noted magazine editor comment pontifically on the possibilities of Negro literature:

Nobody has yet written a good gambling story; nobody has gone into the curious subject of the divers tribes of the region. . . . There's the servant-girl, for instance. Nobody has ever done the

NEGRO CHARACTER AS SEEN BY WHITE AUTHORS 143

Negro servant-girl, who refuses to "live in." Washing dishes in the day-time, she returns at night to her home in Harlem where she smacks her daddy in the jaw or else dances and makes love. On the whole I should say she has the best time of any domestic servant in the world. . . . The Negro fast set does everything the Long Island fast set does, plays bridge, keeps the bootlegger busy, drives around in Rolls-Royces and commits adultery, but it is vastly more amusing than the Long Island set for the simple reason that it is *amused* . . . . Why, Roy McKain visited Harlem just once and then brought me in a cabaret yarn about a Negro pimp. I don't suppose he even saw the fellow. Probably just made him up, imagined him, but his imagination was based on a background of observation. The milieu is correct. . . .[43]

Although these are merely the offhand comments of an editor, and not to be taken too seriously as final critical pronouncements on *the* Negro, still certain implications are obvious. The best Negro characters for literary purposes are suggested: gamblers, fast set, servant-girl-sweet-mamma, etc. All are similar in their great capacity for enjoyment—and it is that side that must be shown. The eternal playboys of the Western hemisphere! Why even one trip to Harlem will reveal the secret of their mystery. The connection of all of this to the contented slave, comic, local color Negro is patent. Another thing to be noticed is the statement issued by the literary market: Stereotypes wanted.

In *Black Sadie*, T. Bowyer Campbell, whose preference is for the stereotype of the contented slave of the South, ironically accounts for the Harlem fad by the desire of jaded sophisticates for a new thrill. But Campbell does agree in some degree with the Harlem stereotype: "Colored people demand nothing but easy happiness, good nature." Black Sadie, child of a man hanged for raping an old white woman, having become the toast of artistic New York, remaining a kleptomaniac—"it was in her blood"—even in affluence, causing a murder, returns—in the best tradition of minstrel songs—to happy Virginia. "Easy come, easy go, niggers," Campbell closes his book, philosophically.

43. Carl Van Vechten, *Nigger Heaven*. New York: Grosset and Dunlap, 1928, pp. 225 ff.

Sherwood Anderson, in *Dark Laughter*, expresses a genuine Rousseauism. Hostile toward the routine of industrialism and Puritanism, Anderson sets up as a foil the happy-go-lucky sensuality of river-front Negroes, who laugh, with genial cynicism, at the self-lacerations of hypersensitive Nordics. His "dark laughter" lacks the sinister undertone of Llewellyn Powy's "black laughter" heard in Africa. Anderson's Negroes are too formalized a chorus, however, for conviction, and are more the dream-children of a romanticist than actual flesh-and-blood creations. Anderson has drawn some excellent Negro characters; in *Dark Laughter*, however, he characterizes the Negroes too straitly. That the chief response of the Negro to his experience is a series of deep rounds of laughter at white sex-tangles is difficult of credence.

William Seabrook in *Magic Island* and *Jungle Ways* writes sensational travel tales—according to some, in the tradition of Munchausen and Marco [199] Polo. He exploits the exotic and primitive, recording voodoo rites, black magic, strange sexual practices, weird superstitions, and cannibalism. His work brings a sort of vicarious satisfaction to Main Street, and advances the stereotype. He traces back to original sources what downtown playboys come up to Harlem to see.

The stereotype of the exotic-primitive would require more than a dogmatic refutation. Not so patently a "wish-fulfillment," as the "contented slave" stereotype was, nor an expression of unreasoning hatred, as the "brute Negro," it is advanced by novelists realistic in technique and rather convincing, although demonstrably "romantic" in their choice of the sensational. But it would be pertinent to question the three basic assumptions—either insinuated or expressed—underlying the stereotype: that the "natural" Negro is to be found in Harlem cabarets; that the life and character depicted there are representative of Negro life in general; and that the Negro is "himself," and startlingly different in the sensational aspects of his life.

It is strange that the "natural" Negro should be looked for in the most sophisticated of environment. Even the names "Cotton Club," "Plantation Revue," the lavish, though inaccurate, cotton bolls decorating the walls, the choruses in silken overalls and bandanas do not disguise but rather enforce the fact that Negro entertainers, like entertainers everywhere, give the public what clever managers, generally Caucasian, believe the public wants. Unwise as it is to generalize about America, or New York State, or even Queens from the Great White Way, it is no less unwise to generalize about Negro life and character from Harlem. It is even unwise to generalize about Harlem, from *the* Harlem shown in books. Strange to say, there is a Harlem that can be observed by the cold glare of daylight.

The exotic primitives of Mississippi levees and cane-brakes, of Catfish Row and Blue Brook Plantation are more convincing, as examples of frontier communities, and of underprivileged groups who are known to live violent lives. It is surely not impossible, however, to believe that observers with an eye for environmental factors might see an entirely different picture from the one presented by searchers for exotic-primitive innate tendencies.

Harvey Wickham in *The Impuritans* writes:

> On Pacific Street, San Francisco, there used to be, and probably still is, a Negro dance hall called the So-Different Cafe. The name was deceptive. It was not so different from any other slum-hole. [A slum hole] is tediously the same, whether it be in Harlem, lower Manhattan, London, Paris, Berlin, Rome, Athens, Pekin, or Timbuctoo. There is no possible variety in degradation. . . .[44]

Such a comment surely deserves as careful attention as the stereotype of the exotic-primitive.

Attempts at Realization

> "*John Henry said to his captain,*
> *A man ain't nothin' but a man . . . .*"
> "Ballad of John Henry"

It would be a mistake to believe that the works of all white authors bear out these stereotypes. Some of the best attacks upon stereotyping have come from white authors, and [200] from Southerners, just as some of the strongest upholding of the stereotypes has come from Negroes. Moreover, the writer of this essay hopes that he will not

---

44. Harvey Wickham, *The Impuritans*. New York: The Dial Press, 1929, p. 284.

be accused of calling everything a stereotype that does not flatter Negro character, or of insisting that the stereotypes have no basis in reality. Few of the most apologistic of "race" orators could deny the presence of contented slaves, of wretched freemen, in our past; nor of comic Negroes (even in the joke-book tradition), of self-pitying mulattoes, of brutes, of exotic primitives in our present. Negro life does have its local color, and a rich, glowing color it can be at times. What this essay has aimed to point out is the obvious unfairness of hardening racial character into fixed moulds. True in some particulars, each of these popular generalizations is dangerous when applied to the entire group. Furthermore, most of these generalizations spring from a desire to support what is considered social expediency rather than from a sincere attempt at interpretation, and are therefore bad art.

Attempts at sincere "realization" rather than imitation of set patterns can be found in the early works of Eugene O'Neill, whose plays first brought a tragic Negro to Broadway. Ridgeley Torrence saw another side to the familiar guitar-playing clown—showing him to be a dreamer of dreams like the other Playboy of the Western World—and saw dignity in his long suffering, hard-working wife. *The Rider of Dreams*, in its quiet way, did much to demolish the old stereotypes.

Julia Peterkin, for all of her tendency to local color (*Bright April* is a storehouse of Negro superstitions and folk customs) and her emphasis on sex and violence, [45] is still of importance in her departure from the stereotypes.

In a simple, effective manner, she reveals the winning humanity of the Gullah people, whom she obviously loves and respects. If critics would refuse to call her the interpreter of *the* Negro, and realize that she writes of a very limited segment of life from a very personal point of view, they would do a service to her and to their own reputations. She has well-nigh surmounted the difficulty of being a plantation owner.

Du Bose Heyward has given us some of the best Negro characterizations in *Porgy* and *Mamba's Daughters*. Though the first is naturalistic with a flair for the exotic-primitive, Heyward does show in it essential humanity: Porgy reveals himself as capable of essen-

---

45. *Vide: Black April, Scarlet Sister Mary* for examples of extreme promiscuity, and *Bright Skin* for violent deaths.

tial fineness, and even Bess is not completely past reclaiming. *Mamba's Daughters* reveals that Negroes, too, can be provident as Mamba was, or heroic as Hagar was, for the sake of the young. The travesty of Southern justice toward the Negro, the difficulties of the aspiring Negro, the artistic potentialities and actualities of Negroes, receive ample attention. Except for certain forgivable slips into the "comic," the book is an excellent illustration of the dignity and beauty that can be found in some aspects of lowly Negro life.

E. C. L. Adams, because he seems to let Negro characters speak for themselves, in their own idiom, and [201] as if no white man was overhearing, has been very successful in his interpretation of Negro folk-life. Here the humor expressed by the Negro is miles away from Cohen's buffoonery. There is a sharp, acid flavor to it; in the Negroes' condemnation of the Ben Bess case there is the bitterness that has been stored up for so very long. These folk are not happy-go-lucky, nor contented; they are shrewd, realistic philosophers, viewing white pretense and injustice with cynicism—though not with Sherwood Anderson's "Dark Laughter." Illiterate they may be, but they are not being fooled.

Howard Odum, by letting the Negro speak for himself, presents a similarly convincing folk-Negro, in this case, the rambling man, who has been everywhere, and seen everybody. Many of the stereotypes are overthrown in *Rainbow Round My Shoulder,* although comic, and brutal, and submissive Negroes may be seen there. These are viewed, however, "in the round," not as walking generalizations about *the* Negro, and Odum is intent on making us understand how they got to be what they are.

Evelyn Scott and T. S. Stribling, historical novelists of the Civil War, as different as may be in technique, agree in giving us rounded pictures of antebellum Negroes. Slavery is not a perpetual Mardi Gras in their novels, nor are Negroes cast in the old, rigid mould. They are characterized as human beings, not as representatives of a peculiar species. Paul Green's *In Abraham's Bosom* shows the Negro's handicapped struggles for education during the Reconstruction; Green has brought great dramatic power to bear upon revealing that the Negro is a figure worthy of tragic dignity. In *The House of Connelly* he has disclosed aspects of the so-called "contented slave" that antebellum authors were either ignorant of, or afraid to show.

Erskine Caldwell, George Milburn, William Faulkner, and

Thomas Wolfe, while their métier is the portraiture of poor whites, help in undermining the stereotypes by showing that what have been considered Negro characteristics, such as dialect, illiteracy, superstitions, sexual looseness, violence, etc., are to be found as frequently among poor whites. When they do show Negro characters, they frequently show them to be burdened by economic pressure, the playthings of Southern justice, and the catspaws for sadistic "superiors."

A recent novel, *Amber Satyr*, shows a lynching that follows a white woman's relentless and frenzied pursuit of her hired man, a good-looking Negro. Welbourn Kelley's *Inchin' Along*, although influenced by some stereotypes (his mulatto wife, true to type, is the easy prey of the first white man who rides along), does show the hardworking, provident, stoical Negro. James Knox Millen wrote a powerful attack upon lynching in *Never No More*, showing the precarious hold the Southern Negro has upon peace and happiness. Scott Nearing, with a proletarian emphasis, has presented graphically the new slavery, peonage, in the South, with its horrible concomitant lynchings, and the bitter prejudice of organized labor in the North. And finally, John L. Spivak, in *Georgia Nigger*, has written a second *Uncle Tom's Cabin*, an indictment of peonage, and convict-labor in Georgia, powerful enough to put to shame all the rhapsodists of the folk-Negro's happy state.

To trace the frequency with which the Negro author has stepped out of his conventional picture frame, from the spirituals and satiric folk-rhymes down to Langston Hughes, would exceed the bounds of this paper, and for present purposes is not needed. A reading of only a few of the white authors just mentioned (many of whom are from the South) would effectively illustrate the inadequacy of the familiar stereotypes.

It is likely that, in spite of the willingness of some Negro authors to accept at face value some of these stereotypes, the exploration of Negro life and character rather than its exploitation must come from Negro authors themselves. This, of course, runs counter to the American conviction that the Southern white man knows the Negro best, and can best interpret him. Nan Bagby Stephens states what other Southern authors have insinuated:

> Maybe it was because my slave-owning ancestors were fond of their darkies and treated them as individuals that I see them like

that. It seems to me that no one, not even the negroes themselves, can get the perspective reached through generations of understanding such as we inherited.[46]

The writer of this essay holds to the contrary opinion, agreeing with another Southerner, F. P. Gaines,[47] that when a white man says that he knows the Negro he generally means that he knows the Negro of the joke-book tradition. Stephen Vincent Benét has written:

> Oh, blackskinned epic, epic with the black spear,
> I cannot sing you, having too white a heart,
> And yet, some day a poet will rise to sing you
> And sing you with such truth and mellowness. . .
> That you will be a match for any song . . . .[48]

But whether Negro life and character are to be best interpreted from without or within is an interesting by-path that we had better not enter here. One manifest truth, however, is this: the sincere, sensitive artist, willing to go beneath the clichés of popular belief to get at an underlying reality, will be wary of confining a race's entire character to a half-dozen narrow grooves. He will hardly have the temerity to say that his necessarily limited observation of a few Negroes in a restricted environment can be taken as the last word about some mythical *the* Negro. He will hesitate to do this, even though he had a Negro mammy, or spent a night in Harlem, or has been a Negro all his life. The writer submits that such an artist is the only one worth listening to, although the rest are legion. [203]

46. *Contempo,* Volume II, No. 2, p. 3.
47. F. P. Gaines, *op. cit.,* p. 17.
48. Stephen Vincent Benét, *John Brown's Body.* Garden City, New York: Doubleday Doran and Co., 1928, p. 347.

BLACK BOYS AND NATIVE SONS
Irving Howe

James Baldwin first came to the notice of the American literary public not through his own fiction but as author of an impassioned criticism of the conventional Negro novel. In 1949 he published in *Partisan Review* an essay called "Everybody's Protest Novel," attacking the kind of fiction, from *Uncle Tom's Cabin* to *Native Son*, that had been written about the ordeal of the American Negroes; and two years later he printed in the same magazine "Many Thousands Gone," a tougher and more explicit polemic against Richard Wright and the school of naturalistic "protest" fiction that Wright represented. The protest novel, wrote Baldwin, is undertaken out of sympathy for the Negro, but through its need to present him merely as a social victim or a mythic agent of sexual prowess, it hastens to confine the Negro to the very tones of violence he has known all his life. Compulsively re-enacting and magnifying his trauma, the protest novel proves unable to transcend it. So choked with rage has this kind of writing become, it cannot show the Negro as a unique person or locate him as a member of a community with its own traditions and values, its own "unspoken recognition of shared experience which creates a way of life." The failure of the protest novel "lies in its insistence that it is [man's] categorization alone which is real and which cannot be transcended." [98]

Like all attacks launched by young writers against their famous elders, Baldwin's essays were also a kind of announcement of his own intentions. He wrote admiringly about Wright's courage ("his work was an immense liberation and revelation for me"), but now, precisely because Wright had prepared the way for all the Negro writers to come, he, Baldwin, would go further, transcending the sterile categories of "Negro-ness," whether those enforced by the white world or those defensively erected by the Negroes themselves. No longer mere victim or rebel, the Negro would stand free in a self-achieved humanity. As Baldwin put it some years later, he hoped "to prevent myself from becoming *merely* a Negro; or even, merely a Negro writer." The world "tends to trap and immobilize you in the role you

SOURCE: Irving Howe, "Black Boys and Native Sons," *A World More Attractive* (New York: Horizon Press, 1963), pp. 98–122. Reprinted by permission of the publisher.

play," and for the Negro writer, if he is to be a writer at all, it hardly matters whether the trap is sprung from motives of hatred or condescension.

Baldwin's rebellion against the older Negro novelist who had served him as a model and had helped launch his career, was not of course an unprecedented event. The history of literature is full of such painful ruptures, and the issue Baldwin raised is one that keeps recurring, usually as an aftermath to a period of "socially engaged" writing. The novel is an inherently ambiguous genre: it strains toward formal autonomy and can seldom avoid being a public gesture. If it is true, as Baldwin said in "Everybody's Protest Novel," that "literature and sociology are not one and the same," it is equally true that such statements hardly begin to cope with the problem of how a writer's own experience affects his desire to represent human affairs in a work of fiction. Baldwin's formula evades, through rhetorical sweep, the genuinely difficult issue of the relationship between social experience and literature.

Yet in *Notes of a Native Son,* the book in which his remark appears, Baldwin could also say: "One writes out of one thing only—one's own experience." What, then, was the experience of a man with a black skin, what *could* it be in this [99] country? How could a Negro put pen to paper, how could he so much as think or breathe, without some impulsion to protest, be it harsh or mild, political or private, released or buried? The "sociology" of his existence formed a constant pressure on his literary work, and not merely in the way this might be true for any writer, but with a pain and ferocity that nothing could remove.

James Baldwin's early essays are superbly eloquent, displaying virtually in full the gifts that would enable him to become one of the great American rhetoricians. But these essays, like some of the later ones, are marred by rifts in logic, so little noticed when one gets swept away by the brilliance of the language that it takes a special effort to attend their argument.

Later Baldwin would see the problems of the Negro writer with a greater charity and more mature doubt. Reviewing in 1959 a book of poems by Langston Hughes, he wrote: "Hughes is an American Negro poet and has no choice but to be acutely aware of it. He is not the first American Negro to find the war between his social and artistic responsibilities all but irreconcilable." All but irreconcilable: the phrase strikes a note sharply different from Baldwin's attack upon Wright in the early fifties. And it is not hard to surmise the reasons for this change. In the intervening years Baldwin had been living through some of the experiences that had goaded Richard Wright into rage and driven him into exile; he too, like Wright, had been to hell and back, many times over.

II

Gawd, Ah wish all them white folks was dead.

The day *Native Son* appeared, American culture was changed forever. No matter how much qualifying the book might later need, it made impossible a repetition of the old [100] lies. In all its crudeness, melodrama and claustrophobia of vision, Richard Wright's novel brought out into the open, as no one ever had before, the hatred, fear and violence that have crippled and may yet destroy our culture.

A blow at the white man, the novel forced him to recognize himself as an oppressor. A blow at the black man, the novel forced him to recognize the cost of his submission. *Native Son* assaulted the most cherished of American vanities: the hope that the accumulated injustice of the past would bring with it no lasting penalties, the fantasy that in his humiliation the Negro somehow retained a sexual potency —or was it a childlike good-nature?—that made it necessary to envy and still more to suppress him. Speaking from the black wrath of retribution, Wright insisted that history can be a punishment. He told us the one thing even the most liberal whites preferred not to hear: that Negroes were far from patient or forgiving, that they were scarred by fear, that they hated every moment of their suppression even when seeming most acquiescent, and that often enough they hated *us*, the decent and cultivated white men who from complicity or neglect shared in the responsibility for their plight. If such younger novelists as Baldwin and Ralph Ellison were to move beyond Wright's harsh naturalism and toward more supple modes of fiction, that was possible only because Wright had been there first, courageous enough to release the full weight of his anger.

In *Black Boy*, the autobiographical narrative he published several years later, Wright would tell of an experience he had while working as a bellboy in the South. Many times he had come into a hotel room carrying luggage or food and seen naked white women lounging about, unmoved by shame at his presence, for "blacks were not considered human beings anyway . . . I was a non-man . . . I felt doubly cast out." With the publication of *Native Son,* however, Wright forced his readers to acknowledge his anger, and in that way, if none other, he wrested for himself a sense of dignity as a man. He forced his [101] readers to confront the disease of our culture, and to one of its most terrifying symptoms he gave the name of Bigger Thomas.

Brutal and brutalized, lost forever to his unexpended hatred and his fear of the world, a numbed and illiterate black boy stumbling into a murder and never, not even at the edge of the electric chair, breaking through to an understanding of either his plight or himself, Bigger Thomas was a part of Richard Wright, a part even of the James Baldwin who stared with horror at Wright's Bigger, unable either to absorb him into his consciousness or eject him from it. Enormous courage, a discipline of self-conquest, was required to conceive Bigger Thomas, for this was no eloquent Negro spokesman, no admirable intellectual or formidable proletarian. Bigger was drawn—one would surmise, deliberately—from white fantasy and white contempt. Bigger was the worst of Negro life accepted, then rendered a trifle conscious and thrown back at those who had made him what he was. "No American Negro exists," Baldwin would later write, "who does not have his private Bigger Thomas living in the skull."

Wright drove his narrative to the very core of American phobia: sexual fright, sexual violation. He understood that the fantasy of rape is a consequence of guilt, what the whites suppose themselves to deserve. He understood that the white man's notion of uncontaminated Negro vitality, little as it had to do with the bitter realities of Negro life, reflected some ill-formed and buried feeling that our culture has run down, lost its blood, become febrile. And he grasped the way in which the sexual issue has been intertwined with social relationships, for even as the white people who hire Bigger as their chauffeur are decent and charitable, even as the girl he accidentally kills is a liberal of sorts, theirs is the power and the privilege. "We black and they white. They got things and we ain't. They do things and we can't."

The novel barely stops to provision a recognizable social [102] world, often contenting itself with cartoon simplicities and yielding almost entirely to the nightmare incomprehension of Bigger Thomas. The mood is apocalyptic, the tone superbly aggressive. Wright was an existentialist long before he heard the name, for he was committed to the literature of extreme situations both through the pressures of his rage and the gasping hope of an ultimate catharsis.

Wright confronts both the violence and the crippling limitations of Bigger Thomas. For Bigger white people are not people at all, but something more, "a sort of great natural force, like a stormy sky looming overhead." And only through violence does he gather a little meaning in life, pitifully little: "he had murdered and created a new life for himself." Beyond that Bigger cannot go.

At first *Native Son* seems still another naturalistic novel: a novel of exposure and accumulation, charting the waste of the undersides of the American city. Behind the book one senses the molding influence of Theodore Dreiser, especially the Dreiser of *An American Tragedy* who knows there are situations so oppressive that only violence can provide their victims with the hope of dignity. Like Dreiser, Wright wished to pummel his readers into awareness; like Dreiser, to overpower them with the sense of society as an enclosing force. Yet the comparison is finally of limited value, and for the disconcerting reason that Dreiser had a white skin and Wright a black one.

The usual naturalistic novel is written with detachment, as if by a scientist surveying a field of operations; it is a novel in which the writer withdraws from a detested world and coldly piles up the evidence for detesting it. *Native Son*, though preserving some of the devices of the naturalistic novel, deviates sharply from its characteristic tone: a tone Wright could not possibly have maintained and which, it may be, no Negro novelist can really hold for long. *Native Son* is a work of assault rather than withdrawal; the author yields himself [103] in part to a vision of nightmare. Bigger's cowering perception of the world becomes the most vivid and authentic component of the book. Naturalism pushed to an extreme turns here into something other than itself, a kind of expressionist outburst, no longer a replica of the familiar social world but a self-contained realm of grotesque emblems.

That *Native Son* has grave faults anyone can see. The language is often coarse, flat in rhythm, syntactically overburdened, heavy with journalistic slag. Apart from Bigger, who seems more a brute energy than a particularized figure, the characters have little reality, the Negroes being mere stock accessories and the whites either "agitprop" villains or heroic Communists whom Wright finds it easier to admire from a distance than establish from the inside. The long speech by Bigger's radical lawyer Max (again a device apparently borrowed from Dreiser) is ill-related to the book itself: Wright had not achieved Dreiser's capacity for absorbing everything, even the most recalcitrant philosophical passages, into a unified vision of things. Between Wright's feelings as a Negro and his beliefs as a Communist there is hardly a genuine fusion, and it is through this gap that a good part of the novel's unreality pours in.

Yet it should be said that the endlessly repeated criticism that Wright caps his melodrama with a party-line oration tends to oversimplify the novel, for Wright is too honest simply to allow the propagandistic message to constitute the last word. Indeed, the last word is given not to Max but to Bigger. For at the end Bigger remains at the mercy of his hatred and fear, the lawyer retreats helplessly, the projected union between political consciousness and raw revolt has not been achieved—as if Wright were persuaded that, all ideology apart, there is for each Negro an ultimate trial that he can bear only by himself.

Black Boy, which appeared five years after *Native Son*, is a slighter but more skillful piece of writing. Richard Wright [104] came from a broken home, and as he moved from his helpless mother to a grandmother whose religious fanaticism (she was a Seventh-Day Adventist) proved utterly suffocating, he soon picked up a precocious knowledge of vice and a realistic awareness of social power. This autobiographical memoir, a small classic in the literature of self-discovery, is packed with harsh evocations of Negro adolescence in the South. The young Wright learns how wounding it is to wear the mask of a grinning niggerboy in order to keep a job. He examines the life of the Negroes and judges it without charity or idyllic compensation—for he already knows, in his heart and his bones, that to be oppressed means to lose out on human possibilities. By the time he is seventeen, preparing to leave for Chicago, where he will work on a WPA project, become a member of the Communist Party, and publish his first book of stories called *Uncle Tom's Children*, Wright has managed to achieve the beginnings of consciousness, through a slow and painful growth from the very bottom of deprivation to the threshold of artistic achievement and a glimpsed idea of freedom.

III

Baldwin's attack upon Wright had partly been anticipated by the more sophisticated American critics. Alfred Kazin, for example, had found in Wright a troubling obsession with violence:

> If he chose to write the story of Bigger Thomas as a grotesque crime story, it is because his own indignation and the sickness of the age combined to make him dependent on violence and shock, to astonish the reader by torrential scenes of cruelty, hunger, rape, murder and flight, and then enlighten him by crude Stalinist homilies.

The last phrase apart, something quite similar could be said about the author of *Crime and Punishment*; it is disconcerting to reflect upon how few novelists, even the very greatest, [105] could pass this kind of moral inspection. For the novel as a genre seems to have an inherent bias toward extreme effects, such as violence, cruelty and the like. More important, Kazin's judgment rests on the assumption that a critic can readily distinguish between the genuine need of a writer to cope with ugly realities and the damaging effect these realities may have upon his moral and psychic life. But in regard to contemporary writers one finds it very hard to distinguish between a valid portrayal of violence and an obsessive involvement with it. A certain amount of obsession may be necessary for the valid portrayal —writers devoted to themes of desperation cannot keep themselves morally intact. And when we come to a writer like Richard Wright, who deals with the most degraded and inarticulate sector of the Negro world, the distinction between objective rendering and subjective immersion becomes still more difficult, perhaps even impossible. For a novelist who has lived through the searing experiences that Wright has there cannot be much possibility of approaching his subject with the "mature" poise recommended by high-minded critics. What is more, the very act of writing his novel, the effort to confront what

Bigger Thomas means to him, is for such a writer a way of dredging up and then perhaps shedding the violence that society has pounded into him. Is Bigger an authentic projection of a social reality, or is he a symptom of Wright's "dependence on violence and shock"? Obviously both; and it could not be otherwise.

For the reality pressing upon all of Wright's work was a nightmare of remembrance, everything from which he had pulled himself out, with an effort and at a cost that is almost unimaginable. Without the terror of that nightmare it would have been impossible for Wright to summon the truth of the reality—not the only truth about American Negroes, perhaps not even the deepest one, but a primary and inescapable truth. Both truth and terror rested on a gross fact which Wright alone dared to confront: that violence is a central fact in the life [106] of the American Negro, defining and crippling him with a harshness few other Americans need suffer. "No American Negro exists who does not have his private Bigger Thomas living in the skull."

Now I think it would be well not to judge in the abstract, or with much haste, the violence that gathers in the Negro's heart as a response to the violence he encounters in society. It would be well to see this violence as part of an historical experience that is open to moral scrutiny but ought to be shielded from presumptuous moralizing. Bigger Thomas may be enslaved to a hunger for violence, but anyone reading *Native Son* with mere courtesy must observe the way in which Wright, even while yielding emotionally to Bigger's deprivation, also struggles to transcend it. That he did not fully succeed seems obvious; one may doubt that any Negro writer can.

More subtle and humane than either Kazin's or Baldwin's criticism is a remark made by Isaac Rosenfeld while reviewing *Black Boy*: "As with all Negroes and all men who are born to suffer social injustice, part of [Wright's] humanity found itself only in acquaintance with violence, and in hatred of the oppressor." Surely Rosenfeld was not here inviting an easy acquiescence in violence; he was trying to suggest the historical context, the psychological dynamics, which condition the attitudes all Negro writers take, or must take, toward violence. To say this is not to propose the condescension of exempting Negro writers from moral judgment, but to suggest the terms of understanding, and still more, the terms of hesitation for making a judgment.

There were times when Baldwin grasped this point better than anyone else. If he could speak of the "unrewarding rage" of *Native Son*, he also spoke of the book as "an immense liberation." Is it impudent to suggest that one reason he felt the book to be a liberation was precisely its rage, precisely the relief and pleasure that he, like so many other Negroes, must [107] have felt upon seeing those long-suppressed emotions finally breaking through?

The kind of literary criticism Baldwin wrote was very fashionable in America during the post-war years. Mimicking the Freudian corrosion of motives and bristling with dialectical agility, this criticism approached all ideal claims, especially those made by radical and naturalist writers, with a weary skepticism and proceeded to transfer the values such writers were attacking to the perspective from which they attacked. If Dreiser wrote about the power hunger and dream of success corrupting American society, that was because he was really infatuated with them. If Farrell showed the meanness of life in the Chicago slums, that was because he could not really escape it. If Wright portrayed the violence gripping Negro life, that was because he was really obsessed with it. The word "really" or more sophisticated equivalents could do endless service in behalf of a generation of intellectuals soured on the tradition of protest but suspecting they might be pigmies in comparison to the writers who had protested. In reply, there was no way to "prove" that Dreiser, Farrell and Wright were not contaminated by the false values they attacked; probably, since they were mere mortals living in the present society, they were contaminated; and so one had to keep insisting that such writers were nevertheless presenting actualities of modern experience, not merely phantoms of their neuroses.

If Bigger Thomas, as Baldwin said, "accepted a theology that denies him life," if in his Negro self-hatred he "*wants* to die because he glories in his hatred," this did not constitute a criticism of Wright unless one were prepared to assume what was simply preposterous: that Wright, for all his emotional involvement with Bigger, could not see beyond the limitations of the character he had created. This was a question Baldwin never seriously confronted in his early essays. He would describe accurately the limitations of Bigger Thomas [108] and then, by one of those rhetorical leaps at which he is so gifted, would assume that these were also the limitations of Wright or his book.

Still another ground for Baldwin's attack was his reluctance to accept the clenched militancy of Wright's posture as both novelist and man. In a remarkable sentence appearing in "Everybody's Protest Novel," Baldwin wrote, "our humanity is our burden, our life; we need not battle for it; we need only to do what is infinitely more difficult—that is, accept it." What Baldwin was saying here was part of the outlook so many American intellectuals took over during the years of a post-war liberalism not very different from conservatism. Ralph Ellison expressed this view in terms still more extreme: "Thus to see America with an awareness of its rich diversity and its almost magical fluidity and freedom, I was forced to conceive of a novel unburdened by the narrow naturalism which has led after so many triumphs to the final and unrelieved despair which marks so much of our current fiction." This not of willed affirmation—as if one could *decide* one's deepest and most authentic response to society!—was to be heard in many other works of the early fifties, most notably in Saul Bellow's *Adventures of Augie March*. Today it is likely to strike one as a note whistled in the dark. In response to Baldwin and Ellison, Wright would have said (I virtually quote the words he used in talking to me during the summer of 1958) that only through struggle could men with black skins, and for that matter, all the oppressed of the world, achieve their humanity. It was a lesson, said Wright with a touch of bitterness yet not without kindness, that the younger writers would have to learn in their own way and their own time. All that has happened since, bears him out.

One criticism made by Baldwin in writing about *Native Son*, perhaps because it is the least ideological, remains important. He complained that in Wright's novel "a necessary dimension has been cut away; this dimension being the relationship [109] that Negroes bear to one another, that depth of involvement and unspoken recognition of shared experience which creates a way of life." The climate of the book, "common to most Negro protest novels . . . has led us all to believe that in Negro life there exists no tradition, no field of manners, no possibility of ritual or intercourse, such as may, for example, sustain the Jew even after he has left his father's house." It could be urged, perhaps, that in composing a novel verging on expressionism Wright need not be expected to present the Negro world with fullness, balance or nuance; but there can be little doubt that in this respect Baldwin did score a major point: the posture of militancy, no matter how great the need for it, exacts a heavy price from the writer, as indeed from everyone else. For "Even the hatred of squalor / Makes the brow grow stern / Even anger against injustice / Makes the voice grow harsh . . ." All one can ask, by way of reply, is whether the refusal to struggle may not exact a still greater price. It is a question that would soon be tormenting James Baldwin, and almost against his will.

IV

In his own novels Baldwin hoped to show the Negro world in its diversity and richness, not as a mere spectre of protest; he wished to show it as a living culture of men and women who, even when deprived, share in the emotions and desires of common humanity. And he meant also to evoke something of the distinctiveness of Negro life in America, as evidence of its worth, moral tenacity and right to self-acceptance. How can one not sympathize with such a program? And how, precisely as one does sympathize, can one avoid the conclusion that in this effort Baldwin has thus far failed to register a major success?

His first novel, *Go Tell It on the Mountain,* is an enticing but minor work: it traces the growing-up of a Negro boy in [110] the atmosphere of a repressive Calvinism, a Christianity stripped of grace and brutal with fantasies of submission and vengeance. No other work of American fiction reveals so graphically the way in which an oppressed minority aggravates its own oppression through the torments of religious fanaticism. The novel is also striking as a modest *Bildungsroman,* the education of an imaginative Negro boy caught in the heart-struggle between his need to revolt, which would probably lead to his destruction in the jungles of New York, and the miserly consolations of black Calvinism, which would signify that he accepts the denial of his personal needs. But it would be a mistake to claim too much for this first novel, in which a rhetorical flair and a conspicuous sincerity often eat away at the integrity of event and the substance of character. The novel is intense, and the intensity is due to Baldwin's absorption in that religion of denial which leads the boy to become a preacher in his father's church, to scream out God's word from "a merciless resolve to kill my father rather than allow my father to kill me." Religion has of course played a central role in Negro life, yet one may doubt that the special kind of religious experience dominating *Go Tell It on the Mountain* is any more representative of that life, any more advantageous a theme for gathering in the qualities of Negro culture, than the violence and outrage of *Native Son*. Like Wright before him, Baldwin wrote from the intolerable pressures of his own experience; there was no alternative; each had to release his own agony before he could regard Negro life with the beginnings of objectivity.

Baldwin's second novel, *Giovanni's Room*, seems to me a flat failure. It abandons Negro life entirely (not in itself a cause for judgment) and focusses upon the distraught personal relations of several young Americans adrift in Paris. The problem of homosexuality, which is to recur in Baldwin's fiction, is confronted with a notable courage, but also with a disconcerting kind of sentimentalism, a quavering and sophisticated submission [111] to the ideology of love. It is one thing to call for the treatment of character as integral and unique; but quite another for a writer with Baldwin's background and passions to succeed in bringing together his sensibility as a Negro and his sense of personal trouble.

Baldwin has not yet managed—the irony is a stringent one—in composing the kind of novel he counterposed to the work of Richard Wright. He has written three essays, ranging in tone from disturbed affection to disturbing malice, in which he tries to break from his rebellious dependency upon Wright, but he remains tied to the memory of the older man. The Negro writer who has come closest to satisfying Baldwin's program is not Baldwin himself but Ralph Ellison, whose novel *Invisible Man* is a brilliant though flawed achievement, standing with *Native Son* as the major fiction thus far composed by American Negroes.

What astonishes one most about *Invisible Man* is the apparent freedom it displays from the ideological and emotional penalties suffered by Negroes in this country—I say "apparent" because the freedom is not quite so complete as the book's admirers like to suppose. Still, for long stretches *Invisible Man* does escape the formulas of protest, local color, genre quaintness and jazz chatter. No white man could have written it, since no white man could know with such intimacy the life of the Negroes from the inside; yet Ellison writes with an ease and humor which are now and again simply miraculous.

Invisible Man is a record of a Negro's journey through contemporary America, from South to North, province to city, naïve faith to disenchantment and perhaps beyond. There are clear allegorical intentions (Ellison is "literary" to a fault) but with a book so rich in talk and drama it would be a shame to neglect the fascinating surface for the mere depths. The beginning is both nightmare and farce. A timid Negro boy comes to a white smoker in a Southern town: he is to be awarded a scholarship. Together with several other Negro boys [112] he is rushed to the front of the ballroom, where a sumptuous blonde tantalizes and frightens them by dancing in the nude. Blindfolded, the Negro boys stage a "battle royal," a free-for-all in which they pummel each other to the drunken shouts of the whites. Practical jokes, humiliations, terror—and then the boy delivers a prepared speech of gratitude to his white benefactors. At the end of this section, the boy dreams that he has opened the briefcase given him together with his scholarship to a Negro college and that he finds an inscription reading: "To Whom It May Concern: Keep This Nigger-Boy Running."

He keeps running. He goes to his college and is expelled for having innocently taken a white donor through a Negro ginmill which also happens to be a brothel. His whole experience is to follow this pattern. Strip down a pretense, whether by choice or accident, and you will suffer penalties, since the rickety structure of Negro respectability rests upon pretense and those who profit from it cannot bear to have the reality exposed (in this case, that the college is dependent upon the Northern white millionaire). The boy then leaves for New York, where he works in a white-paint factory, becomes a soapboxer for the Harlem Communists, the darling of the fellow-travelling bohemia, and a big wheel in the Negro world. At the end, after witnessing a frenzied race riot in Harlem, he "finds himself" in some not entirely specified way, and his odyssey from submission to autonomy is complete.

Ellison has an abundance of that primary talent without which neither craft nor intelligence can save a novelist: he is richly, wildly inventive; his scenes rise and dip with tension, his people bleed, his language sings. No other writer has captured so much of the hidden gloom and surface gaiety of Negro life.

There is an abundance of superbly rendered speech: a West Indian woman inciting her men to resist an eviction, a Southern sharecropper calmly describing how he seduced his [113] daughter, a Harlem street-vender spinning jive. The rhythm of Ellison's prose is harsh and nervous, like a beat of harried alertness. The observation is expert: he knows exactly how zootsuiters walk, making stylization their principle of life, and exactly how the antagonism between American and West Indian Negroes works itself out in speech and humor. He can accept his people as they are, in their blindness and hope—here, finally, the Negro world does exist, seemingly apart from plight or protest. And in the final scene Ellison has created an unforgettable image: "Ras the Destroyer," a Negro nationalist, appears on a horse dressed in the costume of an Abyssinian chieftain, carrying spear and shield, and charging wildly into the police—a black Quixote, mad, absurd, unbearably pathetic.

But even Ellison cannot help being caught up with *the idea* of the Negro. To write simply about "Negro experience" with the esthetic distance urged by the critics of the 'fifties, is a moral and psychological impossibility, for plight and protest are inseparable from that experience, and even if less political than Wright and less prophetic than Baldwin, Ellison knows this quite as well as they do.

If *Native Son* is marred by the ideological delusions of the 'thirties, *Invisible Man* is marred, less grossly, by those of the 'fifties. The middle section of Ellison's novel, dealing with the Harlem Communists, does not ring quite true, in the way a good portion of the writings on this theme during the post-war years does not ring quite true. Ellison makes his Stalinist figures so vicious and stupid that one cannot understand how they could ever have attracted him or any other Negro. That the party leadership manipulated members with deliberate cynicism is beyond doubt, but this cynicism was surely more complex and guarded than Ellison shows it to be. No party leader would ever tell a prominent Negro Communist, as one of them does in *Invisible Man*: "You were not hired [as a functionary] to think"—even if that were what he felt. Such [114] passages are almost as damaging as the propagandist outbursts in *Native Son*.

Still more troublesome, both as it breaks the coherence of the novel and reveals Ellison's dependence on the post-war *Zeitgeist*, is the sudden, unprepared and implausible assertion of unconditioned freedom with which the novel ends. As the hero abandons the Communist Party he wonders, "Could politics ever be an expression of love?" This question, more portentous than profound, cannot easily be reconciled to a character who has been presented mainly as a passive victim of his experience. Nor is one easily persuaded by the hero's discovery that "my world has become one of infinite possibilities," his refusal to be the "invisible man" whose body is manipulated by various social groups. Though the unqualified assertion of self-liberation was a favorite strategy among American literary people in the 'fifties, it is also vapid and insubstantial. It violates the reality of social life, the interplay between external conditions and personal will, quite as much as the determinism of the 'thirties. The unfortunate fact remains that to define one's individuality is to stumble upon social barriers which stand in the way, all too much in the way, of "infinite possibilities." Freedom can be fought for, but it cannot always be willed or asserted into existence. And it seems hardly an accident that even as Ellison's hero asserts the "infinite possibilities" he makes no attempt to specify them.

Throughout the 'fifties Richard Wright was struggling to find his place in a world he knew to be changing but could not grasp with the assurance he had felt in his earlier years. He had resigned with some bitterness from the Communist Party, though he tried to preserve an independent radical outlook, tinged occasionally with black nationalism. He became absorbed in the politics and literature of the rising African nations, but when visiting them he felt hurt at how great was the distance between an American Negro and an African. He [115] found life in America intolerable, and he spent his last fourteen years in Paris, somewhat friendly with the intellectual group around Jean-Paul Sartre but finally a loner, a man who stood by the pride of his rootlessness. And he kept writing, steadily experimenting, partly, it may be, in response to the younger men who had taken his place in the limelight and partly because he was truly a dedicated writer.

These last years were difficult for Wright, since he neither made a true home in Paris nor kept in imaginative touch with the changing life of the United States. In the early 'fifties he published a very poor novel, *The Outsider*, full of existentialist jargon applied but not really absorbed to the Negro theme. He was a writer in limbo, and his better fiction, such as the novelette "The Man Who Lived Underground," is a projection of that state.

In the late 'fifties Wright published another novel, *The Long*

Dream, which is set in Mississippi and displays a considerable recovery of his powers. This book has been criticized for presenting Negro life in the South through "old-fashioned" images of violence, but one ought to hesitate before denying the relevance of such images or joining in the criticism of their use. For Wright was perhaps justified in not paying attention to the changes that have occurred in the South these past few decades. When Negro liberals write that despite the prevalence of bias there has been an improvement in the life of their people, such statements are reasonable and necessary. But what have these to do with the way Negroes feel, with the power of the memories they must surely retain? About this we know very little and would be well advised not to nourish preconceptions, for their feelings may be much closer to Wright's rasping outbursts than to the more modulated tones of the younger Negro novelists. *Wright remembered,* and what he remembered other Negroes must also have remembered. And in that way he kept faith with the experience [116] of the boy who had fought his way out of the depths, to speak for those who remained there.

His most interesting fiction after *Native Son* is to be found in a posthumous collection of stories, *Eight Men,* written during the last 25 years of his life. Though they fail to yield any clear line of chronological development, these stories give evidence of Wright's literary restlessness, his often clumsy efforts to break out of the naturalism which was his first and, I think, necessary mode of expression. The unevenness of his writing is highly disturbing: one finds it hard to understand how the same man, from paragraph to paragraph, can be so brilliant and inept. Time after time the narrative texture is broken by a passage of sociological or psychological jargon; perhaps the later Wright tried too hard, read too much, failed to remain sufficiently loyal to the limits of his talent.

Some of the stories, such as "Big Black Good Man," are enlivened by Wright's sardonic humor, the humor of a man who has known and released the full measure of his despair but finds that neither knowledge nor release matters in a world of despair. In "The Man Who Lived Underground," Wright shows a sense of narrative rhythm, which is superior to anything in his full-length novels and evidence of the seriousness with which he kept working.

The main literary problem that troubled Wright in recent years was that of rendering his naturalism a more terse and supple instrument. I think he went astray whenever he abandoned naturalism entirely: there are a few embarrassingly bad experiments with stories employing self-consciously Freudian symbolism. Wright needed the accumulated material of circumstance which naturalistic detail provided his fiction; it was as essential to his ultimate effect of shock and bruise as dialogue to Hemingway's ultimate effect of irony and loss. But Wright was correct in thinking that the problem of detail is the most vexing technical problem the naturalist writer must face, since the accumulation that makes for depth and solidity [117] can also create a pall of tedium. In "The Man Who Lived Underground" Wright came close to solving this problem, for here the naturalistic detail is put at the service of a radical projective image—a Negro trapped in a sewer; and despite some flaws, the story is satisfying both for its tense surface and elasticity of suggestion.

Richard Wright died at 52, full of hopes and projects. Like many of us, he had somewhat lost his intellectual way but he kept struggling toward the perfection of his craft and toward a comprehension of the strange world that in his last years was coming into birth. In the most fundamental sense, however, he had done his work: he had told his contemporaries a truth so bitter, they paid him the tribute of trying to forget it.

V

Looking back to the early essays and fiction of James Baldwin, one wishes to see a little further than they at first invite—to see past their brilliance of gesture, by which older writers could be dismissed, and past their aura of gravity, by which a generation of intellectuals could be enticed. After this hard and dismal decade, what strikes one most of all is the sheer pathos of these early writings, the way they reveal the desire of a greatly talented young man to escape the scars—and why should he not have wished to escape them?—which he had found upon the faces of his elders and knew to be gratuitous and unlovely.

Chekhov once said that what the aristocratic Russian writers assumed as their birthright, the writers who came from the lower orders had to pay for with their youth. James Baldwin did not want to pay with his youth, as Richard Wright had paid so dearly. He wanted to move, as Wright had not been able to, beyond the burden or bravado of his stigma; he wanted to enter the world of freedom, grace, and self-creation. One would need a heart of stone, or be a brutal moralist, to [118] feel anything but sympathy for this desire. But we do not make our circumstances; we can, at best, try to remake them. And all the recent writing of Baldwin indicates that the wishes of his youth could not be realized, not in *this* country. The sentiments of humanity which had made him rebel against Richard Wright have now driven him back to a position close to Wright's rebellion.

Baldwin's most recent novel, *Another Country,* is a "protest novel" quite as much as *Native Son,* and anyone vindictive enough to make the effort could score against it the points Baldwin scored against Wright. No longer is Baldwin's prose so elegant or suave as it was once; in this book it is harsh, clumsy, heavy-breathing with the pant of suppressed bitterness. In about half of *Another Country*—the best half, I would judge—the material is handled in a manner somewhat reminiscent of Wright's naturalism: a piling on of the details of victimization, as the jazz musician Rufus Scott, a sophisticated distant cousin of Bigger Thomas, goes steadily down the path of self-destruction, worn out in the effort to survive in the white man's jungle and consumed by a rage too extreme to articulate yet too amorphous to act upon. The narrative voice is a voice of anger, rasping and thrusting, not at all "literary" in the somewhat lacquered way the earlier Baldwin was able to achieve. And what that voice says, no longer held back by the proprieties of literature, is that the nightmare of the history we have made allows us no immediate escape. Even if all the visible tokens of injustice were erased, the Negroes would retain their hatred and the whites their fear and guilt. Forgiveness cannot be speedily willed, if willed at all, and before it can even be imagined there will have to be a fuller discharge of those violent feelings that have so long been suppressed. It is not a pretty thought, but neither is it a mere "unrewarding rage"; and it has the sad advantage of being true, first as Baldwin embodies it in the disintegration of Rufus, which he portrays with a ferocity quite new in his [119] fiction, and then as he embodies it in the hard-driving ambition of Rufus' sister Ida, who means to climb up to success even if she has to bloody a good many people, whites preferably, in order to do it.

Another Country has within it another novel: a nagging portrayal of that entanglement of personal relationships—sterile, involuted, grindingly rehearsed, pursued with quasi-religious fervor, and cut off from any dense context of social life—which has come to be a standard element in contemporary fiction. The author of *this* novel is caught up with the problem of communication, the emptiness that seeps through the lives of many cultivated persons and in response to which he can only reiterate the saving value of true and lonely love. These portions of *Another Country* tend to be abstract, without the veined milieu, the filled-out world, a novel needs: as if Baldwin, once he moves away from the Negro theme, finds it quite as hard to lay hold of contemporary experience as do most other novelists. The two pulls upon his attention are difficult to reconcile, and Baldwin's future as a novelist is decidedly uncertain.

During the last few years James Baldwin has emerged as a national figure, the leading intellectual spokesman for the Negroes, whose recent essays, as in *The Fire Next Time*, reach heights of passionate exhortation unmatched in modern American writing. Whatever his ultimate success or failure as a novelist, Baldwin has already secured his place as one of the two or three greatest essayists this country has ever produced. He has brought a new luster to the essay as an art form, a form with possibilities for discursive reflection and concrete drama which make it a serious competitor to the novel, until recently almost unchallenged as the dominant literary genre in our time. Apparently drawing upon Baldwin's youthful experience as the son of a Negro preacher, the style of these essays is a remarkable instance of the way in which a grave and sustained eloquence—the rhythm of oratory, but that rhythm held firm and hard—can be employed in an age deeply suspicious of rhetorical prowess. And in pieces like the reports on Harlem and the account of his first visit South, Baldwin realizes far better than in his novel the goal he had set himself of presenting Negro life through an "unspoken recognition of shared experience." Yet it should also be recognized that these essays gain at least some of their resonance from the tone of unrelenting protest in which they are written, from the very anger, even the violence Baldwin had begun by rejecting.

Like Richard Wright before him, Baldwin has discovered that to assert his humanity he must release his rage. But if rage makes for power it does not always encourage clarity, and the truth is that Baldwin's most recent essays are shot through with intellectual confusions, torn by the conflict between his assumption that the Negro must find an honorable place in the life of American society and his apocalyptic sense, mostly fear but just a little hope, that this society is beyond salvation, doomed with the sickness of the West. And again like Wright, he gives way on occasion to the lure of black nationalism. Its formal creed does not interest him, for he knows it to be shoddy, but he is impressed by its capacity to evoke norms of discipline from followers at a time when the Negro community is threatened by a serious inner demoralization.

In his role as spokesman, Baldwin must pronounce with certainty and struggle with militancy; he has at the moment no other choice; yet whatever may have been the objective inadequacy of his polemic against Wright a decade ago, there can be no question but that the refusal he then made of the role of protest reflected faithfully some of his deepest needs and desires. But we do not make our circumstances; we can, at best, try to remake them; and the arena of choice and action always proves to be a little narrower than we had supposed. One generation passes its dilemmas to the next, black boys on to native sons. [121]

"It is in revolt that man goes beyond himself to discover other people, and from this point of view, human solidarity is a philosophical certainty." The words come from Camus; they might easily have been echoed by Richard Wright; and today one can imagine them being repeated, with a kind of rueful passion, by James Baldwin. No more important words could be spoken in our century, but it would be foolish, and impudent, not to recognize that for the men who must live by them the cost is heavy. [122]

ELLISON IN DIALOGUE WITH THE TRADITION

THE WORLD AND THE JUG
Ralph Ellison

"The World and the Jug" is actually a combination of two separate pieces. The first, bearing the original title, was written at the suggestion of Myron Kolatch of *The New Leader*, who was interested in my reactions, via telephone, to an essay by Irving Howe titled "Black Boys and Native Sons," which appeared in the Autumn 1963 issue of Howe's magazine, *Dissent*.

Usually such a reply would have appeared in the same magazine in which the original essay was published, but in this instance, and since it hadn't occurred to me to commit my reactions to paper, they went to the editor who asked for them. The second section of the essay, originally entitled "A Rejoinder," was written after Irving Howe had consented to reply, in *The New Leader*, of February 3, 1964, to my attack. There is, unfortunately, too little space here to do justice to Howe's arguments, and it is recommended that the interested reader consult Mr. Howe's book of essays, *A World More Attractive*—a book worthy of his attention far beyond the limits of our exchange—published by Horizon Press in 1963.

SOURCE: Ralph Ellison, "The World and the Jug," 1964, pp. 107–43. Copyright © 1963, 1964 by Ralph Ellison. Reprinted from *Shadow and Act* by permission of Random House, Inc.

> *What runs counter to the revolutionary convention is, in revolutionary histories, suppressed more imperiously than embarrassing episodes in private memoirs, and by the same obscure forces. . . .*
>
> ANDRÉ MALRAUX

I

First, three questions: Why is it so often true that when critics confront the American as *Negro* they suddenly drop their advanced critical armament and revert with an air of confident superiority to quite primitive modes of analysis? [107] Why is it that sociology-oriented critics seem to rate literature so far below politics and ideology that they would rather kill a novel than modify their presumptions concerning a given reality which it seeks in its own terms to project? Finally, why is it that so many of those who would tell us the meaning of Negro life never bother to learn how varied it really is?

These questions are aroused by "Black Boys and Native Sons," an essay by Irving Howe, the well-known critic and editor of *Dissent*, in the Autumn 1963 issue of that magazine. It is a lively piece, written with something of the Olympian authority that characterized Hannah Arendt's "Reflections on Little Rock" in the Winter 1959 *Dissent* (a dark foreshadowing of the Eichmann blowup). And in addition to a hero, Richard Wright, it has two villains, James Baldwin and Ralph Ellison, who are seen as "black boys" masquerading as false, self-deceived "native sons." Wright himself is given a diversity of roles (all conceived by Howe): He is not only the archetypal and true-blue black boy—the "honesty" of his famous autobiography established this for Howe—but the spiritual father of Ellison, Baldwin and all other Negroes of literary bent to come. Further, in the platonic sense he is his own father and the culture hero who freed Ellison and Baldwin to write more "modulated" prose.

Howe admires Wright's accomplishments, and is frankly annoyed by the more favorable evaluation currently placed upon the works of the younger men. His claims for *Native Son* are quite broad:

> The day [it] appeared, American culture was changed forever . . . it made impossible a repetition of the old lies . . . it

brought into the open . . . the fear and violence that have crippled and may yet destroy our culture. . . . A blow at the white man, the novel forced him to recognize himself as an oppressor. A blow at the black man, the novel forced him to recognize the cost of his submission. *Native* [108] *Son* assaulted the most cherished of American vanities: the hope that the accumulated injustices of the past would bring with it no lasting penalties, the fantasy that in his humiliation the Negro somehow retained a sexual potency . . . that made it necessary to envy and still more to suppress him. Speaking from the black wrath of retribution, Wright insisted that history can be a punishment. He told us the one thing even the most liberal whites preferred not to hear: that Negroes were far from patient or forgiving, that they were scarred by fear, that they hated every moment of their suppression even when seeming most acquiescent, and that often enough they hated *us*, the decent and cultivated white men who from complicity or neglect shared in the responsibility of their plight. . . .

There are also negative criticisms: that the book is "crude," "melodramatic" and marred by "claustrophobia" of vision, that its characters are "cartoons," etc. But these defects Howe forgives because of the book's "clenched militancy." One wishes he had stopped there. For in his zeal to champion Wright, it is as though he felt it necessary to stage a modern version of the Biblical myth of Noah, Ham, Shem and Japheth (based originally, I'm told, on a castration ritual), with first Baldwin and then Ellison acting out the impious role of Ham: Baldwin by calling attention to Noah—Wright's artistic nakedness in his famous essays, "Everybody's Protest Novel" (1949) and "Many Thousands Gone" (1951); Ellison by rejecting "narrow naturalism" as a fictional method, and by alluding to the "diversity, fluidity and magical freedom of American life" on that (for him at least) rather magical occasion when he was awarded the National Book Award. Ellison also offends by having the narrator of *Invisible Man* speak of his life (Howe either missing the irony or assuming that *I* did) as one of "infinite possibilities" while living in a hole in the ground.

Howe begins by attacking Baldwin's rejection in "Everybody's Protest Novel" of the type of literature he labeled [109] "protest fiction" (*Uncle Tom's Cabin* and *Native Son* being prime examples), and which he considered incapable of dealing adequately with the complexity of Negro experience. Howe, noting that this was the beginning of Baldwin's career, sees the essay's underlying motive as a declaration of Baldwin's intention to transcend "the sterile categories of 'Negroness,' whether those enforced by the white world or those defensively erected by the Negroes themselves. No longer mere victim or rebel, the Negro would stand free in a self-achieved humanity. As Baldwin put it some years later, he hoped to 'prevent himself from becoming merely a Negro; or even, merely, a Negro writer.'" Baldwin's elected agency for self-achievement would be the novel—as it turns out, it was the essay *and* the novel—but the novel, states Howe, "is an inherently ambiguous genre: it strains toward formal autonomy and can seldom avoid being public gesture."

I would have said that it is *always* a public gesture, though not necessarily a political one. I would also have pointed out that the American Negro novelist is himself "inherently ambiguous." As he strains toward self-achievement as artist (and here he can only "integrate" and free himself), he moves toward fulfilling his dual potentialities as Negro and American. While Howe agrees with Baldwin that "literature and sociology are not one and the same," he notes nevertheless that, "it is equally true that such statements hardly begin to cope with the problem of how a writer's own experience affects his desire to represent human affairs in a work of fiction." Thus Baldwin's formula evades "through rhetorical sweep, the genuinely difficult issue of the relationship between social experience and literature." And to Baldwin's statement that one writes "out of one thing only—one's own experience" (I would have added, for the novelist, this qualification: one's own experience as understood and ordered [110] through one's knowledge of self, culture and literature), Howe, appearing suddenly in blackface, replies with a rhetorical sweep of his own:

> What, then, was the experience of a man with a black skin, what *could* it be here in this country? How could a Negro put pen to paper, how could he so much as think or breathe, without some impulse to protest, be it harsh or mild, political or private, released or buried? . . . The "sociology" of his existence forms a constant pressure on his literary work, and not merely in the

way this might be true of any writer, but with a pain and ferocity that nothing could remove.

I must say that this brought a shock of recognition. Some twelve years ago, a friend argued with me for hours that I could not possibly write a novel because my experience as a Negro had been too excruciating to allow me to achieve that psychological and emotional distance necessary to artistic creation. Since he "knew" Negro experience better than I, I could not convince him that he might be wrong. Evidently Howe feels that unrelieved suffering is the only "real" Negro experience, and that the true Negro writer must be ferocious.

But there is also an American Negro tradition which teaches one to deflect racial provocation and to master and contain pain. It is a tradition which abhors as obscene any trading on one's own anguish for gain or sympathy; which springs not from a desire to deny the harshness of existence but from a will to deal with it as men at their best have always done. It takes fortitude to be a man and no less to be an artist. Perhaps it takes even more if the black man would be an artist. If so, there are no exemptions. It would seem to me, therefore, that the question of how the "sociology of his existence" presses upon a Negro writer's work depends upon how much of his life the individual writer is able to transform [111] into art. What moves a writer to eloquence is less meaningful than what he makes of it. How much, by the way, do we know of Sophocles' wounds?

One unfamiliar with what Howe stands for would get the impression that when he looks at a Negro he sees not a human being but an abstract embodiment of living hell. He seems never to have considered that American Negro life (and here he is encouraged by certain Negro "spokesmen") is, for the Negro who must live it, not only a burden (and not always that) but also a *discipline*—just as any human life which has endured so long is a discipline teaching its own insights into the human condition, its own strategies of survival. There is a fullness, even a richness here; and here *despite* the realities of politics, perhaps, but nevertheless here and real. Because it is *human* life. And Wright, for all of his indictments, was no less its product than that other talented Mississippian, Leontyne Price. To deny in the interest of revolutionary posture that such possibilities of human richness exist for others, even in Mississippi, is not only to deny us our humanity but to betray the critic's commitment to social reality. Critics who do so should abandon literature for politics.

For even as his life toughens the Negro, even as it brutalizes him, sensitizes him, dulls him, goads him to anger, moves him to irony, sometimes fracturing and sometimes affirming his hopes; even as it shapes his attitudes toward family, sex, love, religion; even as it modulates his humor, tempers his joy—it *conditions* him to deal with his life and with himself. Because it is *his* life and no mere abstraction in someone's head. He must live it and try consciously to grasp its complexity until he can change it; must live it *as* he changes it. He is no mere product of his socio-political predicament. He is a product of the interaction between his racial predicament, his individual will and the broader American cultural freedom in which he finds his ambiguous existence. [112] Thus he, too, in a limited way, is his own creation.

In his loyalty to Richard Wright, Howe considers Ellison and Baldwin guilty of filial betrayal because, in their own work, they have rejected the path laid down by *Native Son,* phonies because, while actually "black boys," they pretend to be mere American writers trying to react to something of the pluralism of their predicament.

In his myth Howe takes the roles of both Shem and Japheth, trying mightily (his face turned backward so as not see what it is he's veiling) to cover the old man's bare belly, and then becoming Wright's voice from beyond the grave by uttering the curses which Wright was too ironic or too proud to have uttered himself, at least in print:

> In response to Baldwin and Ellison, Wright would have said (I virtually quote the words he used in talking to me during the summer of 1958) that only through struggle could men with black skins, and for that matter, all the oppressed of the world, achieve their humanity. It was a lesson, said Wright, with a touch of bitterness yet not without kindness, that the younger writers would have to learn in their own way and their own time. All that has happened since, bears him out.

What, coming eighteen years after *Native Son* and thirteen years after World War II, does this rather limp cliché mean? Nor is it clear what is meant by the last sentence—or is it that today Baldwin has come to out-Wrighting Richard? The real questions seem to be: How does the Negro writer participate *as a writer* in the struggle for human freedom? To whom does he address his work? What values emerging from Negro experience does he try to affirm?

I started with the primary assumption that men with black skins, having retained their humanity before all of the conscious efforts made to dehumanize them, especially following the Reconstruction, are unquestionably human. Thus [113] they have the obligation of freeing themselves—whoever their allies might be—by depending upon the validity of their own experience for an accurate picture of the reality which they seek to change, and for a gauge of the values they would see made manifest. Crucial to this view is the belief that their resistance to provocation, their coolness under pressure, their sense of timing and their tenacious hold on the ideal of their ultimate freedom are indispensable values in the struggle, and are at least as characteristic of American Negroes as the hatred, fear and vindictiveness which Wright chose to emphasize.

Wright believed in the much abused idea that novels are "weapons"—the counterpart of the dreary notion, common among most minority groups, that novels are instruments of good public relations. But I believe that true novels, even when most pessimistic and bitter, arise out of an impulse to celebrate human life and therefore are ritualistic and ceremonial at their core. Thus they would preserve as they destroy, affirm as they reject.

In *Native Son*, Wright began with the ideological proposition that what whites think of the Negro's reality is more important than what Negroes themselves know it to be. Hence Bigger Thomas was presented as a near-subhuman indictment of white oppression. He was designed to shock whites out of their apathy and end the circumstances out of which Wright insisted Bigger emerged. Here environment is all—and interestingly enough, environment conceived solely in terms of the physical, the non-conscious. Well, cut off my legs and call me Shorty! Kill my parents and throw me on the mercy of the court as an orphan! Wright could imagine Bigger, but Bigger could not possibly imagine Richard Wright. Wright saw to that.

But without arguing Wright's right to his personal vision, I would say that he was himself a better argument for my approach than Bigger was for his. And so, to be fair and as [114] inclusive as Howe, is

James Baldwin. Both are true Negro Americans, and both affirm the broad possibility of personal realization which I see as a saving aspect of American life. Surely, this much can be admitted without denying the injustice which all three of us have protested.

Howe is impressed by Wright's pioneering role and by the ". . . enormous courage, the discipline of self-conquest required to conceive Bigger Thomas. . . ." And earlier: "If such younger novelists as Baldwin and Ralph Ellison were able to move beyond Wright's harsh naturalism toward more supple modes of fiction, that was only possible because Wright had been there first, courageous enough to release the full weight of his anger."

It is not for me to judge Wright's courage, but I must ask just why it was possible for me to write as I write "only" because Wright released his anger? Can't I be allowed to release my own? What does Howe know of my acquaintance with violence, or the shape of my courage or the intensity of my anger? I suggest that my credentials are at least as valid as Wright's, even though he began writing long before I did, and it is possible that I have lived through and committed even more violence than he. Howe must wait for an autobiography before he can be responsibly certain. Everybody wants to tell us what a Negro is, yet few wish, even in a joke, to be one. But if you would tell me who I am, at least take the trouble to discover what I have been.

Which brings me to the most distressing aspect of Howe's thinking: his Northern white liberal version of the white Southern myth of absolute separation of the races. He implies that Negroes can only aspire to contest other Negroes (this at a time when Baldwin has been taking on just about everyone, including Hemingway, Faulkner and the United States Attorney General!), and must wait for the appearance of a Black Hope before they have the courage to move. [115] Howe is so committed to a sociological vision of society that he apparently cannot see (perhaps because he is dealing with Negroes—although not because he would suppress us socially or politically, for in fact he is anxious to end such suppression) that whatever the efficiency of segregation as a socio-political arrangement, it has been far from absolute on the level of *culture*. Southern whites cannot walk, talk, sing, conceive of laws or justice, think of sex, love, the family or freedom without responding to the presence of Negroes.

Similarly, no matter how strictly Negroes are segregated socially and politically, on the level of the imagination their ability to achieve freedom is limited only by their individual aspiration, insight, energy and will. Wright was able to free himself in Mississippi because he had the imagination and the will to do so. He was as much a product of his reading as of his painful experiences, and he made himself a writer by subjecting himself to the writer's discipline—as he understood it. The same is true of James Baldwin, who is not the product of a Negro store-front church but of the library, and the same is true of me.

Howe seems to see segregation as an opaque steel jug with the Negroes inside waiting for some black messiah to come along and blow the cork. Wright is his hero and he sticks with him loyally. But if we are in a jug it is transparent, not opaque, and one is allowed not only to see outside but to read what is going on out there; to make identifications as to values and human quality. So in Macon County, Alabama, I read Marx, Freud, T. S. Eliot, Pound, Gertrude Stein and Hemingway. Books which seldom, if ever, mentioned Negroes were to release me from whatever "segregated" idea I might have had of my human possibilities. I was freed not by propagandists or by the example of Wright—I did not know him at the time and was earnestly trying to learn enough to write a symphony and have it performed by the time I was twenty-six, because Wagner had done so and I [116] admired his music—but by composers, novelists, and poets who spoke to me of more interesting and freer ways of life.

These were works which, by fulfilling themselves as works of art, by being satisfied to deal with life in terms of their own sources of power, were able to give me a broader sense of life and possibility. Indeed, I understand a bit more about myself as Negro because literature has taught me something of my identity as Western man, as political being. It has also taught me something of the cost of being an individual who aspires to conscious eloquence. It requires real poverty of the imagination to think that this can come to a Negro *only* through the example of *other Negroes*, especially after the performance of the slaves in re-creating themselves, in good part, out of the images and myths of the Old Testament Jews.

No, Wright was no spiritual father of mine, certainly in no sense I recognize—nor did he pretend to be, since he felt that I had started writing too late. It was Baldwin's career, not mine, that Wright proudly advanced by helping him attain the Eugene Saxton Fellowship, and it was Baldwin who found Wright a lion in his path. Being older and familiar with quite different lions in quite different paths, I simply stepped around him.

But Wright was a friend for whose magazine I wrote my first book review and short story, and a personal hero in the same way Hot Lips Paige and Jimmy Rushing were friends and heroes. I felt no need to attack what I considered the limitations of his vision because I was quite impressed by what he had achieved. And in this, although I saw with the black vision of Ham, I was, I suppose, as pious as Shem and Japheth. Still I would write my own books and they would be in themselves, implicitly, criticisms of Wright's; just as all novels of a given historical moment form an argument over the nature of reality and are, to an extent, criticisms each of the other. [117]

While I rejected Bigger Thomas as any *final* image of Negro personality, I recognized *Native Son* as an achievement; as one man's essay in defining the human condition as seen from a specific Negro perspective at a given time in a given place. And I was proud to have known Wright and happy for the impact he had made upon our apathy. But Howe's ideas notwithstanding, history is history, cultural contacts ever mysterious, and taste exasperatingly personal. Two days after arriving in New York I was to read Malraux's *Man's Fate* and *The Days of Wrath,* and after these how could I be impressed by Wright as an ideological novelist? Need my skin blind me to all other values? Yet Howe writes:

> When Negro liberals write that despite the prevalence of bias there has been an improvement in the life of their people, such statements are reasonable and necessary. But what have these to do with the way Negroes feel, with the power of the memories they must surely retain? About this we know very little and would be well advised not to nourish preconceptions, for their feelings may well be closer to Wright's rasping outbursts than to the more modulated tones of the younger Negro novelists. *Wright remembered,* and what he remembered other Negroes must also have remembered. And in that way he kept faith with experience of the boy who had fought his way out of the depths, to speak for those who remained there.

Wright, for Howe, is the genuine article, the authentic Negro writer, and his tone the only authentic tone. But why strip Wright of his individuality in order to criticize other writers? He had his memories and I have mine, just as I suppose Irving Howe has his—or has Marx spoken the final word for him? Indeed, very early in *Black Boy*, Wright's memory and his contact with literature come together in a way revealing, at least to the eye concerned with Wright the literary man, that his manner of keeping faith with the Negroes who remained in the depths is quite interesting: [118]

> (After I had outlived the shocks of childhood, after the habit of reflection had been born in me, I used to mull over the strange absence of real kindness in Negroes, how unstable was our tenderness, how lacking in genuine passion we were, how void of great hope, how timid our joy, how bare our traditions, how hollow our memories, how lacking we were in those intangible sentiments that bind man to man and how shallow was even our despair. After I had learned other ways of life I used to brood upon the unconscious irony of those who felt that Negroes led so passional an existence! I saw that what had been taken for our emotional strength was our negative confusions, our flights, our fears, our frenzy under pressure.
>
> (Whenever I thought of the essential bleakness of black life in America, I knew that Negroes had never been allowed to catch the full spirit of Western civilization, that they lived somehow in it but not of it. And when I brooded upon the cultural barrenness of black life, I wondered if clean, positive tenderness, love, honor, loyalty and the capacity to remember were native with man. I asked myself if these human qualities were not fostered, won, struggled and suffered for, preserved in ritual from one generation to another.)

Must I be condemned because my sense of Negro life was quite different? Or because for me keeping faith would never allow me to even raise such a question about any segment of humanity? *Black Boy* is not a sociological case history but an autobiography, and therefore a work of art shaped by a writer bent upon making an ideological point. Doubtlessly, this was the beginning of Wright's exile, the making of a decision which was to shape his life and writing thereafter. And it is precisely at this point that Wright is being what I would call, in Howe's words, "literary to a fault."

For just as *How Bigger Was Born* is Wright's Jamesian preface to *Native Son*, the passage quoted above is his paraphrase of Henry James' catalogue of those items of a high civilization which were absent from American life during Hawthorne's day, and which seemed so necessary in order [119] for the novelist to function. This, then, was Wright's list of those items of high humanity which he found missing among Negroes. Thank God, I have never been quite that literary.

How awful that Wright found the facile answers of Marxism before he learned to use literature as a means for discovering the forms of American Negro humanity. I could not and cannot question their existence, I can only seek again and again to project that humanity as I see it and feel it. To me Wright as *writer* was less interesting than the enigma he personified: that he could so dissociate himself from the complexity of his background while trying so hard to improve the condition of black men everywhere; that he could be so wonderful an example of human possibility but could not for ideological reasons depict a Negro as intelligent, as creative or as dedicated as himself.

In his effort to resuscitate Wright, Irving Howe would designate the role which Negro writers are to play more rigidly than any Southern politician—and for the best of reasons. We must express "black" anger and "clenched militancy"; most of all we should not become too interested in the problems of the art of literature, even though it is through these that we seek our individual identities. And between writing well and being ideologically militant, we must choose militancy.

Well, it all sounds quite familiar and I fear the social order which it forecasts more than I do that of Mississippi. Ironically, during the 1940s it was one of the main sources of Wright's rage and frustration.

II

I am sorry Irving Howe got the impression that I was throwing beanballs when I only meant to pitch him a hyperbole. It would seem, however, that he approves of angry Negro [120] writers only until one questions his ideas; then he reaches for his honor, cries "misrepresentation" and "distortion," and charges the writer with being both out of control of himself and with fashioning a "strategy calculated to appeal, ready-made, to the preconceptions of the liberal audience." Howe implies that there are differences between us which I disguised in my essay, yet whatever the validity of this attempt at long-distance psychoanalysis, it was not his honor which I questioned but his thinking; not his good faith but his critical method.

And the major differences which these raised between us I tried to describe. They are to be seen by anyone who reads Howe's "Black Boys and Native Sons" not as a collection of thematically related fragments but as the literary exposition of a considered point of view. I tried to interpret this essay in the light of the impact it made upon my sense of life and literature, and I judged it through its total form—just as I would have Howe base his judgments of writers and their circumstances on as much of what we know about the actual complexity of men living in a highly pluralistic society as is possible. I realize that the *un*common sense of a critic, his special genius, is a gift to be thankful for whenever we find it. The very least I expected of Howe, though, was that he would remember his *common* sense, that he would not be carried away by that intellectual abandon, that lack of restraint, which seizes those who regard blackness as an absolute and who see in it a release from the complications of the real world.

Howe is interested in militant confrontation and suffering, yet evidently he recognizes neither when they involve some act of his own. He *really* did not know the subject was loaded. Very well, but I was brought into the booby-trapped field of his assumptions and finding myself in pain, I did not choose to "hold back from the suffering" inflicted upon me there. Out of an old habit I yelled—without seeking Howe's [121] permission, it is true—where it hurt the most. For oddly enough, I found it far less painful to have to move to the back of a Southern bus, or climb to the peanut gallery of a movie house—matters about which I could do nothing except walk, read, hunt, dance, sculpt, cultivate ideas, or seek other uses for my time—than to tolerate concepts which distorted the actual reality of my situation or my reactions to it.

I could escape the reduction imposed by unjust laws and customs, but not that imposed by ideas which defined me as no more than the *sum* of those laws and customs. I learned to outmaneuver those who interpreted my silence as submission, my efforts at self-control as fear, my contempt as awe before superior status, my dreams of faraway places and room at the top of the heap as defeat before the barriers of their stifling, provincial world. And my struggle became a desperate battle which was usually fought, though not always, in silence; a guerrilla action in a larger war in which I found some of the most treacherous assaults against me committed by those who regarded themselves either as neutrals, as sympathizers, or as disinterested military advisers.

I recall this not in complaint, for thus was I disciplined to endure the absurdities of both conscious and unconscious prejudice, to resist racial provocation and, before the ready violence of brutal policemen, railroad "bulls," and casual white citizens, to hold my peace and bide my time. Thus was I forced to evaluate my own self-worth, and the narrow freedom in which it existed, against the power of those who would destroy me. In time I was to leave the South, although it has never left me, and the interests which I discovered there became my life.

But having left the South I did not leave the battle—for how could I leave Howe? He is a man of words and ideas, and since I, too, find my identity in the world of ideas and words, where would I flee? I still endure the nonsense of fools with a certain patience, but when a respected critic distorts [122] my situation in order to feel comfortable in the abstractions he would impose upon American reality, then it is indeed "in accordance with my nature" to protest. Ideas are important in themselves, perhaps, but when they are interposed between me and my sense of reality I feel threatened; they are too elusive, they move with missile speed and are too often fired from altitudes rising high above the cluttered terrain upon which I struggle. And too often those with a facility for ideas find themselves in the councils of power representing me at the double distance of racial alienation and inexperience.

Taking leave of Howe for a moment—for his lapse is merely symptomatic—let me speak generally. Many of those who write of Negro life today seem to assume that as long as their hearts are in the right place they can be as arbitrary as they wish in their formulations. Others seem to feel that they can air with impunity their most private

Freudian fantasies as long as they are given the slightest camouflage of intellectuality and projected as "Negro." They have made of the no-man's land created by segregation a territory for infantile self-expression and intellectual anarchy. They write as though Negro life exists only in light of their belated regard, and they publish interpretations of Negro experience which would not hold true for their own or for any other form of human life.

Here the basic unity of human experience that assures us of some possibility of empathic and symbolic identification with those of other backgrounds is blasted in the interest of specious political and philosophical conceits. Prefabricated Negroes are sketched on sheets of paper and superimposed upon the Negro community; then when someone thrusts his head through the page and yells, "Watch out there, Jack, there're people living under here," they are shocked and indignant. I am afraid, however, that we shall hear much more [123] of such protest as these interpositions continue. And I predict this, not out of any easy gesture of militancy (and what an easy con-game for ambitious, publicity-hungry Negroes this stance of "militancy" has become!) but because as Negroes express increasingly their irritation in this critical area, many of those who make so lightly with our image shall find their own subjected to a most devastating scrutiny.

One of the most insidious crimes occurring in this democracy is that of designating another, politically weaker, less socially acceptable people as the receptacle for one's own self-disgust, for one's own infantile rebellions, for one's own fears of, and retreats from, reality. It is the crime of reducing the humanity of others to that of a mere convenience, a counter in a banal game which involves no apparent risk to ourselves. With us Negroes it started with the appropriation of our freedom and our labor; then it was our music, our speech, our dance and the comic distortion of our image by burnt-corked, cotton-gloved corn-balls yelling, "Mammy!" And while it would be futile, non-tragic, and un-Negro American to complain over the processes through which we have become who and what we are, it is perhaps permissible to say that the time for such misappropriations ran out long ago.

For one thing, Negro American consciousness is not a product (as so often seems true of so many American groups) of a will to historical forgetfulness. It is a product of our memory, sustained and constantly reinforced by events, by our watchful waiting, and by our hopeful suspension of final judgment as to the meaning of our grievances. For another, most Negroes recognize themselves as themselves despite what others might believe them to be. Thus, although the sociologists tell us that thousands of light-skinned Negroes become white each year undetected, most Negroes can spot a paper-thin "white Negro" every time simply because those who masquerade missed what others were forced to pick up along the way: discipline— a discipline [124] which these heavy thinkers would not undergo even if guaranteed that combined with their own heritage it would make of them the freest of spirits, the wisest of men and the most sublime of heroes.

The rhetorical strategy of my original reply was not meant, as Howe interprets it, to strike the stance of a "free artist" against the "ideological critic," although I *do* recognize that I can be free only to the extent that I detect error and grasp the complex reality of my circumstances and work to dominate it through the techniques which are my means of confronting the world. Perhaps I am only free enough to recognize those tendencies of thought which, actualized, would render me even less free.

Even so, I did not intend to take the stance of the "knowing Negro writer" against the "presuming white intellectual." While I am without doubt a Negro, and a writer, I am also an *American* writer, and while I am more knowing than Howe where my own life and its influences are concerned, I took the time to question his presumptions as one responsible for contributing as much as he is capable to the clear perception of American social reality. For to think unclearly about that segment of reality in which I find my existence is to do myself violence. To allow others to go unchallenged when they distort that reality is to participate not only in that distortion but to accept, as in this instance, a violence inflicted upon the art of criticism. And if I am to recognize those aspects of my role as writer which do not depend primarily upon my racial identity, if I am to fulfill the writer's basic responsibilities to his craft, then surely I must insist upon the maintenance of a certain level of precision in language, a maximum correspondence between the form of a piece of writing and its content, and between words and ideas and the things and processes of his world.

Whatever my role as "race man" (and it knocks me out whenever anyone, black or white, tries to tell me—and [125] the white Southerners have no monopoly here—how to become their conception of a "good Negro"), I am as writer no less a custodian of the American language than is Irving Howe. Indeed, to the extent that I am a writer—I lay no claims to being a thinker—the American language, including the Negro idiom, is all that I have. So let me emphasize that my reply to Howe was neither motivated by racial defensiveness nor addressed to his own racial identity.

It is fortunate that it was not, for considering how Howe identifies himself in this instance, I would have missed the target, which would have been embarrassing. Yet it would have been an innocent mistake, because in situations such as this many Negroes, like myself, make a positive distinction between "whites" and "Jews." Not to do so could be either offensive, embarrassing, unjust or even dangerous. If I would know who I am and preserve who I am, then I must see others distinctly whether they see me so or no. Thus I feel uncomfortable whenever I discover Jewish intellectuals writing as though *they* were guilty of enslaving my grandparents, or as though the *Jews* were responsible for the system of segregation. Not only do they have enough troubles of their own, as the saying goes, but Negroes know this only too well.

The real guilt of such Jewish intellectuals lies in their facile, perhaps unconscious, but certainly unrealistic, identification with what is called the "power structure." Negroes call that "passing for white." Speaking personally, both as writer and as Negro American, I would like to see the more positive distinctions between whites and Jewish Americans maintained. Not only does it make for a necessary bit of historical and social clarity, at least where Negroes are concerned, but I consider the United States freer politically and richer culturally because there are Jewish Americans to bring it the benefit of their special forms of dissent, their humor and their gift for ideas which are based upon the uniqueness [126] of their experience. The diversity of American life is often painful, frequently burdensome and always a source of conflict, but in it lies our fate and our hope.

To Howe's charge that I found his exaggerated claims for Richard Wright's influence upon my own work presumptuous, I plead guilty. Was it necessary to impose a line of succession upon Negro writers simply because Howe identified with Wright's cause? And why, since he grasps so readily the intentional absurdity of my question regarding his relationship to Marx, couldn't he see that the notion of an intellectual or artistic succession based upon color or racial background is no less absurd than one based upon a common religious background? (*Of course, Irving, I know that you haven't believed in final words for twenty years—not even your own—and I know, too, that the line from Marx to Howe is as complex and as dialectical as that from Wright to Ellison. My point was to try to see to it that certain lapses in your thinking did not become final.*) In fact, this whole exchange would never have started had I not been dragged into the discussion. Still, if Howe could take on the role of man with a "black skin," why shouldn't I assume the role of critic-of-critic?

But how surprising are Howe's ideas concerning the ways of controversy. Why, unless of course he holds no respect for his opponent, should a polemicist be expected to make things *hard* for himself? As for the "preconceptions of the liberal audience," I had not considered them, actually, except as they appear in Howe's own thinking. Beyond this I wrote for anyone who might hesitate to question his formulations, especially very young Negro writers who might be bewildered by the incongruity of such ideas coming from such an authority. Howe himself rendered complicated rhetorical strategies unnecessary by lunging into questionable territory with his flanks left so unprotected that any schoolboy sniper could have routed him with a bird gun. Indeed, his reaction to my [127] reply reminds me of an incident which occurred during the 1937 Recession when a companion and I were hunting the country outside Dayton, Ohio.

There had been a heavy snowfall and we had just put up a covey of quail from a thicket which edged a field when, through the rising whirr of the rocketing, snow-shattering birds, we saw, emerging from a clump of trees across the field, a large, red-faced, mackinawed farmer, who came running toward us shouting and brandishing a rifle. I could see strands of moisture tearing from his working mouth as he came on, running like a bear across the whiteness, the brown birds veering and scattering before him; and standing there against the snow, a white hill behind me and with no tree nor foxhole for cover I felt as exposed as a Black Muslim caught at a meeting of the K.K.K.

He had appeared as suddenly as the quail, and although the rifle was not yet to his shoulder, I was transfixed, watching him zooming up to become the largest, loudest, most aggressive-sounding white man I'd seen in my life, and I was, quite frankly, afraid. Then I was measuring his approach to the crunching tempo of his running and praying silently that he'd come within range of my shotgun before he fired; that I would be able to do what seemed necessary for me to do; that, shooting from the hip with an old twelve-gauge shotgun, I could stop him before he could shoot either me or my companion; and that, though stopped effectively, he would be neither killed, nor blinded, nor maimed.

It was a mixed-up prayer in an icy interval which ended in a smoking fury of cursing, when, at a warning from my companion, the farmer suddenly halted. Then we learned that the reckless man had meant only to warn us off of land which was not even his but that of a neighbor—my companion's foster father. He stood there between the two shotguns pointing short-ranged at his middle, his face quite drained of color now by the realization of how close to death he'd come, [128] sputtering indignantly that we'd interpreted his rifle, which wasn't loaded, in a manner other than he'd intended. He truly did not realize that situations can be more loaded than guns and gestures more eloquent than words.

Fortunately, words are not rifles, but perhaps Howe is just as innocent of the rhetorical eloquence of situations as the farmer. He does not see that the meaning which emerges from his essay is not determined by isolated statements, but by the juxtaposition of those statements in a context which creates a larger statement. Or that contributing to the judgment rendered by that larger statement is the one in which it is uttered. When Howe pits Baldwin and Ellison against Wright and then gives Wright the better of the argument by using such emotionally weighted terms as "remembered" and "kept faith," the implication to me is that Baldwin and Ellison did *not* remember or keep faith with those who remained behind. If this be true, then I think that in this instance "villain" is not too strong a term.

Howe is not the first writer given to sociological categories who has had unconscious value judgments slip into his "analytical" or "scientific" descriptions. Thus I can believe that his approach was meant to be "analytic, not exhortatory; descriptive, not prescriptive." The results, however, are something else again. And are we to believe that he simply does not recognize rhetoric when he practices it? That when he asks, "What *could* [his italics] the experience of a a man with a black skin be . . ." etc., he thinks he is describing a situation as viewed by each and every Negro writer rather than expressing, yes, and in the mode of "exhortation," the views of Irving Howe? Doesn't he recognize that just as the anti-Negro stereotype is a command to Negroes to mold themselves in its image, there sounds through his descriptive "thus it is" the command "thus you become"? And doesn't he realize that in this emotion-charged area definitive description is, in effect, prescription? If he does not, [129] how then can we depend upon his "analysis" of politics or his reading of fiction?

Perhaps Howe could relax his views concerning the situation of the writers with a "black skin" if he examined some of the meanings which he gives to the word "Negro." He contends that I "cannot help being caught up with *the idea* of the Negro," but I have never said that I could or wished to do so—only Howe makes a problem for me here. When he uses the term "Negro" he speaks of it as a "stigma," and again, he speaks of "Negroness" as a "sterile category." He sees the Negro writer as experiencing a "constant pressure upon his literary work" from the "sociology of his existence . . . not merely in the way this might be true of any writer, but with a *pain* and *ferocity* that nothing could remove." [1]

Note that this is a condition arising from a *collective* experience which leaves no room for the individual writer's unique existence. It leaves no room for that intensity of personal anguish which compels the artist to seek relief by projecting it into the world in conjunction with other things; that anguish which might take the form of an acute sense of inferiority for one, homosexuality for another, an overwhelming sense of the absurdity of human life for still another. Nor does it leave room for the experience that might be caused by humiliation, by a harelip, by a stutter, by epilepsy—indeed, by any and everything in this life which plunges the talented individual into solitude while leaving him the will to transcend his condition through art. The individual Negro writer must create out of his own special needs and through his own sensibilities, and these alone. Otherwise, all those who suffer in anonymity would be creators.

Howe makes of "Negroness" a metaphysical condition, one that is a state of irremediable agony which all but engulfs the [130] mind. Happily, the view from inside the skin is not so dark as it appears to

1. Italics mine.

be from Howe's remote position, and therefore my view of "Negroness" is neither his nor that of the exponents of *negritude*. It is not skin color which makes a Negro American but cultural heritage as shaped by the American experience, the social and political predicament; a sharing of that "concord of sensibilities" which the group expresses through historical circumstance and through which it has come to constitute a subdivision of the larger American culture. Being a Negro American has to do with the memory of slavery and the hope of emancipation and the betrayal by allies and the revenge and contempt inflicted by our former masters after the Reconstruction, and the myths, both Northern and Southern, which are propagated in justification of that betrayal. It involves, too, a special attitude toward the waves of immigrants who have come later and passed us by.

It has to do with a special perspective on the national ideals and the national conduct, and with a tragicomic attitude toward the universe. It has to do with special emotions evoked by the details of cities and countrysides, with forms of labor and with forms of pleasure; with sex and with love, with food and with drink, with machines and with animals; with climates and with dwellings, with places of worship and places of entertainment; with garments and dreams and idioms of speech; with manners and customs, with religion and art, with life styles and hoping, and with that special sense of predicament and fate which gives direction and resonance to the Freedom Movement. It involves a rugged initiation into the mysteries and rites of color which makes it possible for Negro Americans to suffer the injustice which race and color are used to excuse without losing sight of either the humanity of those who inflict that injustice or the motives, rational or irrational, out of which they act. It imposes the uneasy burden and occasional joy of a complex [131] double vision, a fluid, ambivalent response to men and events which represents, at its finest, a profoundly civilized adjustment to the cost of being human in this modern world.

More important, perhaps, being a Negro American involves a *willed* (who wills to be a Negro? I do!) affirmation of self as against all outside pressures—an identification with the group as extended through the individual self which rejects all possibilities of escape that do not involve a basic resuscitation of the original American ideals of social and political justice. And those white Negroes (and I do not mean Norman Mailer's dream creatures) are Negroes too—if they wish to be.

Howe's defense against my charge that he sees unrelieved suffering as the basic reality of Negro life is to quote favorable comments from his review of *Invisible Man*. But this does not cancel out the restricted meaning which he gives to "Negroness," or his statement that "the sociology of [the Negro writer's] existence forms a constant pressure with a *pain* and *ferocity* that nothing could remove." He charges me with unfairness for writing that he believes ideological militancy is more important than writing well, yet he tells us that "there may of course be times when one's obligation as a human being supersedes one's obligation as a writer. . . ." I think that the writer's obligation in a struggle as broad and abiding as the one we are engaged in, which involves not merely Negroes but all Americans, is best carried out through his role as writer. And if he chooses to stop writing and take to the platform, then it should be out of personal choice and not under pressure from would-be managers of society.

Howe plays a game of pitty-pat with Baldwin and Ellison. First he throws them into the pit for lacking Wright's "pain," "ferocity," "memory," "faithfulness" and "clenched militance," then he pats them on the head for the quality of [132] their writing. If he would see evidence of this statement, let him observe how these terms come up in his original essay when he traces Baldwin's move toward Wright's position. Howe's rhetoric is weighted against "more modulated tones" in favor of "rasping outbursts," the Baldwin of *Another Country* becomes "a voice of anger, rasping and thrusting," and he is no longer "held back" by the "proprieties of literature." The character of Rufus in that novel displays a "ferocity" quite new in Baldwin's fiction, and Baldwin's essays gain resonance from "the tone of unrelenting protest . . . from [their] very anger, even the violence," etc. I am afraid that these are "good" terms in Howe's essay and they led to part of my judgment.

In defense of Wright's novel *The Long Dream*, Howe can write:

> . . . This book has been attacked for presenting Negro life in the South through "old-fashioned" images of violence, but [and now we have "prescription"] one ought to hesitate before denying

the relevance of such images or joining in the criticism of their use. *For Wright was perhaps justified* in not paying attention to the changes that have occurred in the South these past few decades.[2]

If this isn't a defense, if not of bad writing at least of an irresponsible attitude toward good writing, I simply do not understand the language. I find it astonishing advice, since novels exist, since the fictional spell comes into existence precisely through the care which the novelist gives to selecting the details, the images, the tonalities, the specific social and psychological processes of specific characters in specific milieus at specific points in time. Indeed, it is one of the main tenets of the novelist's morality that he should write of that which he knows, and this is especially crucial for novelists who deal with a society as mobile and rapidly changing as ours. To justify ignoring this basic obligation is to encourage [133] the downgrading of literature in favor of other values, in this instance "anger," "protest" and "clenched militancy." Novelists create not simply out of "memory" but out of memory modified, extended, transformed by social change. For a novelist to heed such advice as Howe's is to commit an act of artistic immorality. Amplify this back through society and the writer's failure could produce not order but chaos.

Yet Howe proceeds on the very next page of his essay to state, with no sense of contradiction, that Wright failed in some of the stories which comprise *Eight Men* ("The Man Who Lived Underground" was first published, by the way, in 1944), because he needed the "accumulated material of circumstance." If a novelist ignores social change, how can he come by the "accumulated material of circumstance"? Perhaps if Howe could grasp the full meaning of that phrase he would understand that Wright did not report in *Black Boy* much of his life in Mississippi, and he would see that Ross Barnett is not the whole state, that there is also a Negro Mississippi which is much more varied than that which Wright depicted.

For the critic there simply exists no substitute for the knowledge of history and literary tradition. Howe stresses Wright's comment that when he went into rooms where there were naked white women he felt like a "non-man . . . doubly cast out." But had Howe thought

---

2. Italics mine.

about it he might have questioned this reaction, since most young men would have been delighted with the opportunity to study, at first hand, women usually cloaked in an armor of taboos. I wonder how Wright felt when he saw Negro women acting just as shamelessly? Clearly this was an ideological point, not a factual report. And anyone aware of the folk sources of Wright's efforts to create literature would recognize that the situation is identical with that of the countless stories which Negro men tell of the male slave called in to wash the [134] mistress' back in the bath, of the Pullman porter invited in to share the beautiful white passenger's favors in the berth, of the bellhop seduced by the wealthy blond guest.

It is interesting that Howe should interpret my statement about Mississippi as evidence of a loss of self-control. So allow me to repeat it coldly: I fear the implications of Howe's ideas concerning the Negro writer's role as actionist more than I do the State of Mississippi. Which is not to deny the viciousness which exists there but to recognize the degree of freedom which also exists there precisely because the repression is relatively crude, or at least it was during Wright's time, and it left the world of literature alone. William Faulkner lived neither in Jefferson nor Frenchman's Bend but in Oxford. He, too, was a Mississippian, just as the boys who helped Wright leave Jackson were the sons of a Negro college president. Both Faulkner and these boys must be recognized as part of the social reality of Mississippi. I said nothing about Ross Barnett, and I certainly did not say that Howe was a "cultural authoritarian," so he should not spread his honor so thin. Rather, let him look to the implications of his thinking.

Yes, and let him learn more about the South and about Negro Americans if he would speak with authority. When he points out that "the young Ralph Ellison, even while reading these great writers, could not in Macon County attend the white man's school or movie house," he certainly appears to have me cornered. But here again he does not know the facts and he underplays choice and will. I rode freight trains to Macon County, Alabama, during the Scottsboro trial because I desired to study with the Negro conductor-composer William L. Dawson, who was, and probably still is, the greatest classical musician in that part of the country. I had no need to attend a white university when the master I wished to study with was available at Tuskegee. Besides, [135] why sould I have wished to attend the white state-controlled university where the works of the great writers might not have been so easily available.

As for the movie-going, it is ironic but nonetheless true that one of the few instances where "separate but equal" was truly separate and equal was in a double movie house in the town of Tuskegee, where Negroes and whites were accommodated in parallel theaters, entering from the same street level through separate entrances and with the Negro side viewing the same pictures shortly after the showing for whites had begun. It was a product of social absurdity and, of course, no real relief from our resentment over the restriction of our freedom, but the movies were just as enjoyable or boring. And yet, is not knowing the facts more interesting, even as an isolated instance, and more stimulating to real thought than making abstract assumptions? I went to the movies to see pictures, not to be with whites. I attended a certain college because what I wanted was there. What is more, I *never* attended a white school from kindergarten through my three years of college, and yet, like Howe, I have taught and lectured for some years now at Northern, predominantly white, colleges and universities.

Perhaps this counts for little, changes little of the general condition of society, but it *is* factual and it does form a part of my sense of reality because, though it was not a part of Wright's life, it is my own. And if Howe thinks mine is an isolated instance, let him do a bit of research.

I do not really think that Howe can make a case for himself by bringing up the complimentary remarks which he made about *Invisible Man*. I did not quarrel with them in 1952, when they were first published, and I did not quarrel with them in my reply. His is the right of any critic to make judgment of a novel, and I do not see the point of arguing that I achieved an aesthetic goal if it did not work for him. (I can only ask that my fiction be judged as art; if it fails, it fails [136] aesthetically, not because I did or did not fight some ideological battle.) I repeat, however, that Howe's strategy of bringing me into the public quarrel between Baldwin and Wright was inept. I simply did not belong in the conflict, since I knew, even then, that protest is *not* the source of the inadequacy characteristic of most novels by Negroes, but the simple failure of craft, bad writing; the desire to have protest perform the difficult tasks of art; the belief that racial suffering, social injustice or ideologies of whatever mammy-made variety, is enough. I know, also, that when the work of Negro writers has been rejected they have all too often protected their egos by blaming racial discrimination, while turning away from the fairly obvious fact that good art—and Negro musicians are ever present to demonstrate this—commands attention of itself, whatever the writer's politics or point of view. And they forget that publishers will publish almost anything which is written with even a minimum of competency, and that skill is developed by hard work, study and a conscious assault upon one's own fear and provincialism.

I agree with Howe that protest is an element of all art, though it does not necessarily take the form of speaking for a political or social program. It might appear in a novel as a technical assault against the styles which have gone before, or as protest against the human condition. If *Invisible Man* is even "apparently" free from "the ideological and emotional penalties suffered by Negroes in this country," it is because I tried to the best of my ability to transform these elements into art. My goal was not to escape, or hold back, but to work through; to transcend, as the blues transcend the painful conditions with which they deal. The protest is there, not because I was helpless before my racial condition, but because I *put* it there. If there is anything "miraculous" about the book it is the result of hard work undertaken in the belief that the work of art is important in itself, that it is a social action in itself. [137]

I cannot hope to persuade Irving Howe to this view, for it seems quite obvious that he believes there are matters more important than artistic scrupulousness. I will point out, though, that the laws of literary form exert their validity upon all those who write, and that it is his slighting of the formal necessities of his essay which makes for some of our misunderstanding. After reading his reply, I gave in to my ear's suggestion that I had read certain of his phrases somewhere before, and I went to the library, where I discovered that much of his essay was taken verbatim from a review in the *Nation* of May 10, 1952, and that another section was published verbatim in the *New Republic* of February 13, 1962; the latter, by the way, being in its original context a balanced appraisal and warm farewell to Richard Wright.

But when Howe spliced these materials together with phrases from an old speech of mine, swipes at the critics of the *Sewanee* and *Kenyon* reviews (journals in which I have never published), and the

Baldwin-Wright quarrel, the effect was something other than he must have intended. A dialectical transformation into a new quality took place and despite the intention of Howe's content, the form made its own statement. If he would find the absurdities he wants me to reduce to a quotation, he will really have to read his essay whole. One gets the impression that he did a paste-and-scissors job and, knowing what he intended, knowing how the separated pieces had operated by themselves, did not bother to read very carefully their combined effect. It could happen to anyone; nevertheless, I'm glad he is not a scientist or a social engineer.

I do not understand why Howe thinks I said anything on the subject of writing about "Negro experience" in a manner which excludes what he calls "plight and protest"; he must have gotten his Negroes mixed. But as to answering his question concerning the "ways a Negro writer can achieve personal [138] realization apart from the common effort of his people to win their full freedom," I suggest that he ask himself in what way shall a Negro writer achieve personal realization (as writer) *after* his people shall have won their full freedom? The answer appears to be the same in both instances: He will have to go it alone! He must suffer alone even as he shares the suffering of his group, and he must write alone and pit his talents against the standards set by the best practitioners of the craft, both past and present, in any case. For the writer's real way of sharing the experience of his group is to convert its mutual suffering into lasting value. Is Howe suggesting, incidentally, that Heinrich Heine did not exist?

His question is silly, really, for there is no such thing as "full freedom" (Oh, how Howe thirsts and hungers for the absolute for *Negroes!*), just as the notion of an equality of talent is silly. I am a Negro who once played trumpet with a certain skill, but alas, I am no Louis Armstrong or Clark Terry. Willie Mays has realized himself quite handsomely as an individual despite coming from an impoverished Negro background in oppressive Alabama; and Negro Americans, like most Americans who know the value of baseball, exult in his success. I am, after all, only a minor member, not the whole damned tribe; in fact, most Negroes have never heard of me. I could shake the nation for a while with a crime or with indecent disclosures, but my pride lies in earning the right to call myself quite simply "writer." Perhaps if I write well enough the children of today's Negroes will be proud that I did, and so, perhaps, will Irving Howe's.

Let me end with a personal note: Dear Irving, I have no objections to being placed beside Richard Wright in any estimation which is based not upon the irremediable ground of our common racial identity, but upon the quality of our achievements as writers. I respected Wright's work and I knew him, but this is not to say that he "influenced" me as [139] significantly as you assume. Consult the text! I *sought out* Wright because I had read Eliot, Pound, Gertrude Stein and Hemingway, and as early as 1940 Wright viewed me as a potential rival, partially, it is true, because he feared I would allow myself to be used against him by political manipulators who were not Negro and who envied and hated him. But perhaps you will understand when I say he did not influence me if I point out that while one can do nothing about choosing one's relatives, one can, as artist, choose one's "ancestors." Wright was, in this sense, a "relative"; Hemingway an "ancestor." Langston Hughes, whose work I knew in grade school and whom I knew before I knew Wright, was a "relative"; Eliot, whom I was to meet only many years later, and Malraux and Dostoievsky and Faulkner, were "ancestors"—if you please or don't please!

Do you still ask why Hemingway was more important to me than Wright? Not because he was white, or more "accepted." But because he appreciated the things of this earth which I love and which Wright was too driven or deprived or inexperienced to know: weather, guns, dogs, horses, love *and* hate and impossible circumstances which to the courageous and dedicated could be turned into benefits and victories. Because he wrote with such precision about the processes and techniques of daily living that I could keep myself and my mother alive during the 1937 Recession by following his descriptions of wing-shooting; because he knew the difference between politics and art and something of their true relationship for the writer. Because all that he wrote—and this is very important—was imbued with a spirit beyond the tragic with which I could feel at home, for it was very close to the feeling of the blues, which are, perhaps, as close as Americans can come to expressing the spirit of tragedy. (And if you think Wright knew anything about the blues, listen to a "blues" he composed with Paul Robeson singing, a *most* unfortunate collaboration!; and read his introduction [140] to Paul Oliver's *Blues Fell This Morning*.) But most important, because Hemingway was a greater artist than Wright, who although a

Negro like myself, and perhaps a great man, understood little if anything of these, at least to me, important things. Because Hemingway loved the American language and the joy of writing, making the flight of birds, the loping of lions across an African plain, the mysteries of drink and moonlight, the unique styles of diverse peoples and individuals come alive on the page. Because he was in many ways the true father-as-artist of so many of us who came to writing during the late thirties.

I will not dwell upon Hemingway's activities in Spain or during the liberation in Paris, for you know all of that. I will remind you, however, that any writer takes what he needs to get his own work done from wherever he finds it. I did not need Wright to tell me how to be a Negro, or how to be angry or to express anger—Joe Louis was doing that very well—or even to teach me about socialism; my mother had canvassed for the socialists, not the communists, the year I was born. No, I had been a Negro for twenty-two or twenty-three years when I met Wright, and in more places and under a greater variety of circumstances than he had then known. He was generously helpful in sharing his ideas and information, but I needed instruction in other values and I found them in the works of other writers—Hemingway was one of them, T. S. Eliot initiated the search.

I like your part about Chekhov arising from his sickbed to visit the penal colony at Sakhalin Island. It was, as you say, a noble act. But shouldn't we remember that it was significant only because Chekhov was *Chekhov,* the great writer? You compliment me truly, but I have not written so much or so well, even though I *have* served a certain apprenticeship in the streets and even touch events in the Freedom Movement in a modest way. But I can also recall the story of a certain writer who succeeded with a great fanfare of publicity in [141] having a talented murderer released from prison. It made for another very short story which ended quite tragically—though not for the writer: A few months after his release the man killed the mother of two young children. I also know of another really quite brilliant writer who, under the advice of certain wise men who were then managing the consciences of artists, abandoned the prison of his writing to go to Spain, where he was allowed to throw away his life defending a worthless hill. I have not heard his name in years but I remember it vividly; it was Christopher Cauldwell, *né* Christopher St. John Sprigg. There are many such stories, Irving. It's heads you win, tails you lose, and you are quite right about my not following Baldwin, who is urged on by a nobility—or is it a demon—quite different from my own. It has cost me quite a pretty penny, indeed, but then I was always poor and not (and I know this is a sin in our America) too uncomfortable.

Dear Irving, I am still yakking on and there's many a thousand gone, but I assure you that no Negroes are beating down my door, putting pressure on me to join the Negro Freedom Movement, for the simple reason that they realize that I am enlisted for the duration. Such pressure is coming only from a few disinterested "military advisers," since Negroes want no more fairly articulate would-be Negro leaders cluttering up the airways. For, you see, my Negro friends recognize a certain division of labor among the members of the tribe. Their demands, like that of many whites, are that I publish more novels—and here I am remiss and vulnerable perhaps. You will recall what the Talmud has to say about the trees of the forest and the making of books, etc. But then, Irving, they recognize what you have not allowed yourself to see; namely, that my reply to your essay is in itself a small though necessary action in the Negro struggle for freedom. You should not feel unhappy about this or think that I regard you either as dishonorable or an enemy. I hope, rather, that [142] you will come to view this exchange as an act of, shall we say, "antagonistic co-operation"? [143]

CRITICAL REACTIONS TO *INVISIBLE MAN*

Ralph Ellison and *Invisible Man* have both occasioned a great deal of critical commentary. It is wise to recognize that these are two separate subjects. In the context of the recent Black Arts movement, a movement that dismisses the traditional divisions between art and politics, Ralph Ellison's example is anything but charismatic. Much of the commentary on Ellison therefore deals with his failure to be a more active participant in the black liberation movement. Ellison's answer to these charges appears in "The World and the Jug." Robert Bone's essay "Ralph Ellison and the Uses of Imagination" establishes perspective on Ellison's argument with the Black Arts movement. The appeal of "Negro Nationalism" is as limited as the illusion of "assimilationism." What is needed is some new understanding of the concept of cultural pluralism. And, as Bone suggests, "to this end, Ellison offers what might be called some Notes toward a Redefinition of American Culture."

While the attacks on Ellison's politics continue, young black intellectuals cannot, as Harold Cruse has pointed out, "attack Ellison on craftsmanship, or even content any more . . . because none of them has written anything even remotely comparable to Ellison's achievements."[1] Another kind of criticism, that occasioned by critical engagement with the novel proper, has been diverse and extremely prolific. Recently, two literary journals—*Black World* XX (December, 1970) and *CLA Journal* XIII No. 3 (1970)—have devoted a whole issue to critical articles on *Invisible Man*. The selections chosen for this handbook represent the range of critical approaches possible. William Schafer discusses "The Birth of the Anti-Hero" and connects Ellison's protagonist to epic and mythic patterns, particularly Joseph Campbell's conception of the myth of the hero. Ellin Horowitz establishes Ellison's use of the "portrait of the artist" theme and then moves on to consider the psychological themes of castration and Oedipal ri-

---

1. Harold Cruse, *The Crisis of the Negro Intellectual* (New York: William Morrow & Co., 1967), p. 508.

valry. Earl Rovit points to the national and cosmic joke at the heart of *Invisible Man* and illustrates, by his discussion of writers like Emerson, that Ellison is firmly within the American comic tradition.

More specialized critical approaches may be found in the next three articles. Alice Bloch presents a concise treatment of the "Sight Imagery in *Invisible Man*." Marvin Mengeling, echoing Rovit's suggestion that Ellison is firmly within the mainstream of the American literary tradition, illustrates how Ellison has used that tradition through ironic allusions to Whitman in Homer A. Barbee's speech. Floyd R. Horowitz has shown how Ellison has utilized black folklore to good advantage. And finally, Richard Kostelanetz, reading *Invisible Man* as symbolic history, traces the intellectual history that parallels the novel. As Ellison would say, "the end is in the beginning." But serving as a kind of "Epilogue" to this book is Ellison's acceptance speech for the National Book Award. Here Ellison affirms his commitment to the craft of the artist and to the kind of novel that renders the theme of "personal moral responsibility for democracy." These are "brave words" indeed, but the achievement of *Invisible Man* suggests that such words are not for a "startling occasion."

RALPH ELLISON AND THE USES OF IMAGINATION
Robert Bone

We live only in one place at one time, but far from being bound by it, only through it do we realize our freedom. We do not have to abandon our familiar and known to achieve distinction; rather in that place, if only we make ourselves sufficiently aware of it, do we join with others in other places.
WILLIAM CARLOS WILLIAMS

Some fourteen years ago an unknown writer, no longer young, published a first novel and, to no one's astonishment more than his own, won the National Fiction Award for 1953. There, suddenly, was the novel, and it spoke eloquently enough, but who was the author of *Invisible Man*? We knew only that the curve of his life was a parabola, moving from Oklahoma City to New York by way of Alabama. In the intervening years we have had some fleeting glimpses of the man and his ideas: the acceptance speech itself, an occasional interview, a fragment of his work in progress. We might have noticed his music criticism in the *Saturday Review* or the recent exchange with Irving Howe in *The New Leader*. But basically the man behind the mask remained invisible.

Now, with the publication of *Shadow and Act*,[1] this remarkable [86] man emerges, at least in silhouette, to the public view. The book contains most of Ellison's essays, from the beginning of his literary career to the present. There are seven apprentice pieces, written in the Forties, which reflect the author's social and political concerns, and seven essays on jazz and the blues, which appeared principally in the late Fifties. There are three interviews of the *Paris Review* genre, and three first-rate essays on literary topics. Along the way, we learn a good deal about the author and the forces that have shaped his sense of life.

SOURCE: Robert Bone, "Ralph Ellison and the Uses of the Imagination," *Tri-Quarterly*, VI (1966). Reprinted in *Anger and Beyond*, ed. Herbert Hill (New York: Harper & Row, 1969), pp. 86–111. Copyright by Robert Bone. Reprinted by permission of the author.

1. New York: Random House, 1964.

The formative years in Oklahoma City are sketched in some detail. Ellison was born in 1914, just seven years after Oklahoma was admitted to the Union. In the early days, his adopted grandfather had led a group of settlers from Tennessee to the Oklahoma Territory. Containing such elements, the Negro community of Oklahoma City developed more a Western than a Southern tone. Race relations, like all social relations, were more fluid than in established communities. Frontier attitudes persisted well into the present century, and Ellison was raised in a tradition of aggressiveness and love of freedom. He is proud of his frontier heritage, and to it may be traced his fierce individualism and his sense of possibility.

Oklahoma City was a boomtown in the postwar years—a swirling vortex of social styles and human types. There were many masks which an imaginative adolescent might try on:

> Gamblers and scholars, jazz musicians and scientists, Negro cowboys and soldiers from the Spanish-American and First World Wars, movie stars and stunt men, figures from the Italian Renaissance and literature, both classical and popular, were combined with the special virtues of some local bootlegger, the eloquence of some Negro preacher, the strength and grace of some local athlete, the ruthlessness of some businessman-physician, the elegance in dress and manners of some headwaiter or hotel doorman.[2]

If there was no local writer for a model, there was access to a rich oral literature in the churches, schoolyards, barbershops, [87] and cotton-picking camps. And there was a curious double exposure to the exacting habits of artistic discipline. Through one of the ironies of segregation, the Negro school system placed particular stress on training in classical music. Ellison took up the trumpet at the age of eight and studied four years of harmony in high school. Meanwhile he was exposed to the driving beat of Southwestern jazz, of which Kansas City, Dallas, and Oklahoma City were acknowledged centers. From his boyhood onward, he was caught up in that creative tension between the folk and classical traditions which has remained the richest resource of his art.

In 1933 Ellison enrolled at Tuskegee Institute to study com-

2. *Shadow and Act,* pp. xv–xvi.

position under William Dawson, the Negro conductor and composer. In his sophomore year, however, he came upon a copy of *The Waste Land*, and the long transition from trumpet to typewriter had begun. He read widely in American fiction and, initially scorning the moderns, developed a lifelong devotion to the nineteenth-century masters. On coming to New York in 1936 he met Richard Wright, who introduced him on the one hand to the prefaces of Conrad and the letters of Dostoevski, and on the other to the orbit of the Communist party. One evening he accompanied Wright to a fund-raising affair for the Spanish Loyalists, where he met both Malraux and Leadbelly for the first time. It was a notable occasion, symbolic of the times and of the cross-pressures exerted from the first upon his art.

From these cross-pressures Ellison derived his most enduring themes. How could he interpret and extend, define and yet elaborate upon the folk culture of the American Negro and, at the same time, assimilate the most advanced techniques of modern literature? How could he affirm his dedication to the cause of Negro freedom without succumbing to the stridencies of protest fiction, without relinquishing his complex sense of life? In *Shadow and Act*, Ellison returns again and again to these tangled themes: the relationship of Negro folk culture to American culture as a whole, and the responsibility of the Negro artist to his ethnic group.

As instrumentalist and composer, Ellison had faced these issues for the better part of two decades. When he began to write, it was natural for him to draw upon his musical experience for guidelines and perspectives. Not that his approach to writing is merely an extension of an earlier approach to jazz and the blues; they tend, in fact, to reinforce each other. But his experience with jazz was formative; it left a permanent mark upon his style. His controlling metaphors are musical, and if we are to grasp his thought, we must trace his language to its source. There, in the world of Louis Armstrong and Charlie Parker, Bessie Smith and Jimmy Rushing, we may discover the foundations of Ellison's aesthetic.

Music

The essence of jazz is group improvisation. Its most impressive effects are achieved, according to Ellison, when a delicate balance is maintained between the individual performer and the group. The form itself, consisting of a series of solo "breaks" with a framework of standard chord progressions, encourages this balance. "Each true jazz moment," Ellison explains, "springs from a contest in which each artist challenges all the rest; each solo flight, or improvisation, represents (like the successive canvases of a painter) a definition of his identity: as individual, as member of the collectivity, and as a link in the chain of tradition." "True jazz," he concludes, "is an art of individual assertion within and against the group."

Here is a working model for the Negro writer. By balancing conflicting claims upon his art, he can solve his deepest problems of divided loyalty. As an artist with a special function to perform within the Negro group, the writer must be careful to preserve his individuality. He must learn to operate "within and against the group," allowing neither claim to cancel out the [89] other. Similarly on the cultural plane, where the Negro's group identity is at stake. Here the writer can affirm whatever is uniquely Negro in his background while insisting precisely on the American quality of his experience. "The point of our struggle," writes Ellison, "is to be both Negro and American and to bring about that condition in American society in which this would be possible."

Closely related to the question of individual and group identity is that of personal and traditional styles. Every jazz musician must strike a balance between tradition and experimentation, for "jazz finds its very life in an endless improvisation upon traditional materials." It follows that no jazzman is free to repudiate the past. The jam session, where he must display a knowledge of traditional techniques, will see to that. He must master "the intonations, the mute work, manipulation of timbre, the body of traditional styles" before he can presume to speak in his own voice. The path, in short, to self-expression lies through what is given, what has gone before.

As an American Negro writer, Ellison inherits a double obligation to the past. He must become familiar with a folk tradition which is his alone, and with a wider literary culture which he shares. Moreover, he must strive in both dimensions for a proper blend of past and present, given and improvised. In describing his response to his folk tradition, Ellison draws a parallel to the work of Picasso: "Why, he's the greatest wrestler with forms and techniques of them all. Just the same, he's never abandoned the old symbolic forms of Spanish art: the guitar, the bull, daggers, women, shawls, veils, mirrors." Similarly,

Ellison appropriates folkloristic elements from Negro culture, embroiders on them, adapts them to his literary aims, and lifts them to the level of a conscious art.

In the wider context of American literature, the same principles apply. Consider Ellison's experimental idiom. Not since Jean Toomer has a Negro novelist been so inventive of new forms, new language, new technical devices. And yet none has been so deeply immersed in the American literary past. As Ellison [90] struggles toward the realization of a personal style, he is *improvising* on the achievement of our nineteenth-century masters. It is this body of writing, he insists, "to which I was most attached and through which . . . I would find my own voice, and to which I was challenged, by way of achieving myself, to make some small contribution, and to whose composite picture of reality I was obligated to offer some necessary modifications."

Still a third balance must be struck between constraint and spontaneity, discipline and freedom. For the jazzman owes his freedom to the confident possession of technique. From his own struggles with the trumpet, Ellison learned how much the wild ecstatic moment depends on patient hours of practice and rehearsal. Freedom, he perceived, is never absolute, but rooted in its opposite. The game is not to cast off all restraint but to achieve, within the arbitrary limits of a musical tradition, a transcendent freedom. Jazz taught Ellison a respect for limits, even as it revealed the possibility of overcoming limits through technique. It was the blues, however, that taught him to discern in this paradox an emblem of the human condition.

The blues arise out of a tension between circumstance and possibility. The grim reality that gives them birth bespeaks the limits and restrictions, the barriers and thwartings, which the universe opposes to the human will. But the tough response that is the blues bespeaks a moral courage, a spiritual freedom, a sense of human possibility, which more than balances the scales. In Ellison's words, "The blues is an art of ambiguity, an assertion of the irrepressibly human over all circumstance whether created by others or by one's own human failings. They are the only consistent art in the United States which constantly reminds us of our limitations while encouraging us to see how far we can actually go."

The blues begin with personal disaster. They speak of flooded farmlands and blighted crops, of love betrayed and lovers parted, of the black man's poverty and the white man's justice. But what matters is the human response to these events. For the blues are a poetic confrontation of reality. They are a form of [91] spiritual discipline, a means of transcending the painful conditions with which they deal. The crucial feature of the blues response is the margin of freedom it proclaims. To call them an art of ambiguity is to assert that no man is entirely the victim of circumstance. Within limits, there is always choice and will. Thinking of this inner freedom, Ellison speaks of "the secular existentialism of the blues."

This sense of possibility lies at the center of Ellison's art. It explains his devotion to his craft, for what is technique but another name for possibility? It explains his attitude toward protest fiction, for the propaganda novel, in portraying the Negro primarily as victim, gives more weight to circumstance than possibility. Ellison's is a more plastic sensibility. His heroes are not victims but adventurers. They journey toward the possible in all ignorance of accepted limits. In the course of their travels, they shed their illusions and come to terms with reality. They are, in short, picaresque heroes, full of "rash efforts, quixotic gestures, hopeful testings of the complexity of the known and the given."

If circumstance often enough elicits tears, possibility may release a saving laughter. This blend of emotion, mixed in some ancient cauldron of the human spirit, is characteristic of the blues. It is a lyricism better sampled than described. Note in Ellison's example how the painful humiliation of the bird is controlled, or absorbed, or even converted into triumph by a kind of grudging laughter:

> Oh they picked poor robin clean
> They picked poor robin clean
> They tied poor robin to a stump
> Lord, they picked all the feathers
> Round from robin's rump
> Oh they picked poor robin clean.

The blues have nothing to do with the consolations of philosophy. They are a means of neutralizing one emotion with another, [92] in the same way that alkalies can neutralize an acid stomach. For the American Negro, they are a means of prophylaxis, a specific for the prevention of spiritual ulcers. It is not a question of laughing away one's troubles in any superficial sense, but of gazing steadily at pain while perceiving its comic aspect. Ellison regards this tragicomic sensibility as the most precious feature of his Negro heritage. From it stems his lyrical intensity and the complex interplay of tragic and comic elements which is the distinguishing mark of his fiction.

If the blues are primarily an expression of personal emotion, they also serve a group need. Perhaps the point can best be made through a comparison with gospel singing. When Mahalia Jackson sings in church, she performs a ritual function. Her music serves "to prepare the congregation for the minister's message, to make it receptive to the spirit and, with effects of voice and rhythm, to evoke a shared community of experience." Similarly in the secular context of the blues. When Jimmy Rushing presided over a Saturday night dance in Oklahoma City, he was acting as the leader of a public rite: "It was when Jimmy's voice began to soar with the spirit of the blues that the dancers—and the musicians—achieved that feeling of communion which was the true meaning of the public jazz dance."

We are dealing here with substitute rituals. During an epoch which has witnessed the widespread breakdown of traditional religious forms, Ellison finds in jazz and the blues, as Hemingway found in the bullfight, a code of conduct and a ceremonial framework for his art. "True novels," he insists, "arise out of an impulse to celebrate human life and therefore are ritualistic and ceremonial at their core." Ellison perceives, in short, the priestly office of the modern artist and assumes the role of celebrant in his own work. Like the blues singer, he is motivated by an impulse to restore to others a sense of the wholeness of their lives.

Finally, specific features of Ellison's literary style may be traced to his musical background. His fondness for paradox and ambiguity, for example, derives from the blues: "There is a [93] mystery in the whiteness of blackness, the innocence of evil and the evil of innocence, though being initiates Negroes express the joke of it in the blues." The changing styles of *Invisible Man* (from naturalism to expressionism to surrealism, as Ellison describes the sequence) are based on the principle of modulation. Chord progressions in jazz are called "changes"; they correspond in speed and abruptness to Ellison's sense of American reality, the swift flow of sound and sudden changes of key suggesting the fluidity and discontinuity of American life.

Literature

Let us now turn from Ellison's musical to his literary heritage. We must begin with the picaresque novel and attempt to explain why this form, which first appeared in Renaissance Spain, should be revived by a contemporary Negro novelist. We must then consider Ellison's affinity for the American transcendentalists, in light of his commitment to the picaresque. Finally, we must examine in some detail two devices that are central to his art.

The picaresque novel emerged toward the end of the feudal and the beginning of the bourgeois epoch. Its characteristic hero, part rogue and part outlaw, transcended all established norms of conduct and violated all ideas of social hierarchy. For with the breakdown of static social relations, a testing of personal limits, a bold confrontation with the new and untried became necessary. Hence the picaresque journey, no longer a religious quest or pilgrimage but a journey toward experience, adventure, personal freedom. It was the journey of the bourgeois soul toward possibility, toward a freedom possessed by neither serf nor lord under the old regime.

It can hardly be an accident that *Invisible Man* and *The Adventures of Augie March* should win the National Fiction Award within two years of one another. Nor that Ellison and Bellow should each acknowledge a major debt to Twain. For *Huckleberry Finn* is the last great picaresque novel to be written by a [94] white Anglo-Saxon American. The genre has been abandoned to the Negro and the Jew who, two generations from slavery or the *shtetl*, experience for the first time and in full force what Ellison calls the magical fluidity of American life. A century after Hawthorne wrote *The Scarlet Letter*, our minority groups are re-enacting the central drama of that novel: the break with the institutions and authorities of the past and the emergence into an epoch of personal freedom and individual moral responsibility.

Ellison's revival of the picaresque reflects his group's belated access to the basic conditions of bourgeois existence. These consist economically of the freedom to rise and psychologically of "the right and opportunity to dilate, deepen, and enrich sensibility." The Southern Negro who is taught from childhood to "know his place" is denied these basic freedoms. He is deprived of individuality as thoroughly as any serf: "The pre-individualistic black community discourages individuality out of self-defense. . . . Within the ambit of the black family this takes the form of training the child away from curiosity and adventure, against reaching out for those activities lying beyond the borders."

The Great Migration of the Negro masses from Southern farm to Northern city was picaresque in character. In terms of Negro personality, it was like uncorking a bottle of champagne. Traditionally the journey has been made by railroad, and it is no accident that the blues are associated with freight yards, quick getaways and long journeys in "a side door Pullman car." No accident either that Ellison should emphasize his own wanderings: "To attempt to express that American experience which has carried one back and forth and up and down the land and across, and across again the great river, from freight train to Pullman car, from contact with slavery to contact with the world of advanced scholarship, art and science, is simply to burst such neatly understated forms of the novel asunder."

The bursting forth of Negro personality from the fixed boundaries [95] of Southern life is Ellison's essential theme. And it is this, at bottom, that attracts him to the transcendentalists. For what was the central theme of Thoreau, Emerson and Whitman, if not the journeying forth of the soul? These writers were celebrating their emancipation from the Custom House, from the moral and political authority of old Europe. Their romantic individualism was a response to the new conditions created by the Revolution, conditions calling for *self*-government in both the political and moral sphere. Their passion for personal freedom, moreover, was balanced by a sense of personal responsibility for the future of democracy.

Ellison's debt to transcendentalism is manifold, but what is not acknowledged can easily be surmised. He is named, to begin with, for Ralph Waldo Emerson. In this connection he mentions two specific influences: the "Concord Hymn" and "Self-Reliance." The poem presumably inspires him with its willingness to die that one's children may be free; the essay, as we shall see, governs his attitude toward Negro culture. He admires Thoreau, plainly enough, for his stand on civil disobedience and his militant defense of John Brown. Whitman he finds congenial, for such poems as "The Open Road" and "Passage to India" are squarely in the picaresque tradition.

In broader terms, it may be said that Ellison's ontology derives from transcendentalism. One senses in his work an unseen reality behind the surfaces of things. Hence his fascination with guises and disguises, with the con man and the trickster. Hence the felt dichotomy between visible and invisible, public and private, actual and fictive modes of reality. His experience as a Negro no doubt reinforces his ironic awareness of "the joke that always lies between appearance and reality," and turns him toward an inner world that lies beyond the reach of insult or oppression. This world may be approached by means of the imagination; it is revealed during the transcendent moment in jazz or the epiphany in literature. *Transcend* is thus a crucial word in Ellison's aesthetic. [96]

Above all, Ellison admires the transcendentalists for their active democratic faith. They were concerned not only with the slavery question but with the wider implications of cultural pluralism, with the mystery of the one and the many. To these writers, the national motto, *e pluribus unum*, was a serious philosophical concern. Emerson discerned a cosmic model for American democracy in the relationship of soul to Oversoul. Whitman, however, made the classic formulation:

> One's self I sing, a simple separate person,
> Yet utter the word Democracy, the word En-Masse.

Ellison reveals, in his choice of ancestors, the depth of his commitment to American ideals. When he describes jazz as "that embodiment of a superior democracy in which each individual cultivated his uniqueness and yet did not clash with his neighbors," he is affirming the central values of American civilization.

It remains to place Ellison in his twentieth-century tradition. What is involved is a rejection of the naturalistic novel and the philosophical assumptions on which it rests. From Ellison's allusions to certain of his contemporaries—to Stein and Hemingway, Joyce and Faulkner, Eliot and Yeats—one idea emerges with persistent force: *Man is the creator of his own reality*. If a culture shapes its artists, the converse is equally the case: "The American novel is in this sense a conquest of the frontier; as it describes our experience, it creates it." This turn toward subjectivity, this transcendence of determinism, this insistence on an existential freedom, is crucial to Ellison's conception of the artist. It finds concrete expression in his work through the devices of masking and naming.

Masking has its origin in the psychological circumstances of Southern life: "In the South the sensibilities of both blacks and whites are inhibited by the rigidly defined environment. For the Negro there is relative safety as long as the impulse toward individuality is suppressed." As soon, however, as this forbidden [97] impulse seeks expression, an intolerable anxiety is aroused. Threatened by his own unfolding personality as much as by the whites, the Negro learns to camouflage, to dissimulate, to retreat behind a protective mask. There is magic in it: the mask is a means of warding off the vengeance of the gods.

Consider the jazz solo, one of the few means of self-expression permitted to the southern Negro. Precisely because it is a solo, and the musician must go it alone, it represents potential danger. Ellison writes of certain jazz musicians: "While playing in ensemble, they carried themselves like college professors or high church deacons; when soloing they donned the comic mask." Louis Armstrong, as Ellison reminds us, has raised masking to the level of a fine art. Musical trickster, con man with a cornet, Elizabethan clown, "he takes liberties with kings, queens, and presidents." In a later development, the bearded mask of the bopster appeared, frankly expressive of hostility, rudeness and contempt. It is a pose which still finds favor among certain Negro writers of the younger generation.

In his own prose, Ellison employs various masking devices, including understatement, irony, *double-entendre* and calculated ambiguity. There is something deliberately elusive in his style, something secret and taunting, some instinctive avoidance of explicit statement which is close in spirit to the blues. His fascination with masquerade gives us two memorable characters in *Invisible Man*: the narrator's grandfather, whose mask of meekness conceals a stubborn resistance to white supremacy, and Rinehart, whom Ellison describes as "an American virtuoso of identity who thrives on chaos and swift change." A master of disguise, Rinehart survives by manipulating the illusions of society, much in the tradition of Melville's Confidence Man, Twain's Duke and Dauphin and Mann's Felix Krull.

Masking, which begins as a defensive gesture, becomes in Ellison's hands a means of altering reality. For if reality is a process of becoming, that process can be partially controlled through manipulation of a ritual object or mask. "Masking," Ellison [98] remarks, "is a play upon possibility," and possibility is precisely the domain of art.

To clarify the matter he summons Yeats, a man not ignorant of masks: "If we cannot imagine ourselves as different from what we are and assume the second self, we cannot impose a discipline upon ourselves, though we may accept one from others. Active virtue, as distinct from the passive acceptance of a current code, is the wearing of a mask." Yeats is speaking of morality, of active virtue, but the function of the artist is implicit in his words. Before pursuing the point, however, we must come to terms with a second feature of Ellison's art.

Naming likewise has its origin in negation, in the white man's hypocritical denial of his kinship ties. For the African slaves received from their Christian masters not only European names but a massive infusion of European blood, under circumstances so brutal and degrading as to have been virtually expunged from the national consciousness. At once guilty and proud, the white man has resorted to a systematic *misnaming* in an effort to obscure his crime. Thus the use of the matronymic to conceal the slave's paternity. Thus the insulting epithets which deny not merely kinship but humanity. In some obscene rite of exorcism, the white man says "nigger" when he should say "cousin." And yet the family names persist as symbols of that hidden truth, that broken connection which will have to be restored before the nation, sick from the denial of reality, can regain its mental health.

Having been misnamed by others, the American Negro has attempted from the first to define himself. This persistent effort at self-definition is the animating principle of Negro culture. The earliest appearance of Negro folklore, for example, "announced the Negro's willingness to trust his own experience, his own sensibilities as to the definition of reality, rather than allow his masters to define these crucial matters for him." Similarly with musical expression: the jazzman who rejects classical technique is affirming his right to define himself in sound. Cultural autonomy, [99] to Ellison, is an elementary act of self-reliance. We have listened too long, he seems to say, to the courtly Muses of white America. "Our names, being the gift of others, must be made our own."

For personal as well as historical reasons, Ellison is fascinated by the distinction between one's given and achieved identity. Named for a famous poet, it was half a lifetime before he could define, let alone accept, the burden of his given name. Acknowledging in retrospect the prescience of his father, he speaks of "the suggestive power of names and the magic involved in naming." We are dealing here with the ritual use of language, with the pressure which language can exert upon reality. This is the special province of the poet, and, broadly speaking, Ellison claims it as his own. He regards the novel as an act of ritual naming; the novelist, as a "moralist-designate" who *names* the central moral issues of his time.

"The poet," writes Ralph Waldo Emerson, "is the Namer or Language-maker." As such, he is the custodian of his language and the guarantor of its integrity. In performance of this function, Ellison has discovered that the language of contemporary America is in certain ways corrupt. "With all deliberate speed," for example, does not mean what it seems to mean when uttered by the Supreme Court of the United States. He proposes a rectification of the language and, therefore, of the nation's moral vision. For accurate naming is the writer's first responsibility: "In the myth, God gave man the task of naming the objects of the world; thus one of the functions of the poet is to insist upon a correspondence between words and ever-changing reality, between ideals and actualities."

As with naming, so with the image-making function as a whole. The artist, or image-maker, is guardian of the national iconography. And since the power of images for good or evil is immense, he bears an awesome responsibility. If his images are false, if there is no bridge between portrayal and event, no correspondence between the shadow and the act, then the emotional life of the nation is to that extent distorted, and its daily conduct [100] is rendered ineffectual or even pathological. This is the effect of the anti-Negro stereotype, whether in song or statuary, novel or advertising copy, comic strip or film. Images, being ritual objects, or masks, may be manipulated by those who have a stake in the preservation of caste lines. What is required is a recitification of the nation's icons, a squaring of the shadow and the act.

Nor can this be accomplished through the use of counterstereotypes. Protest fiction, by portraying sociological types, holds its readers at a distance from the human person. But the problem is precisely one of identification. To identify, in the psychological sense, is to become one with. For this process to occur between white reader and Negro character, the writer must break through the outer crust of racial conflict to the inner core of common humanity. He must evoke, by his imaginative power, an act of "painful identification." To succeed requires the utmost in emotional maturity, craftsmanship and skill. For what the artist undertakes, in the last analysis, is the rectification of the human heart.

Politics

If Ellison had remained a jazz musician, he might have been spared a series of political attacks upon his art. No one would have complained, if he had spoken in a jazz idiom, that his riffs were lacking in protest content. No one would have accused him, as he blew up there on the bandstand, of abandoning a posture of clenched militancy. For it is not expected of a Negro jazzman that, like the first trumpet in the Dodger Fan Club, he should sit in the stands during every civil-rights contest and play at appropriate moments, "Da da da datta da: Charge!" So long as he refuses to play for segregated audiences, accepts no gigs from the State Department and does an occasional benefit for SNCC, he is allowed to go about the very difficult business of interpreting Negro experience in sound.

Not so with the Negro novelist, who works in the medium of [101] words. For words have a variety of uses, political exhortation being one. The ideologists, therefore, move in. The question of militancy is raised, bearing not on the novelist's conduct as a citizen or political man but precisely on his creative work, his function as an artist. To those who feel above all else the urgency of the Negro's political struggle, it is not enough that a writer demonstrate his solidarity; he must enlist his image-making powers in the service of the cause. Since no writer who understands the proper uses of imagination can acquiesce in this perversion of his talent, he must prepare to walk that lonesome valley during much of his career, and to accept a good deal of abuse from those who do not recognize the value of his art.

It was predictable enough, given the rising tempo of the civil-rights struggle, that Ellison should be under pressure from the political activists. The Freedom Movement, like all great movements of social liberation, is lacking neither in demagogues nor Philistines. But that so sophisticated a critic and humane a man as Irving Howe should join the attack is scandalous. In an article called "Black Boys and Native Sons," [3] Howe takes Baldwin and Ellison to task for abandoning the "rasping outbursts," "black anger," and "clenched militancy" of Richard Wright. While he sees some signs of hope in Baldwin's recent work, he plainly regards Ellison as unregenerate. Howe's essay prompted a reply from Ellison, and the result was a sharp exchange in *The New Leader*.[4]

One's chief impression of this debate is that the antagonists are arguing at cross-purposes. They shout at one another, but little or no dialogue occurs. Howe's original piece is a monument to tactlessness, and Ellison is understandably provoked into a sometimes angry response. It is a bad show all around, and the issues deserve to be aired in a calmer atmosphere. It is [102] not my intent to mediate, however, for in my opinion Howe is overwhelmingly in the wrong. Nor do I wish to repeat Ellison's arguments which—tone aside—make most of the essential points. I should like rather to explore the philosophical foundations of the controversy. If my argument seems elementary, it is best that we proceed with caution, since, plainly, each of the contestants feels threatened by the other at the center of his being.

Let me begin with a parable. Imagine a Negro writer in the late 1950's (I choose the period advisedly, for Howe describes it as a conservative decade) attempting to decide on a subject for a novel. He has before him two projects, each based on the life of a Dodger baseball hero. The one—call it the Jackie Robinson story—is alive with racial drama: the first Negro ballplayer to make the big time, the insults from the stands, the spikings by opposing players, the mixed reception from his teammates. The other—call it the Roy Campanella story—concerns an athlete who, at the height of his career, spun his car around a curve one icy morning and spent the rest of his life in a wheelchair. Within a year or two his wife divorced him, she, too, a victim of her human frailty.

Suppose, for purposes of argument, that our writer chose to tell the second story. Would that choice suggest to Howe that he

3. *Dissent*, Autumn, 1963.
4. Dec. 9, 1963, and Feb. 3, 1964. Howe's original piece has been reprinted in *A World More Attractive* (New York: Horizon Press, 1963); Ellison's rejoinder appears in *Shadow and Act* under the title "The World and the Jug."

was running from reality, the reality of the sharpened spikes? Or is it possible that the Campanella story also contains a reality sufficiently sharp? Nor is there a refusal to confront injustice, for the theme of the second story would have to be injustice on a cosmic scale. Perhaps Howe would attempt a political explanation of our writer's choice. He might propose that during the militant decade of the Thirties such a writer would have turned at once to Jackie Robinson, but that out of his "dependence on the postwar *Zeitgeist*" he turned instead to a subject that was safe. But perhaps these political categories are beside the point. Perhaps our writer chose as he did simply because he felt in that story a deeper sense of human life. [103]

Not all human suffering is racial in origin, that is our initial point. Being Negro, unfortunately, does not release one from the common burdens of humanity. It is for this reason that the blues singer so often deals with other than his racial woes. And it is to this dimension of human, as opposed to racial, pain that Howe gives insufficient attention. Ultimately, Ellison and Howe are divided over the *locus* of human suffering. One stresses man's position in society; the other, his position in the universe at large.

At issue is a crucial distinction between remediable and irremediable evil. The first, roughly speaking, is the domain of politics and science; the second, of art and religion. One's sense of tragedy is linked to one's perception of irremediable evil. What we have, therefore, in the Howe-Ellison exchange, is a confrontation between Howe's political optimism and Ellison's tragic sensibility. Howe, who still believes in Progress, concentrates on the evil that can be changed to the neglect of that which must be borne.

To the white liberal, racial injustice is a remediable evil. The Negro, however, experiences it in both modes simultaneously. In historical time, things are no doubt getting better, but in one's own lifetime, white oppression is a bitter fact to which one must adjust. The Negro, as Ellison points out, must live with and suffer under the present reality even as he works to change it. Entirely apart from the Movement, he must concern himself with the strategies and techniques of personal survival. It is precisely with this necessity of Negro life that Ellison's art is engaged.

Because of Howe's bias toward remediable evil, it is difficult for him to understand redemptive suffering. Speaking of Richard Wright, he remarks, "He examines the life of the Negroes and judges it without charity or idyllic compensation—for he already knows, in his heart and his bones, that to be oppressed means to lose out on human possibilities." This half-truth, it seems to me, dehumanizes the Negro by depriving him of his [104] human triumph over pain. For as Ellison insists, Negro life is not only a burden but a discipline. Is it idyllic to suggest that Campanella's experience as a Negro might have prepared him in some way for coping with his accident? Was it in any way relevant? Was it, in short, an emotional resource?

If one attends primarily to remediable evil, one may be tempted to make larger claims for politics than history can justify. One may end by making politics the touchstone of a man's humanity: "In response to Baldwin and Ellison, Wright would have said . . . that only through struggle could men with black skins, and for that matter, all the oppressed of the world, achieve their humanity." Perhaps the question of humanity is after all more complex. It would be impertinent to remind Howe, who is a close student of the subject, that in recent Russian history many struggled and were brutalized thereby. But the memoirs of Victor Serge suggest to me that even in the midst of revolution the artist has a special function to perform: to remind the revolution of its human ends.

It will be clear, I trust, that I am speaking out of no hostility to the Freedom Movement or to politics as such. I am arguing not for the abandonment of militancy but for the autonomy of art. There is no need for literature and politics to be at odds. It is only when the aesthete approaches politics as if it were a poem, or when the political activist approaches the poem as if it were a leaflet, that the trouble starts. Phrases like "only through struggle" urge the subordination of art to politics. We must stifle these imperialistic impulses and foster a climate of mutual respect. Emerson distinguishes between the Doer and the Sayer, and refuses to honor one at the expense of the other. "Homer's words," he observes, "are as costly to Homer as Agamemnon's victories are to Agamemnon."

And I would add that Homer's words are as valuable as Agamemnon's victories *to the Greeks*. For I am arguing throughout for the social value of art. When Howe touches on this aspect of the question, he tries invariably to pre-empt all social [105] value for his own position. Ellison, he charges, is pursuing the essentially antisocial goal of "personal realization," while Wright is fulfilling his responsibility to the Negro community. It is a false dichotomy. The

Negro writer, who is surely not free of social responsibility, must yet discharge it *in his own fashion,* which is not the way of politics but art; not the lecture platform but the novel and the poem. Without repudiating his sense of obligation to the group, Ellison has tried to express it through services which only the imagination can perform.

What is at issue is the role of the imagination in that complex process which we call civilization. The visionary power, the power of naming, the power of revealing a people to itself are not to be despised. If those who can command these powers are diverted from their proper task, who will celebrate the values of the group, who create those myths and legends, those communal rites which alone endow the life of any group with meaning? These gifts are no less precious to a people (and if you like, no more) than those of personal charisma, theoretical analysis and political organization which are the special province of the revolutionary. Let us therefore give the imaginative faculty its due, concede its social value and respect its unique contribution to the process of becoming man.

Culture

At least as important as Ellison's defense of the imagination is his contribution to a theory of American Negro culture. Previous work in the field, whether by Negro or white intellectuals, has stressed the autonomous character of Negro culture, viewing it as an alien or exotic tributary to the mainstream of American life. Ellison proposes a more integrated view. Negro folk culture, to his way of thinking, is an indestructible monument to the national past. Embodying as it does three centuries of American history, it is a bittersweet reminder of what we were and are as a people. Far from being isolated from the mainstream, [106] it marks the channel where the river runs deepest to the sea.

Given the complex interplay of culture and personality, race and social class that shapes the lives of American Negroes, some degree of theoretical clarity, some modicum of sophistication in these matters is essential. Not only racial strategies but one's own sanity and peace of mind are at stake. For every American Negro responds, at some level of his being, to two apparently disjunctive cultural traditions. If this can be shown to be an arbitrary division, false to the realities of American history, not only will the personal tensions ease but the Freedom Movement will be seen in new perspective. Integration will now appear as a mutual attempt, by American whites as well as Negroes, to restore a splintered culture to a state of wholeness.

The problem of dual identity is particularly acute for members of the Negro middle class. Suspended between two cultural traditions, each with its own claims and loyalties, the educated Negro has been caught on the horns of a dilemma. To identify closely with the life-style of the white middle class has generally led to a rejection of Negro folk culture. Conversely, to identify closely with the life-style of the Negro masses has implied a disaffection with the dominant values of American civilization. This conflicting pattern of identification and rejection has produced two broad currents of thought and feeling which I have elsewhere called assimilationism and Negro nationalism. Let me describe them briefly, for purposes of contrast with Ellison's point of view.

Assimilationism is a natural response to the experience of upward mobility. As the Negro middle class becomes differentiated from the masses by virtue of income, education and social status, it looks back upon its origins with embarrassment and shame. Negro folk culture, this rising middle class would argue, is the creation of an illiterate peasantry. It is vulgar and often shocking, permeated with the smell of poverty, reminiscent of our degradation and our pain. However well it may attest to what [107] we were, it contains nothing of enduring value for us or for our children. On the contrary, it is a major obstacle to integration. The white middle class will accept us only to the extent that we become like them. It is therefore necessary to expunge every trace of "Negroness" from our behavior.

To these arguments Ellison would counterpose the richness of his folk tradition. He insists upon the relevance of folk experience to the conditions of modern urban life and, more important still, to the condition of being man. The assimilationist demands that in the name of integration the Negro self be put to death. But Ellison regards this proposal as a projection of self-hatred. To integrate means to make whole, not to lop off or mutilate; to federate as equals, not to merge and disappear. Anything else is a denial not only of one's racial identity but of one's national identity as well. For slavery really happened on American soil, and it has made us both, Negro and white alike, what we are today.

Negro nationalism is a natural response to the experience of rejection. Rebuffed by the whites, the Negro nationalist rebuffs in turn. Rejecting the white man's civilization as thoroughly corrupt, visibly in decay and hopelessly compromised by its oppression of the blacks, he asks in anger and despair, "Why should we integrate into a burning house?" From this mood of separatism and alienation flows his attitude toward the folk culture. For here is a system of values to oppose to those of the white middle class. All that is distinctive in Negro life is thus exalted as a matter of racial pride. Traditionally, this point of view has been fortified by some sort of African mystique, the current version being the concept of *Négritude*.

Here Ellison would counter with the richness of the dominant tradition. European civilization, of which he is a part, cannot be written off so lightly. Emerson and Einstein, Mozart and Michelangelo, Jefferson and Joyce are part of his tradition, and he has paid for them in blood. He is not about to bargain them away in exchange for *Négritude*. The Negro nationalist demands that [108] for the sake of injured pride the Western self be put to death. But if the injury is real, the remedy is disastrous. What is separatism but the sulking of a rejected child? The American Negro, after all, is no stranger to the affairs of this nation. Nor can he stand aside from its appointed destiny. For if the house burns, one thing is certain: the American Negro will not escape the conflagration.

Assimilationism and Negro nationalism both involve a maiming of the self, an unnecessary loss. Why not combine the best of both traditions? Between these opposite and symmetrical errors, Ellison steers a steady course. On the one hand, he wants in: no one, white or colored, will persuade him that he is an outsider. Talk about the mainstream! He's been swimming in it since 1619. On the other hand, he is not about to trade in his tested techniques of survival on some white man's vague promise: "Be like us and we will accept you, maybe." When he comes in, he brings his chitlins with him. If, in the process, he transforms America into a nation of chitlin eaters, so much the better for our ethnic cooking.

While assimilationism and Negro nationalism make opposite evaluations of Negro folk culture, they both regard it as in some sense un-American. To all such formulations Ellison objects that they abstract distinctive Negro qualities from the concrete circumstances of American life. The American Negro *is* different from his white countrymen, but American history and that alone has made him so. Any serious attempt to understand these differences will, therefore, lead, by a thousand devious paths, across the tracks to white America. Always there is a connection, however hidden; always a link, however brutally severed. It follows that "any viable theory of Negro American culture obligates us to fashion a more adequate theory of American culture as a whole."

To this end, Ellison offers what might be called some Notes toward a Redefinition of American Culture. There is a gross distortion, he suggests, in America's self-image. It begins with the [109] white man's artificial attempt to isolate himself from Negro life. But Negro life is not sealed off hermetically from the historical process. On the contrary, it is the most authentic expression of that process as it has actually unfolded on the North American continent. Ellison argues, in effect, that the life-style of the Negro ghetto is *more* American than the so-called standard American culture of white suburbia because the latter, in the very impulse that gave it birth, denies a vital dimension of American experience. There is no possibility, he warns, of escaping from the past. What is required is that we bring our distorted image of ourselves into line with the historical reality.

Paradoxically, what is most distinctive in Negro life is often most American. Jazz, for example, is not simply Negro music, but the definitive rendering of American experience in sound. Similarly with folklore: "In spilling out his heart's blood in his contest with the machine, John Henry was asserting a national value as well as a Negro value." Where do we turn for the truth about American slavery: to Negro spirituals or the songs of Stephen Collins Foster? Why is the current slang of American teen-agers drawn from the speech of the Negro ghetto? Why the persistent vogue for Negro dance forms, unless we have been growing, from Charleston to Watusi, steadily less inhibited as a nation?

American culture is still in process of becoming. It is not a finished form, a house that one day will be rented out to Negroes. On the contrary, in the process of racial integration the culture will be radically transformed. This transformation will amount to a correction of perspective. By degrees, the white man's truncated version of

American reality will be enlarged. The American eye will be retrained to see sights hitherto ignored or, if seen, misconstrued for venal ends. Connections formerly obscure will now be plain; the essential oneness of American civilization will emerge. Ultimately Americans will develop a new image of themselves as a nation.

"I was taken very early," Ellison remarks, "with a passion to [110] link together all I loved within the Negro community and all those things I felt in the world which lay beyond." This passion is the driving force of his career. It can be felt in his response to jazz as well as his approach to fiction. It accounts, moreover, for his views on politics and art. For the linking together which he has in mind can barely begin in courthouse and in workshop, neighborhood and school. It must be consummated in some inner realm, where all men meet on common ground. Such are the links that Ellison would forge, the new reality he would create, the shattered psyche of the nation that he would make whole. [111]

RALPH ELLISON AND THE BIRTH OF THE ANTI-HERO
William J. Schafer

... on a farm in Vermont where I was reading *The Hero* by Lord Raglan and speculating on the nature of Negro leadership in the U.S., I wrote the first paragraph of *Invisible Man*, and was soon involved in the struggle of creating the novel.[1]

From the vantage point of the sixties, Ralph Ellison's *Invisible Man*[2] seems frighteningly prophetic. The convulsive street warfare of the last summers proves the tragic truth we have refused to face, and those episodes of the novel which may seem fantastic or morbidly hyperbolic are daily confirmed by front-page statistics. Ellison's novel, which may once have seemed limited to the special conditions of the Negro at midcentury (as a "Negro novel") is above all an *American* novel about us all, black and white together. It simply extends and develops Richard Wright's aphorism, "The Negro is America's metaphor." The riot episodes and the figure of Ras the Destroyer are no longer paper chimeras, impossible in the light of day. The cultural explosive which Ellison described in imaginative terms now shatters our cities.

The gnomic question which concludes *Invisible Man* reveals the scope of Ellison's vision: "Who knows but that, on the lower frequencies, I speak for you?" (503) This is spoken out of that tangible darkness the nameless narrator has intensified with 1,369 [81] light bulbs, and while it is as double-edged and ironic as the rest of his story, it clearly conveys Ellison's intent. Although his story is founded in observed reality and experienced truth and Ellison answers the street cry—"Tell it like it is, baby!"—he avoids Richard Wright's bare naturalism on the one hand and James Baldwin's hypertense

1. *Writers at Work* (The *Paris Review* Interviews, Second Series) (New York, 1965), p. 328.
2. All page references are to the paperback edition (New York, 1953).

SOURCE: William J. Schafer, "Ralph Ellison and the Birth of the Anti-Hero," *Critique: Studies in Modern Fiction*, X, No. 2 (1968), 81–93. Reprinted by permission of *Critique: Studies in Modern Fiction*.

polemic on the other. Ellison subsumes local and temporal questions of human insight and social justice to more profound inquiries into the human mind and the justice of the heart. The story is basically a quest for identity that describes America in the twentieth century—an epic journey through a labyrinth of freedom, conformity, denial and possibility. Ultimately Ellison's imagination transforms and illuminates the mingled tragedy and comedy, enslavement and freedom inherent in us all.

Technically *Invisible Man* is a *tour de force*, using a whole spectrum of fictional techniques to convey a complex authorial attitude and build a fictional world which transcends realistic description or simple probability. The action shifts from nitty-gritty realism to hallucinatory fantasy without a break in the seams of style. It is a virtuoso performance, moving from unsophisticated methods to highly complex and subtle modes of narration; Ellison especially reveals his craftsmanship in his language, which builds from colloquial idioms and maintains the rhythm and texture of speech throughout. It is an extended jazz performance—the voice used as an instrument (as in Louis Armstrong's finest work), with fluid improvisations on simple themes coalescing into a polished and organic unity.[3] But the shape of the story itself reveals Ellison's skill most clearly. The story of *Invisible Man* is fairly simple—the archetypal migration and metamorphosis of a southern rural Negro progressing to the new found land of Harlem. The tale is related by a man invisible in his impotent self-knowledge, looking back at his visible innocence—an emergent adult human looking back at the broken chrysalis.

But Ellison transforms the story into a parable, breaking with the predictable patterns of the social protest novel by blending fantasy and naturalism, moving without transition from one level of ideas to another and skillfully telescoping the episodes of the novel by concentrating closely on his protagonist's spiritual and psychological evolution. By using a relatively simple plot structure, Ellison is able to concentrate on the *quality* of the experience at hand. [82]

The plot structure of *Invisible Man* is schematic. The novel uses a cumulative plot (in M. C. Bradbrook's illuminating terminology[4]),

3. This idea is developed at length by Richard Kostelanetz, "*Invisible Man* as Symbolic History," *Chicago Review*, 19, No. 2 (1967), 5–26.
4. *Themes and Conventions of Elizabethan Tragedy* (Cambridge, 1960), pp. 41–42.

developing the same basic episode over and over in an emotional crescendo: the protagonist struggles idealistically to live by the commandments of his immediate social group, then is undone by the hypocrisy built into the social structure and is plunged into despair. This happens in four large movements: 1) the struggle into college, the failure with Norton and expulsion from the "paradise" of the college; 2) job-hunting in New York, Emerson's disillusioning lecture and the battle and explosion at Liberty Paints; 3) the "resurrection" or reconstruction of the protagonist, his plunge into radical activism and his purge by the Brotherhood; 4) the meeting with Rinehart, the beginning of the riots and the protagonist's confrontation and defeat of Ras, ending in the flight underground. Each episode is a development to a climax followed by a peripeteia. The novel's prologue and epilogue simply frame this series of climaxes and reversals and interpret the emotional collapse of the invisible man in the present tense. While this structure has been cited as a "technical flaw," it moves the reader from individual Negro experience to the convulsion of a whole society:

> The constant technical flaw in *Invisible Man* is that it so frequently comes to an end and Ellison is put at every point to a greater muscularity to make the next scene more intense, more thoroughly revealing of what has already been largely revealed. It is the concomitant of that flaw that *Invisible Man* is a death-driven novel. Its movement is to confirm again and again that the hero doesn't exist, and Ellison's difficulty . . . is to resurrect the hero for each subsequent adventure.[5]

This shattered effect of death, rebirth and redeath makes the novel work, illustrates completely the erasure of an individual, the process by which a man becomes invisible. The novel repeats the essential Negro experience in several ways: the overall four-part pattern might be read (albeit overly allegorically) as "emancipation," "industrialization," "organization" and "disintegration"; or the pattern may portray the violent urbanization of a rural Negro consciousness; but the linking of general Negro experience with an individual view-

5. Marcus Klein, "Ralph Ellison's *Invisible Man*," in *Images of the Negro in American Literature*, ed. Seymour L. Gross and John Edward Hardy (Chicago, 1966), p. 264.

point and voice is accomplished through the repetition of the invisible man's failure and his cumulative descent into despair. [83]

Every effect in the novel is aimed at showing the *inside* of the nameless invisible man; we are well below the skin level, and Ellison does not attempt to explain the Negro's experiences or to blame society for them but to show *how* he is affected, what the view is from inside the prison of blackness and invisibility. Therefore, Ellison eschews the cataloging devices of social protest fiction as well as the meticulous references to history and place—the time and place are the present landscape of the Negro mind, as it has become fused in American consciousness over 350 years. Ellison blurs the scenery to prevent the reader from absorbing the novel either in simple realistic or symbolic terms. The characters are nearly types, never probed deeply by the narrator, and the milieu is significant only insofar as it reflects and refracts the invisible man's mind.

For primarily *Invisible Man* is a study in the psychology of oppression. It is the story of an internal quest—a journey of the soul. The migration is from innocence to experience, not just from sunny south to ghetto and the underground. Ellison develops this story along mythic lines, incorporating elements of common cultural experience in the parable to generalize it further, and the protagonist's progress is finally a pilgrimage of the self. Ellison simply worked from observable American rituals:

> . . . the patterns were already there in society so that all I had to do was present them in a broader context of meaning. In any society there are many rituals of situation which, for the most part, go unquestioned. They can be simple or elaborate, but they are the connective tissue between the work of art and the audience.[6]

The story, then, describes the birth of a hero—in this case, an antihero—retold in only slightly shaded terms; the novel is, in fact, a fragment of an epic in form.

The anti-hero of *Invisible Man*, though we come to know him intimately, remains nameless. He is no-man and everyman on a mod-

---

6. *Writers at Work*, pp. 326–27.

ern epic quest, driven by the message his grandfather reveals in a dream: "To Whom It May Concern . . . Keep This Nigger-Boy Running." (35) His primary search is for a name—or for the self it symbolizes. During his search he is given another name by the Brotherhood, but it is no help. When he becomes a "brother," he finds that brotherhood does not clarify his inner mysteries. [84]

In creating his anti-hero, Ellison builds on epic and mythic conventions. The nameless voyager passes through a series of ordeals or trials to demonstrate his stature. First, he passes through the initiation-rites of our society—the battle royal (exposing the sadistic sexuality of the white southern world) and speechmaking that sends him to college are parts of this rite of passage, and he is tormented into the adult world. He passes this test by demonstrating his servility and naively interpreting his grandfather's dictum: "Live with your head in the lion's mouth. I want you to overcome 'em with yeses, undermine 'em with grins, agree 'em to death and destruction, let 'em swoller you till they vomit or bust wide open." (19-20) This is the first outlook of the invisible man—the paranoia fostered by "them," the white oppressors; the boy here is Buckeye the Rabbit, the swift clever animal living by its wits beneath the jaws of the killer.

When he arrives at college, he is confronted by the deceit and duplicity of Negroes who have capitulated to a white world; he is broken by the powerful coalition of Bledsoe the Negro president and Norton the white trustee. His second trial shows him that the struggle is not a simple one of black against white, that "they" are more complex than his first experiences showed. He finds that both black and white can be turned against him.

The second phase of his career commences in the trip to New York, an exile from "paradise"; in the city, he finds Bledsoe's seven magic passports to success in the white world, the letters of recommendation, are actually betrayals, variations of the dream-letter: "Keep This Nigger-Boy Running." Thus, his primary illusions are shattered, but there are many more layers to the cocoon in which he sleeps.

For he is first of all a dreamer, a somnambulist, and sleep and dreams figure significantly in his image of himself. As he reassesses himself, his metaphor for new discoveries is the same: ". . . it was as though I had been suddenly awakened from a deep sleep." (365) Yet each sleep and each awakening (little deaths and births) prove to be interlocked layers of his existence, a set of never-ending Chinese boxes. One climactic section of the novel details his second crucial awakening—the "descent into the underworld" which occurs in chapters 10 and 11. [85]

Like the hero of myth and ritual, Ellison's invisible man finally descends from life on the mortal plane into an underworld of death. This is the substance of the entire New York section of the novel. On arriving in the city, he recalls the plucked robin of the old song and imagines himself the victim of a fantasy-letter: "My dear Mr. Emerson . . . The Robin bearing this letter is a former student. Please hope him to death, and keep him running." (171) Then he takes the job at Liberty Paints, keeping white paint white by adding drops of pure black, under the ironic slogan, "If It's Optic White, It's The Right White" (190), which (like "If you're white, all right, if you're black, stay black") has been invented by a Negro, the ancient and malevolent Lucius Brockway. The anti-hero becomes a machine within the machines, and he finds that Brockway, an illiterate "janitor" is the heart of the whole industry. In the boiler room, in inferno, he is betrayed again by a Negro and "killed" through his treachery. But the death is the ritual death of the hero's career—a death which leads to resurrection and a new identity.

After the explosion, the anti-hero awakens in a hospital, where he is resurrected by white doctors using an electroshock machine. Chapter 11 opens with a monstrous image of the demons of this underworld: "I was sitting in a cold, white rigid chair and a man was looking at me out of a bright third eye that glowed from the center of his forehead." (202) The doctors revive him ("We're trying to get you started again. Now shut up!" [203]) to the accompaniment of fantastic effects—Beethoven motifs and a trumpet playing "The Holy City" and dreamlike dialogue from the surgeons:

"I think I prefer surgery. And in this case especially, with this, uh . . . background. I'm not so sure that I don't believe in the effectiveness of simple prayer." (203)

"The machine will produce the results of a prefrontal lobotomy without the negative effects of the knife." (203)

"Why not castration, doctor?" (204)

Then, as he is revived, the doctors construct an heroic identity for him, recapitulating his existence as a Negro, starting with the first folkmyth guises of the clever Negro—Buckeye the Rabbit and Brer Rabbit: ". . . they were one and the same: 'Buckeye' when you were very young and hid yourself behind wide innocent eyes; 'Brer' [86] when you were older." (211) The electrotherapy machine is an emblem of the mechanical society imprisoning the anti-hero: "I could no more escape than I could think of my identity. Perhaps, I thought, the two things are involved with each other. When I discover who I am, I'll be free." (212) This lesson of the resurrection is carried through the rest of the anti-hero's journey.

The apparatus which resurrects the invisible man is a mechanical womb, complete with umbilical cord attached to his stomach which is finally cut by the doctors; he is delivered of the machine, and the doctors pronounce his new name—yet he remains nameless. The doctors, who follow a "policy of enlightened humanitarianism" (215–16) declare that this New Adam will remain a social and economic victim of the machine: "You just aren't prepared for work under our industrial conditions. Later, perhaps, but not now." (215)

The anti-hero sallies forth after his revival in the underworld "overcome by a sense of alienation and hostility" when he revisits the scene of the middleclass Negro arrivals in New York (223). He is now painfully aware of the hostility of his world, and he reacts not passively ("in the lion's mouth") but aggressively. In a symbolic gesture, he dumps a spittoon on a stranger whom he mistakes for his first nemesis, Bledsoe. The act is that of a crazed messiah: "You really baptized ole Rev!" (225) Then he goes forth for a harrowing of hell.

He joins the Brotherhood, an infernal organization which meets at the Chthonian club. In the Brotherhood, he rises to authority, becomes a respected leader and demagogue and is finally again betrayed by the wielders of power, whites who manipulate Negro stooges for their own ends. But at the end of this episode, the penultimate phase of the hero's career, he meets two important emblematic figures: Ras the Destroyer and Rinehart the fox. Ras, the black nationalist leader, is his crazed counterpart, and he harasses the invisible man until the night of the riots, when he attempts to hang and spear the anti-hero as a scapegoat for the mob—a dying god to appease the violence Ras releases. A contrast is Rinehart, who like

Reynard is a master of deception and multiple identities: "Rine the runner and Rine the gambler and Rine the briber and Rine the lover and Rine the reverend." (430) He is a tempter, and the invisible man nearly succumbs to his temptation to freedom without [87] responsibility; he strolls through Harlem disguised as Rinehart, the visible-invisible man who passes undetected through many identities. Ras offers the assurance of one undivided black identity and Rinehart the assurance of many shifting amoral identities—the faces of stability and flux. But the anti-hero avoids both traps, turning Ras's spear on him and shucking the dark glasses and wide hat of Rinehart, then finally dropping literally out of sight underground at the climax of the riot. Ellison has said that he took Rinehart's name from the "suggestion of inner and outer," seeming and being, and that he is an emblem of chaos—"He has lived so long with chaos that he knows how to manipulate it."[7] So Rinehart and Ras both represent chaos, two versions of disorder.

Loss of identity, sleeping and blindness are the figures that express the invisible man's confusion and despair as his world disintegrates. Then, after the cultural malaise climaxes in the riot, the final phase of the anti-hero's progress begins, a descent into the tomb—the netherworld across the Styx where heroes rest: "It's a kind of death without hanging, I thought, a death alive. . . . I moved off over the black water, floating, sighing . . . sleeping invisibly." (490) So he remains immortal and waiting, like the heroes of myth who disappear and are believed to wait should the world require them —like King Arthur and Finn MacCool, sleeping giants blended into the landscape. The invisible man, now grown into Jack-the-Bear, turns to New York's sewer system, a black and labyrinthine underground—a fitting anti-hero's mausoleum.

In this black crypt he destroys his old selves one by one as he searches for light, erasing his past—burning his high school diploma, a doll which is a bitter totem of Tod Clifton's demise, the name given him by the Brotherhood, a poison-pen note, all the tokens of his identity. Then he dreams of castration and sees that the retreat has been his crucifixion—he has been cut off from the world of possibility: "Until some gang succeeds in putting the world in a strait jacket, its definition is possibility. Step outside the narrow

---

7. *Ibid.*, p. 333.

borders of what men call reality and you step into chaos—ask Rinehart, he's a master of it—or imagination." (498) Imagination in the end redeems the anti-hero and makes his flight from battle a victory, for it gives us his story. In his tomb he is not dead but hibernating, preparing for a spring of the heart, a return which may be either death or resurrection: [88]

> There's a stench in the air, which, from this distance underground, might be the smell either of death or of spring—I hope of spring. But don't let me trick you, there *is* a death in the smell of spring and in the smell of thee as in the smell of me. (502)

The Easter of the spirit may be the emergence of the new man—no longer an anti-hero, invisible, nameless and dispossessed, but a true hero—or it may be the death of our culture.

The resurrection motif ties the story in the frame of prologue and epilogue, in the voice from underground:

> . . . don't jump to the conclusion that because I call my home a "hole" it is damp and cold like a grave; there are cold holes and warm holes. Mine is a warm hole. And remember, a bear retires to his hole for the winter and lives until spring; then he comes strolling out like the Easter chick breaking from its shell. I say all this to assure you that it is incorrect to assume that, because I'm invisible and live in a hole, I am dead. I am neither dead nor in a state of suspended animation. Call me Jack-the-Bear, for I am in a state of hibernation. (9)

Buckeye the Rabbit has grown into the formidable Jack-the-Bear (recalling the Bear's Son of the sagas) as the anti-hero has passed his trials and journeyed on his downward path, reliving the recent history of the Negro. He lies in wait beneath the inferno, under the underworld, listening for the hero's call.

The power of *Invisible Man* comes, as I have said, not from realistic description nor from the probability of the story but from metaphoric or symbolic elements linking the episodes of the anti-hero's progress. A skein of metaphor is joined with the outline of the hero's life to unify Ellison's vision of the American dilemma.

The central metaphor is, of course, that of invisibility—light, darkness and transparency. The novel gives shape to the inside of invisibility—the obverse of white America's distorted mythos of Negro life. The whites "see only my surroundings, themselves, or figments of their imagination, everything and anything except me." (7) Blackness and nil are the Negro's position—*nothing nowhere*. And the novel's metaphor leads to the dilemma of identity, for the black man cannot resign himself to nothingness or embrace invisibility: "Why, if they follow this conformity business they'll end up by forcing me, an invisible man, to become white, which is not a [89] color but the lack of one." (499) Both black and white are negative; Ellison, like Melville, has used the black and white of Manichaeism ambiguously so that the "power of black" is a moral consideration, not a matter of genetics or pigmentation.

A second kind of key imagery is a series of emblems of southern Negro life invoked to describe the history of oppression since 1863. In chapter 13, the newly resurrected anti-hero faces his mythic past and the first demonstration of his new identity when he leads a demonstration against an eviction. He first finds that he cannot deny his southern heritage when he encounters a seller of Carolina yams; the food is "forbidden fruit," because it recalls his unsophisticated country ancestry, but he eats it anyway, rebelling against the pressure of conformity: " 'They're my birthmark,' I said, 'I yam what I am.' " (231) Then he sees the old couple being evicted and catalogues their possessions, which chronicle the poor Negro's life for a century:

> . . . "knocking bones," used to accompany music at country dances, used in black-face minstrels . . . a straightening comb, switches of false hair, a curling iron . . . High John the Conqueror, the lucky stone . . . rock candy and camphor . . . a small Ethiopian flag, a faded tintype of Abraham Lincoln . . . In my hand I held three lapsed life insurance policies with perforated seals stamped "Void"; a yellowing newspaper portrait of a huge black man with the caption: MARCUS GARVEY DEPORTED . . . I read: FREE PAPERS. *Be it known to all men that my negro, Primus Provo, has been freed by me on this sixth day of August, 1859.* (235–37)

These bits of folk myth and history permeate the novel; the invisible man, in his new aggressive role, does not renounce this culture but embraces it, dreaming at first of flaying Bledsoe with chitlins to humiliate him, but returning to Louis Armstrong's unanswerable question in the end: "What did I do/To be so black/And blue?" As shoddy and worn as the Negro's past is, it is all that he has, and the anti-hero embraces it in his search for identity.

Several totems the anti-hero carries on his journey link him with his past, also. He carries the shiny briefcase awarded him after the battle royal—a leather bribe given to buy the invisible man's allegiance to the *status quo*. When the school superintendent presents [90] it to him, he says, "Consider it a badge of office. Prize it. Keep developing as you are and some day it will be filled with important papers that will help shape the destiny of your people." (34) He carries it as a passport into the white world of busy-ness; it seems a sprig of moly, a talisman, but it turns out to be an albatross. In the end it is filled only with the invisible man's cancelled identity cards, which he burns. Thus does he find the "destiny of your people."

Along with the briefcase he has carried homelier reminders of his heritage—first, the fragment's of his landlady's bank:

> . . . the cast-iron figure of a very black, red-lipped and wide-mouthed Negro, whose white eyes stared up at me from the floor, his face an enormous grin, his single large black hand held palm up before his chest . . . the kind of bank which, if a coin is placed in the hand and a lever pressed upon the back, will raise its arm and flip the coin into the grinning mouth. (277)

In a fit of rage, of reflex iconoclasm, he smashes the clichéd image of bigotry. But he feels guilty and carries the fragments with him, unable to free himself of this shattered icon of the past. The earlier images of chitlins and hog maws as the emblems of shame are replaced by the bank and its consolidated image of the penny-bribed darky. With it in the briefcase is the paper dancing doll with all its hateful connotations of the Negro who sells himself as the white man's fool. The shameful past intrudes persistently into the invisible man's present.

The imagery and the outline of the hero's life serve to give a classic shape to *Invisible Man*. If we take Joseph Campbell's summary of the hero's career as a standard, we can see how Ellison moved from reading Lord Raglan and pondering Negro leadership to the form of the novel:

> The mythological hero, setting forth from his commonday hut or castle, is lured, carried away, or else voluntarily proceeds to the threshold of adventure. [exile to New York] There he encounters a shadowy presence that guards the passage. [Lucius Brockway] The hero may defeat or conciliate this power and go alive into the kingdom of the dark . . . or be slain by the opposition and descend in death . . . [the explosion and "death"] Beyond the threshold, then, the hero journeys through a world [91] of unfamiliar yet strangely intimate forces, some of which severely threaten him (tests), some of which give magic aid (helpers). When he arrives at the nadir of the mythological round, he undergoes a supreme ordeal and gains his reward. The triumph may be represented as the hero's sexual union with the goddess-mother of the world . . . [the invisible man's seduction by the white woman, who glowed "as though consciously acting a symbolic role of life and feminine fertility" (354)] The final work is that of the return . . . the hero re-emerges from the kingdom of dread . . . The boon that he brings restores the world . . .[8]

Invisible Man follows this loose form. The epic journey from southern oppression to northern invisibility is shaped by the elements of ritual hero; the anti-hero gains stature and universality by his connection with Negro folk-heroes and through his enactment of a ritual role. Only the last part of the myth is incomplete—Ellison does not decide whether the hero will emerge from underground and whether he will bring elixir or destruction. The last question of the novel is posed the reader: will it be death or spring?

Ellison, like Joseph Campbell, probes the unconscious and searches for symbolic representations for states of mind and spirit. He finds in the Negro consciousness the anxieties and problems which Campbell sees as modern man's condition; the invisible man, like all of us, faces the problem of self and other which is the shaping force behind myth:

---

8. *The Hero with a Thousand Faces* (New York, 1949), pp. 245–46.

Man is that alien presence with whom the forces of egoism must come to terms, through whom the ego is to be crucified and resurrected, and in whose image society is to be reformed. Man, understood however not as "I" but as "Thou": for the ideals and temporal institutions of no tribe, race, continent, social class, or century, can be the measure of the inexhaustible and multifariously wonderful divine existence that is the life in all of us.[9]

The problem of identity and existence that Ellison poses transcends the issues of social justice and equity; it is not a question of "the Negro problem" or "race issues." As this novel shows in its prophecy, we must all know who we are before we can be free—and there is no freedom for a white "I" until there is freedom for a black "Thou." [92]

9. *Ibid.*, p. 391.

THE REBIRTH OF THE ARTIST
Ellin Horowitz

> *Welcome O Life! I go to encounter for the millionth time the reality of experience and to forge in the smithy of my soul the uncreated conscience of my race.*
>
> JAMES JOYCE, *A Portrait of the Artist as a Young Man*

Invisible Man is another kind of portrait of the artist, the making of an exile. Ralph Ellison's book, like Joyce's, takes its hero through a series of initiatory episodes from which he emerges a new man, an individual with the godlike power to create. The pattern is generally that of a quest for identity, the birth of the individual out of the chaos of man's manifold potential. In both stories the narrator's art will arise from the conflicts of his hero's quest.

Ralph Ellison has specifically employed the pattern of man's mythic descent into the pit, or womb, and his emergence with the power to prophesy—the ancient initiation of the great going down into the darkness of symbolic death and the resulting resurrection. *Invisible Man* is cyclical in form and resembles the ritual cycle it re-enacts. The narrator begins his story in an underground hole. The underground, as in Dostoyevsky, is identified with the subsconscious, the world outside of time and reason. His hole however is warm and fantastically lit, neither dark, damp nor cold as a grave.

> And remember, a bear retires to his hole for the winter and lives until spring; then he comes strolling out like the Easter chick breaking from its shell. I say all this [330] to assure you that it is incorrect to assume that, because I'm invisible and live in a hole, I am dead. I am neither dead nor in a state of suspended animation. Call me Jack-the-Bear, for I am in a state of hibernation.

The artist tells us that his hero is an invisible man; he is unnamed and invisible because people refuse to see him. This book is a search for his identity, denied both by society and himself.

SOURCE: Ellin Horowitz, "The Rebirth of the Artist," *On Contemporary Literature*, ed. Richard Kostelanetz (New York: Avon Books, 1964), pp. 330–46. Copyright © 1964, 1969 by Richard Kostelanetz. Reprinted by permission of Avon Books, New York.

At the onset the hero is seen as a kind of seasonal god whose underground death will cause new life to rise from the earth. The pattern is a variation on the descent of the initiate: he must go down into the pit and face the mystery in order to be reborn. The narrator functions as a Jonah in the womb of the whale, and his prophecy, his book, will be born out of the pit.

The greatest obstacle in the Negro's search for identity arises out of the incompatibility of individual values with a community whose thinking is preindividual, for the Negro is aware that he is seen only in terms of his category. He exists as a specimen of an ostracized group and to wander from the behavior pattern laid down for that group is to disrupt the community's pattern of thinking. Because every American is, in some sense, an outsider, the Negro is a prototype experiencing the national problem of alienation and isolation. As the outsider and stranger, the insulted and injured, he externalizes the darkest part of all our souls. Ellison's conflict belongs to all of us. Even beyond the failure of man to recognize the identity of those about him is the failure of man to exert himself, to become himself, and to run the risk of humanity. Thus we contribute to our own invisibility.

In his article on Richard Wright in the *Antioch Review* (Summer, 1945), Ellison discusses the various strategies with which the Negro confronts his American destiny. He may choose invisibility, and accept the role created for him by the white world, resolving his resulting conflicts in the hope and catharsis of Negro religion. In repressing the hatred for Jim Crow and striving for a middle way of respectability, he consciously or unconsciously becomes the accomplice of the white man in oppressing his brothers. Thus invisibility, as it appears in Ellison's hero, becomes, [331] like Hamlet's madness, both plight and device. The alternative is to reject the stereotype and become the criminal, the revolutionary carrying on a constant psychological, often physical, battle against the white world. Ellison's own hero must make this choice between invisibility and Lucifer's "non serviam."

A profitable method of dealing with *Invisible Man* is to see the action as a series of initiations in which the hero passes through several stages and groups of identification. The changes of identity are accompanied by somewhat formal rituals resembling the primitive's rites of passage. The primitive recognizes that man changes his identity as he passes from one stage or group to another and accompanies this transition by rituals that are essentially symbolic representations of birth, purification and regeneration in nature.

Ellison's narrative is a series of such initiatory experiences set within a cyclical framework of the mystic initiation of the artist. The rites of passage take the hero through several stages in which he acts out his various and conflicting sub-personalities. When he has won his freedom he is reborn as the artist, the only actor in our society whose "end" is a search beneath the label for what is individual.

The narrator begins his story in the pit and in a flashback takes his hero through the experience that led up to his descent. Finally, in the epilogue, there is a union between the innocent hero and the artist who has achieved wisdom; the central duality lies in that juxtaposition between the two I's. The element of confession in the first-person narration of *Invisible Man* suggests its function as a cathartic. The artist tells us his story from the pit so that he may rise at the end.

The hero begins his career in a Southern town as a docile innocent who dreams of becoming educated and pleasing the white community. The narrative is the story of his expulsion from this Eden of illusion.

The first uneasy note in the hero's youthful paradise is the recurring voice of his grandfather, who on his deathbed told the boy that he had been a spy all his life. "I want you to overcome 'em with yesses, undermine 'em with grins, agree 'em to death and destruction, let 'em swaller you 'till they vomit or bust wide open." Though the [332] meekest of men he had spoken of his meekness as something dangerous. This is essentially the ancient Chinese strategy of absorbing the conqueror in order to keep one's own identity. When things go well for the hero he feels guilty, as though he were unconsciously obeying his grandfather's advice. For conduct defined as treachery he is praised by the most "lily-white" men of the town (i.e., "that's pretty white of you"). Throughout the hero is fearful of upsetting white domination, and the meaning of his grandfather's sphinx-like riddle becomes a key problem ("The old man's words were like a curse").

The smoker scene is the crucial initiatory experience of the hero's boyhood. His art will be born out of blood, chaos, and humiliation—the conditions under which he gives his first speech on The Virtue of Humility. At the height of a battle-royal he sees the prostitute who taunts him as a bird girl, and, as in Joyce, this is the moment the hero's art is born. He will suffer anything in order to give his speech. Ironically, the only prophecy born out of the dark bloody arena is a speech on humility, and the reward, a scholarship, is the key to the world of Negro yes-sayers and repressed respectability. It is the first item in the prize briefcase the hero will always carry. He is told: "Keep developing as you are and someday it will be filled with important papers that will help you shape the destiny of your people." The irony is pointed at the articles he will later carry in the briefcase, which is equated throughout with the hero's unconscious; he will continue collecting things in it, the things he wishes to put away, the symbols of his disillusionment. It becomes a record of his being and his "badge of office" like the Shaman's magic bag.

At the second stage the hero is seen at college aspiring to be an educator and identifying with the college president Bledsoe (long suffering bled-so). Bledsoe is one of various types of Negroes pictured here as tempters; others are a Booker T. Washington Negro, the Uncle Tom educator, the kind who "keeps his place," the semi-mythic Founder, and blind Barbee who says "see ahead." Bledsoe himself is the seemingly unctuous servant who is in truth deadly aggressive. Despite power, prestige, white friends, and Cadillacs he somehow arranges his pants so they will sag at the knees and his feet shuffle to suggest a past on [333] a chain gang. Like the hero's grandfather he says, I seem obsequious but really rule them all. For power he will say yes and aid white men in subjugating his people. The hero's grandfather, however, made no claim to rule. He simply allowed himself to be swallowed so that the white man would choke.

The fall from the college paradise occurs when the hero inadvertently shows a Northern trustee do-gooder the seamier side of Negro life outside the Utopian college grounds. The seamy side appears in the countryside's most notorious Negro, a kind of monster described by progressive Negroes with disgust as "field niggerism." The scene itself is a monstrous parody of Southern genre writing about Negroes, highlighted by an Erskine Caldwell account of the Negro's incestuous relations with his daughter. Not so strangely, minorities seem to be traditionally characterized as oversexed and immoral, and here the image of the Negro as an uncivilized instinctive animal and "big black rapist" is clearly the transference of the forbidden on to the scapegoat people. The trustee, Norton (perhaps a nasty pun on Charles Eliot Norton, as the other Northerner is called Emerson), listens with a voyeur's perverse fascination because he has had just these desires towards his own daughter, and he concludes by paying the old Negro for doing it for him.

For this crime, the acceptance of reality and an unconscious revolt against yesing the white man, the hero is expelled from grace and must leave the sanctuary of school. "Here with the quiet greenness I possessed the only identity I had ever known and I was losing it."

The great exodus following the expulsion is a transition from the South to Harlem. Travel itself suggests a symbolic change of identity but in these first days in the North he continues to pattern himself on the old college ideal. Despite the escape by geography he remains invisible in Harlem's black against black. Dreaming of a great future he remembers always to deodorize so "they" won't think "all of us smell bad," and to be on time, "not any c.p. (colored people) time." He rejects pork chops and grits for bacon and eggs, but hearing an ashman's song begins to "go back to things I had long ago shut out of my mind."

The letter of introduction which was to bring him success [334] proves to be the letter his grandfather showed him in a dream—the letter that says, in essence, "keep this nigger boy running." Kenneth Burke speaks of this advice as a Bellerophontic letter, the message the character carries that contains his fate. Now the innocent first sees himself as deceived and betrayed. This is exactly what will happen to him; they all keep this "nigger" running. Everyone, white and black, seems in a conspiracy to keep him on the inexorable journey towards a self.

The following factory scene is a wild vision of the position of the Negro in a black-white world. Seeing the building at a distance "was like watching some vast patriotic ceremony." Flags flutter around a great white sign bearing the company slogan: "Keep America pure with Liberty Paints"; the factory's chief patriotic contribution is their color "optic white," related to the dominant theme of sight and blindness, visibility and invisibility, white and black. The hero's job is to make white paint by putting a drop of seemingly magic solution into a can of black liquid, but he cannot seem to make it white enough and

THE REBIRTH OF THE ARTIST

when it is white he sees only grey (recalling the white campus and the dim Negro cabins nearby).

Again the Negro appears as the victim, the result of the conscious or unconscious torture of one man to another. The hero remains unseen to those about him who see only what they need or want to see. To the unions he is a company fink, while to Lucius Brockway he is an educated Negro who doesn't know his place and probably belongs to the union. Each uses him for his own ends. Lucius, the old Negro who tends the furnace, says he is the one who really makes the paint white; "I dips my finger in and sweets it." This black finger and the black liquid are needed to make the paint white. It is the Negro who keeps America pure by acting as the scapegoat for all sins (a deliberately grim joke for purity is identified with whiteness).

Lucius Brockway is the Negro who maintains his invisibility, going underground (he works in the basement), and worshipping the boss and white supremacy. He created the company slogan: "If it's optic white it's the right white," reminiscent of the folk song's refrain, "If you're white you're right, but if you're black, get back, get back, get back." [335]

The hero's first act of revolt is his unconscious inability to make white paint, for implicit in his failure is the overthrow of Lucius Brockway, one of the dominant authority images. The act of rebellion culminates in a furnace explosion with its images of the inferno, and a loss of consciousness which functions as the ritualistic death of the initiate.

The scene that follows in the factory hospital is clearly a strange vision of birth with suggestions of lobotomy and castration. The hero lies in a womb-like box as figures in white perform a macabre operation intending to turn him into a "vegetable." During the mock shock therapy he appears as a ludicrous dancing minstrel darky, the harmless silly fellow the white world would like to believe in to allay their fears. Recovering consciousness he feels his limbs amputated; he is like a child, without a past, helpless, and lost in a "vast whiteness." The "delivery" is complete with the literal cutting of an umbilical cord. The old personality is dead and the initiate has a new identity born out of the machine. Because he has lost his past he is considered cured but when questioned about Buckeye the Rabbit he remembers playing this part as a child and is brought back through reversion to the folk tradition of which he is an unacknowledged part: "I could no more escape than I could think of my own identity. Perhaps, I thought, the two things are involved with each other. When I discover who I am I'll be free."

Man is never a constant unified being. Always in a state of transition, he is not one but many multiple sub-identities. Thus duality is essential in the notion of rebirth. The hero, caught in the conflict between old and new, is described in terms of a disassociated personality: "I had the feeling that I had . . . used words and expressed attitudes not my own, that I was in the grip of some alien personality lodged deep within me." The schizophrenic behavior of the tribal shaman is thought to indicate possession by the gods and Ellison's hero displays some of the symptoms of the mad prophet. Later, before his first speech for the Brotherhood he describes his ambivalence:

This was a new phase, I realized, a new beginning, and I would have to take that part of myself that looked on with remote eyes and keep it always at the [336] distance of the campus . . . Perhaps that part of me that observed listlessly but saw all, was still the urging part, the dissenting voice—the traitor self that always threatened internal discord.

Throughout the narrative the hero stands between submission and rebellion like a tragic hero torn between two conflicting necessities. In order to achieve the new life of the ritual, the god, in Freud's terms the father, must be slain. The guilty answering voice demands submission, for parricide is the greatest of man's crimes. The hero's traitor voice is the voice of the rebellious son. A dream in the prologue re-creates the Freudian myth of the primal horde in racial terms. Here a Negro woman poisons her white master-husband to save him from a more brutal sacrifice by their white-hating sons. She tells the hero that she loved her husband but she loved freedom more. While she cries her sons laugh and the hero observes: "I too have become acquainted with ambivalence."

The alternate strategies offered the Negro, to submit or to rebel, reflect the traditional ambivalence of the son. The notion of the great white father and the simple Negro children who must be protected by the parental taboos of white supremacy would suggest that the entire racial division can be seen in terms of the relationship between

THE REBIRTH OF THE ARTIST 245

father and son. The white man's advice to the Negro to "keep his place" is the father's advice and the threat in both cases is sexual. In *Invisible Man* the authoritarian figures consistently play the role of subjugating the hero, punishing him for the crime of asserting his identity, seen as the son's rebellion. The displaced guilt running throughout the narrative can be traced to the desire to overthrow the father and is certainly linked with the dominant castration imagery. Throughout, the hero identifies with authority figures, torn between submission and rebellion, feeling like a criminal but not knowing why he is guilty.

Each of the hero's crimes is essentially the Oedipal crime. At the smoker the town's leading white men watch as a naked prostitute taunts the Negro boys who are alternately threatened if they look and threatened if they don't. The hero submits to the humiliation of watching the woman he cannot have but unconsciously says "equality" instead of "responsibility" in his speech. Bledsoe expels the hero from college because his unconscious defiance threatens Bledsoe's position. He must leave school, the alma mater, and the protection of the father Bledsoe, his only source of identity. He is willing to do anything to stay, obey Bledsoe and worship the godlike Founder, but another expulsion from Eden occurs because the son would not keep his place. The price of freedom is wrath and banishment.

The hero's inability to make white paint and his physical attack on Lucius Brockway are his crimes at the factory. Here again he is feared as a threat to an older man's position and must be punished by castration in the rebirth fantasy. Brockway too had advised the boy to "keep his place." Again in the Brotherhood his crime is the assertion of his individuality, ostensibly called opportunism, that would threaten the communal group. In reality he is expelled by Brother Jack because he has gained too much power and is a rival for his position. When the hero sleeps with a Party leader's wife she is described as a surrogate for Brother Jack's mistress. Here he plays the expected role of "big black rapist" to a masochistic white woman. In effect he is acting out the ultimate crime in terms of both family and racial taboos. The result is the riot and the final destruction.

Such rebellion is punishable by castration. The authoritarian figures in white in the factory hospital are the castrators while in the concluding dream sequence we actually see Bledsoe, Norton, and

Emerson castrating the hero because he will not return to their domination. In both cases castration is equated with the dispelling of illusions. When Bledsoe first smashed his dreams and called him "nigger," it was as shattering as if "I learned the man whom I called father was actually of no relation to me."

It should be made clear that the father-god figures in the narrative are not always white men although white seems to function generally as the image rebelled against. Actually almost every major character in the novel is a variation on this theme. The college Founder, described as part Horatio Alger, part Christ, is called a "cold father symbol" and the narrator derives great pleasure from seeing pigeons soil his statue. Norton is "a god, a force," a "messiah" and a "great white father." Later Brother Jack is called a "great white father" who, for all his seeming liberalism, should really be called "Marse Jack" as he is the field boss in a white supremacy state. He watches his underlings "like a bemused father listening to the performance of his adoring children," and is later compared, in a quite Freudian sense, with a bulldog the hero feared as a child. Finally, at the conclusion, Ras appears as an angry black god wreaking destruction.

After the factory explosion the hero begins a new life mothered by Mary. Not so curiously his family, like Christ's, is fatherless. Mary is a reminder of his past, stable and comforting, but she demands some notable achievement that will benefit the race. As Mary's son he must seek his appointed role. Now he can accept his true identity symbolized in the acceptance of Negro food. He eats yams boldly on the street: "They're my birthmark . . . I yam what I am." This realization, in turn, enables him to deliver the eviction speech (in echo of Antony's address to the Romans) that wins him a position in the Brotherhood.

Even as he is drawn into the Party he suspects that they only wished to use him for something. A drunken member wants him to sing because "all colored people sing" and they wonder if he shouldn't be a little blacker for their purposes. They see him as The Negro, and he, in turn, is unable to see them. He enters the Party only on the assurance that he can become as great as the Founder, and still deluded, strives towards his old identification even at the price of submission.

With the entrance into the Brotherhood comes another transformation. The change in group identification is symbolized by a new set of clothes, a new name, and a new family. (With the concept of maternity conferring rebirth all initiates become brothers.) Despite his new family and role the hero cannot rid himself of a broken bank, the grinning comic Negro image he carries in his briefcase. Brother Jack too speaks of the sacrifice of the old self for new life: "You have not completely shed that old agrarian self, but it's dead and you will throw it off and emerge with something new."

The first speech for the Brotherhood is delivered in an arena reminiscent of the earlier smoker scene. The hero feels curiously unsure of his identity, fearing he will forget [339] his new name, or be recognized. It is a feeling of schizoid disassociation; the hero is seen as the possessed prophet whose magic lies in his speeches and his power to convert. The entire narrative, in fact, is later described as his "raving."

He speaks on blindness and this theme becomes related to the notion of invisibility and the imagery of black and white. In the arena he is blinded by a spot light (white) and looking at the audience sees only a black pit. He says: "They've dispossessed us each of one eye since the day we were born. So now we can see only in straight 'white' lines." The preacher Barbee was blind and Brother Jack has only one eye. The hero tells his audience that under the Brotherhood's leadership the one-eyed men will join and the blind will lead the blind, but the hero himself cannot see and he is invisible to his audience. He speaks of becoming "more human . . . with your eyes upon me I have found my true family . . . I am a citizen of the country of your vision." But he exists only in the vision of the audience and coming off the platform, blinded by the light, "I stumbled as if in a game of blindman's buff." The next time, he decides, he will wear dark glasses. Later, when he affirms his invisibility, dark glasses become his disguise.

The hero does not begin to understand the meaning of his speech but he is reminded of a teacher who told him that we create our race by creating ourselves. He remembers Joyce's *Portrait of the Artist as a Young Man* and thinks, "Stephen's problem, like ours, was not actually one of creating the uncreated conscience of his race, but of creating the uncreated features of his face; our task is that of making ourselves individuals."

The hero's crime in the eyes of the Brotherhood is that of asserting his individuality over the unity of the organization; it is called his striving for personal power. The disillusionment culminates in the betrayal and sacrifice of Tod Clifton. Clifton had turned against the Brotherhood, reverting to the darky notion of the Negro by selling dancing minstrel dolls, mocking self-images like the hero's bank. The doll itself is a hoax; it dances because of a thread tied to its back that is invisible because it is black.

The hero on his own initiative sees this as the time to play up the murdered Clifton as a sacrificial victim [340] to the cause. With the committee's resentment of his tactics comes the realization that the Party does not care for his cause and will exploit the Negro for power. Even they do not see beyond their own ends. Brother Jack has a glass eye which he says he got in discipline to the Party; the price of discipline is blindness.

In the concluding chapters the hero stands between the opposing forces of the Brotherhood and Ras the Exhorter, the Negro nationalist leader; both sides see him as a traitor. To escape, his only recourse is the ultimate invisibility, and his initial move in this last transformation is the disguise of dark glasses in which he can neither see nor be seen. Speaking to a friend he had the feeling "that the old man before me was not Brother Macao at all, but someone else disguised to confuse me." The glasses here function as the blindness of Oedipus.

In the large hat and uniform of a zoot suiter, he no longer has any identity. "It was as though by dressing and walking a certain way, I had enlisted in a fraternity in which I was recognized at a glance—not by features, but by clothes, uniform, by gait."

The key to the novel then is not actually invisibility. In the new disguise "I'd be seen in a snowstorm but they'd think I was someone else." He can be seen but not in his own identity because he is constantly changing. The metaphysical center of the novel is Rinehart, for whom the hero is mistaken. Rinehart is a chameleon: confidence man, runner, gambler, briber, lover and Reverend. Could he himself be both rind and hart? The hero seizes upon this possibility of invisibility through multiple personality. He had never seen the notorious Rinehart who is not invisible but many things, the charlatan-Reverend who advertises, "Let there be light," and "Behold the seen unseen." Perhaps only this man of many possibilities is at home in a world without boundaries where no one is anyone. Freedom, he dis-

THE REBIRTH OF THE ARTIST 249

covers, is not only the recognition of necessity, it is the recognition of possibility. "I was and yet I was invisible, that was the fundamental contradiction. I was and yet I was unseen . . . I sensed another frightening world of possibilities. For now I could agree with Brother Jack without agreeing." Now he understands how to follow his grandfather's advice. This "choke 'em [341] with yesses" strategy is metaphorically the going underground.

The action concludes with a vast apocalyptic image of the end of the world and the destruction of an angry god. The riot grows out of the Party's sacrifice of Harlem and the death of Tod Clifton avenged by Ras in the costume of an Abyssinian chieftain. The hero, caught between the opposing forces, runs through streets flooded with water (anticipating a new creation) as he tries to return to the mother Mary. His glasses are broken and he still carries his briefcase.

The running ceases only when he is driven into the pit—a coal cellar, for a Negro in a coal cellar is invisible. This is the dark womb which will be the source of new life just as the black coal cellar is the source of heat and light. To light his way out of the pit he must literally and symbolically burn the contents of his briefcase—the threatening letter written by Brother Jack, his Brotherhood name and identity, the scholarship, the letter that kept him running, Mary's bank and the dancing doll, Brother Tarp's chain-gang link which he received instead of his grandfather's watch as a son's legacy, the Party pamphlets, and Rinehart's promise to "Behold the seen unseen."

In his dream, Norton, Bledsoe, and Emerson return to demand his submission and castrate him for this final rebellion. The castration acts as the ultimate dispelling of illusions whereby the hero gains the right to see. Like the Fisher King his impotence seems a prerequisite for his life-giving role. Here, as in ancient ritual, the powers of reproduction are sacrificed and scattered on the water for ever-renewing life.

The hero can no longer return to Mary (because he is castrated), or to his old life (because he has no illusions). In the meantime he will remain underground. "The end was in the beginning."

"I am an invisible man and it placed me in a pit." In an epilogue the narrator reviews his experience.

Now I know men are different and that all life is divided and that only in division is there true health. Hence again I have stayed in my hole, because up above there's an increasing passion to make men conform to a pattern. Just as in my nightmare, Jack [342] and the boys are waiting with their knives, looking for the slightest excuse to . . . well, to "ball the Jack," and I do not refer to the old dance step . . .

Apparently castration is necessary for conformity because it is the punishment for rebellion. Diversity becomes the narrator's creed and he warns that there will be no tyrant states if man keeps his many "parts" (in the two-fold sense). "Why if they follow this conformity business they'll end up by forcing me, an invisible man, to become white, which is not a color but a lack of one." The hero himself loves light because he is invisible: "Light confirms my reality, gives birth to my form."

The hibernation is over. I must shake off the old skin and come up for breath. There's a stench in the air which, from this distance underground, might be the smell either of death or of spring—I hope of spring. But don't let me trick you, there *is* a death in the smell of spring and in the smell of thee as in the smell of me. And if nothing more, invisibility has taught my nose to classify the stenches of death.

A brief discussion of a few of Ellison's sources might clarify his novel. *Invisible Man* is the result of a union between the Negro folk culture (blues, jazz, folk tales, the Bible, etc.) and the modern Western art of such men as Joyce and Eliot. Like Eliot among many others, Ellison is concerned with the use of pagan ritual as an objective correlative for his experience, and he has been influenced by Joyce in the use of the initiatory experience as related to the sense of the artist as an exile. The hero, like Stephen Dedalus, is the rejected, isolated figure on the border of human activity who must pass through several stages and survive various tests before winning the freedom to create. He is the modern hero seen in Conrad, Hemingway and Lawrence; the alienated passive hero in a depersonalized world who must become an exile in order to search for the "reality of experience." Like the Faulkner and Hemingway hero he is something of a lonely figure on the shady side of the law; the man with a mystic wound who cannot hunt with the pack. The resemblance to Joyce includes the almost paranoiac sense of deception and betrayal [343] as well as such consciously borrowed symbols as the bird girl.

Images of birds and flight are extremely important in Ellison's work and are more fully developed in his short story published in 1944, "Flying Home." Flight is equated with Daedalus, the mythic figure of the artist whose craftsmanship is potentially the source of his freedom. The augury of the birds in *A Portrait of the Artist* is re-created at several points in *Invisible Man*, notably after the hero has given his successful eviction speech.

For the concept of the underground there is a wealth of background in folk literature and several possible modern sources in the guilty fear-ridden creatures of Kafka's "The Burrow" and Dostoyevsky's *Notes from the Underground*. A more direct source would probably be Richard Wright's story, "The Man Who Lived Underground." Here the hero is specifically an invisible Negro driven into a sewer, where he erects a fantastic world and emerges as the mad prophet of the ritual who speaks with wisdom, although no one will listen to him.

The spirit of the novel is that of the blues, which Ellison has elsewhere defined as the impulse to keep painful details alive, to rub the sore and to transcend it, not by philosophy but by "squeezing from it a near tragic, near comic lyricism." The narrative opens with the ceaseless question of the blues: "What did I do to be so black and blue?" The hero wants to listen to Louis Armstrong play it while he eats a dish of vanilla, his favorite ice cream. "I like Louis because he has made poetry out of being invisible." Ellison's book too is a search for the meaning and experience of being black and blue. It possesses the spirit of the blues in that it tells of the agony of life, and of the possibility of conquering it through sheer toughness of spirit, but like the blues it falls short of tragedy by offering no scapegoat other than the self. *Invisible Man* rubs the sore and probes the festering. It is a blues expression of pain and does not presume an answer. At the conclusion he is enabled to face his experience: "They were me, they defined me, and blind men no matter how powerful they became, even if they conquered the world, could take that, or change a single taunt, laugh, cry, scar, ache, rage, or pain of it."

The half-tragic, half-comic quality of the blues is reflected [344] in the tone of emotional ambivalence in the novel. Through his hero's varied roles the author has acted out the opposing strategies offered the Negro, of being "for" society or "against" it. The new vision born out of the hero's conflict seems to be an attitude of comic ambivalence that allows him to embrace the complexity. Within the paradox of acceptance-rejection the world becomes one of infinite possibility. Thus the hero is neither white nor black but invisible in a world which is neither good nor evil but good-and-evil. "So it is that now I denounce and defend, or feel prepared to defend. I condemn and affirm, say no and say yes, say yes and say no." Ellison's hero is not reborn in traditional triumph. He will emerge with a realistic acceptance of the limitations of society (". . . for all life seen from the hole of invisibility is absurd"), and his own role (". . . and humanity is won by continuing to play in face of certain defeat").

The curious note in this almost neat equation is the stronger emphasis given the sense of limitation and doubt. The narrator's view often appears to have less of the positive quality of union than the tentative quality of hedging. Ellison seems strangely divided about his theme and the sense of hesitancy and confusion in the epilogue would seem to deny the affirmation to be gained by a descent into darkness. The hero has not come very far beyond his initial understanding of invisibility, a fine but limited notion. He has become a prophet but does not have much to prophesy. While the author need not offer us glory and salvation, the structure of the narrative does suggest a rebirth in proportion to the intensity and conviction of the fearsome descent. Ellison's hero, it seems, will emerge simply because he has no real choice and the epilogue, his prophecy, is certainly the least effective piece of writing in the novel. We feel that the author searches for something positive but seems undercut by doubt; significantly, almost all of the writing in the epilogue is qualified or framed as questions. The conclusion is haunted by a curious sense of fear that would deny affirmation and one cannot help but associate this with the castration fear which undercuts all the hero's attempts at rebellion.

Ellison has made poetry out of being invisible by putting it down in black and white, and the hero's failure to find affirmation in his darkness is recompensed by the [345] savage and enlightened vision of that darkness. Ralph Ellison has written an extremely important novel, one that goes far beyond social protest though it is a protest and could scarcely help but be. Ellison neither rises above nor renounces his identity as a Negro, but uses it as the key to an understanding of the meaning and experience of alienation and isolation.

His conflict belongs to all of us. It is externalized in the very real division of our society into white and black; white does not see black and this is all our fates. Having descended into such darkness Ellison has gained the right, the insight and the responsibility to prophesy. The narrator concludes: "Who knows but that, on the lower frequencies, I speak for you?" [346]

RALPH ELLISON AND THE AMERICAN COMIC TRADITION
Earl H. Rovit

The most obvious comment one can make about Ralph Ellison's *Invisible Man* is that it is a profoundly comic work. But the obvious is not necessarily either simple or self-explanatory, and it seems to me that the comic implications of Ellison's novel are elusive and provocative enough to warrant careful examination both in relation to the total effect of the novel itself and the American cultural pattern from which it derives. It is generally recognized that Ellison's novel is a highly conscious attempt to embody a particular kind of experience —the experience of the "outsider" (in this case, a Negro) who manages to come to some sort of temporary acceptance, and thus, definition, of his status in the universe; it is not so generally recognized that *Invisible Man* is an integral link in a cumulative chain of great American creations, bearing an unmistakable brand of kinship to such seemingly incongruous works as *The Divinity School Address, Song of Myself, Moby Dick*, and *The Education of Henry Adams*. But the latter proposition is, I think, at least as valid as the former, and unless it is given proper recognition, a good deal of the value of the novel will be ignored.

First it should be noted that Ellison's commitment to what Henry James has termed "the American joke" has been thoroughly deliberate and undisguised. Ellison once described penetratingly the ambiguous *locus* of conflicting forces within which the American artist has had always to work: "For the ex-colonials, the declaration of an American identity meant the assumption of a mask, and it imposed not only the discipline of national self-consciousness, it gave Americans an ironic awareness of the joke that always lies between appearance and reality, between the discontinuity of social tradition and that sense of the past which clings to the mind. And perhaps even an awareness of the joke that society is man's creation, not God's." This kind of ironic awareness may contain bitterness and may even become susceptible to the heavy shadow of despair, but the art which it produces

SOURCE: Earl H. Rovit, "Ralph Ellison and the American Comic Tradition," *Wisconsin Studies in Contemporary Literature*, I, 34–42. (© 1960 by the Regents of the University of Wisconsin.) Reprinted by permission of the publisher.

has been ultimately comic. It will inevitably probe the masks of [34] identity and value searching relentlessly for some deeper buried reality, but it will do this while accepting the fundamental necessity for masks and the impossibility of ever discovering an essential face beneath a mask. That is to say, this comic stance will accept with the same triumphant gesture both the basic absurdity of all attempts to impose meaning on the chaos of life, and the necessary converse of this, the ultimate significance of absurdity itself.

Ellison's *Invisible Man* is comic in this sense almost in spite of its overtly satirical interests and its excursions into the broadly farcical. Humorous as many of its episodes are in themselves—the surreal hysteria of the scene at the Golden Day, the hero's employment at the Liberty Paint Company, or the expert dissection of political entanglements in Harlem—these are the materials which clothe Ellison's joke and which, in turn, suggest the shape by which the joke can be comprehended. The pith of Ellison's comedy reverberates on a level much deeper than these incidents, and as in all true humor, the joke affirms and denies simultaneously—accepts and rejects with the same uncompromising passion, leaving not a self-cancelling neutralization of momentum, but a sphere of moral conquest, a humanized cone of light at the very heart of the heart of darkness. *Invisible Man*, as Ellison has needlessly insisted in rebuttal to those critics who would treat the novel as fictionalized sociology or as a dramatization of archetypal images, is an artist's attempt to create a *form*. And fortunately Ellison has been quite explicit in describing what he means by *form;* in specific reference to the improvisation of the jazz-musician he suggests that form represents "a definition of his identity: as an individual, as member of the collectivity, and as a link in the chain of tradition." But note that each of these definitions of identity must be individually exclusive and mutually contradictory on any logical terms. Because of its very pursuit after the uniqueness of individuality, the successful definition of an individual must define out the possibilities of generalization into "collectivity" or "tradition." But herein for Ellison in his embrace of a notion of fluid amorphous identity lies the real morality and humor in mankind's art and men's lives—neither of which have much respect for the laws of formal logic.

At one time during the novel when Ellison's protagonist is enthusiastically convinced that his membership in the Brotherhood is the only effective means to individual and social salvation, he recalls these words from a college lecture on Stephen Dedalus: "Stephen's [35] problem, like ours, was not actually one of creating the uncreated conscience of his race, but of creating the *uncreated features of his face*. Our task is that of making ourselves individuals. The conscience of a race is the gift of its individuals who see, evaluate, record.... We create the race by creating ourselves and then to our great astonishment we will have created something far more important: We will have created a culture. Why waste time creating a conscience for something that doesn't exist? For, you see, blood and skin do not think!" This is one of the most significant passages in the novel, and one which must be appreciated within the context of the total form if the subtle pressure of that form is to be adequately weighed. And this can be done only if the Prologue and the Epilogue are viewed as functional elements in the novel which set the tempo for its moral action and modulate ironically upon its emergent meanings.

The Prologue introduces the narrator in his underground hibernation musing upon the events of his life, eating vanilla ice-cream and sloe gin, listening to Louis Armstrong's recording, "What Did I Do to Be So Black and Blue?" and trying to wrest out of the confusions of his experiences some pattern of meaning and/or resilient core of identity. The next twenty-five chapters are a first-person narrative flashback which covers some twenty years of the protagonist's life ending with the beginning, the hero's descent into the underground hole. The concluding Epilogue picks up the tonal patterns of the Prologue, implies that both meaning and identity have been discovered, and dramatically forces a direct identification between the narrator and the reader. Ostensibly this is another novel of the initiation of a boy into manhood—a *Bildungsroman* in the episodic picaresque tradition. The advice of the literature teacher has been realized; the hero has created the features of his face from the malleable stuff of his experience. He who accepts himself as "invisible" has ironically achieved a concrete tangibility, while those characters in the novel who seemed to be "visible" and substantial men (Norton, Brother Jack, and even Tod Clifton) are discovered to be really "invisible" since they are self-imprisoned captives of their own capacities to see and be seen in stereotyped images. However, to read the novel in this way and to go no further is to miss the cream of the jest and the total significance of the whole form which pivots on the ironic fulcrum of the blues theme introduced in the Prologue and given resolution in the Epilogue. As in all seriously comic works the reader [36] is left not with an answer, but with a challenging question—a question which soars beyond the novel on the unanswered notes of Armstrong's trumpet: "What did I do to be so black and blue?"

For the protagonist *is* finally and most comically *invisible* at the end of the novel; he has learned that to create the uncreated features of his face is at best a half-value, and at worst, potentially more self-destructive than not to strive after identity at all. For Ellison ours is a time when "you prepare a face to meet the faces that you meet"—a time when we have learned to shuffle and deal our personalities with a protean dexterity that, as is characterized through Rinehart, is a wholesale exploitation of and surrender to chaos. After the narrator's fall into the coalpit he discovers that his arrogantly naive construction of personality is nothing more than the accumulated fragments in his briefcase: the high-school diploma, Bledsoe's letter, Clifton's dancing doll, Mary's bank, Brother Tarp's iron. And most ironically, even these meager artifacts—the fragments he has shored against his ruin—represent not him, but the world's variegated projections of him. The narrator learns then that his educational romance is a farcical melodrama of the most garish variety; the successive births and rebirths of his life (his Caesarean delivery from college, his birth by electronics at the factory hospital, the christening by the Brotherhood) were not the organic gestations of personality that he idealized so much as they were the cold manipulations of artificial insemination. His final acceptance of his invisibility reminds us of the demand of the Zen Master: "Show me the face you had before you were born."

However, we must note also that this acceptance of invisibility, of amorphous non-identity, is far from a resignation to chaos. The protagonist has successfully rebelled against the imposition of social masks whether externally (like Clifton's) or internally (like Brother Tarp's) bestowed; his is not a surrender of personality so much as a descent to a deeper level of personality where the accent is heavier on possibilities than on limitations. The 1,369 glowing light bulbs in his cellar retreat attest to the increased power and enlightenment which are positive gains from his experience, as well as to the strategic advantages of his recourse to invisibility. The literature teacher unwittingly pointed out the flaw in his exhortation even as he declaimed it: "Blood and skin do not think!" For to think is to be as much concerned with analysis as it is with synthesis; the ironic mind tears radiant unities apart even as it forges them. Accordingly Ellison's [37] narrator assumes the ultimate mask of facelessness and emphasizes the fluid chaos which is the secret substance of form, the dynamic interplay of possibilities which creates limitations. The narrator is backed into the blank corner where he must realize that "the mind that has conceived a plan of living must never lose sight of the chaos against which that pattern was conceived." In accepting himself as the Invisible Man he assumes the historic role which Emerson unerringly assigned to the American poet; he becomes "the world's eye" —something through which one sees, even though it cannot itself be seen.

And here it may be fruitful to investigate briefly the peculiar relationship of Emerson's work to Ellison (whose middle name is propitiously Waldo). In the recently published excerpt from a novel in progress, "And Hickman Arrives," Ellison has his main character, Alonzo Zuber, Daddy Hickman, make some complimentary remarks about Emerson, "a preacher . . . who knew that every tub has to sit on its own bottom." Daddy Hickman, a Negro preacher ("Better known as GOD'S TROMBONE"), is vividly characterized as a wise and shrewd virtuoso of the evangelical circuit who might not unfairly be taken as a modern-day Emerson, preaching eloquently the gospel of humanity. These facts may be significant when we remember that Emerson's work is given short shrift as rhetorical nonsense in *Invisible Man* and his name is bestowed upon a character whose minor function in the novel is to be a self-righteous hypocrite. This shift in attitude may indicate that Ellison has come to realize that there are some major affinities binding him to his famous namesake, and, more important, it may enable us to understand more clearly the remarkable consistency of the American struggle to create art and the relatively harmonious visions which these unique struggles have attained.

Superficially there would seem to be little to link the two men beyond the somewhat labored pun of their names and Ellison's awareness of the pun. The one, an ex-Unitarian minister of respectable, if modest, Yankee background, whose orotund explorations in autobiography gave fullest form to the American dream—whose public pose attained an Olympian serenity and optimistic faith which have caused him to be associated with a wide range of sentimentalities from Mary Baker Eddy to Norman Vincent Peale; the other, an Oklahoma City Negro, born in 1914, ex-Leftist propagandist and editor, who would seem to have belied the Emersonian prophecy of individualism and [38] self-reliance by the very title of his novel, *Invisible Man*. The one, nurtured by the most classical education that America had to offer; the other, a rapt disciple of jazzmen like Charlie Christian and Jimmy Rushing who has attributed to their lyric improvisations his deepest understanding of aesthetic form. The one, white and given to the Delphic utterance; the other, black and adept in the cautery of bitter humor. But in their respective searches for identity, in their mutual concern with defining the possibilities and limitations which give form and shape to that which is human, the poet who called man "a golden impossibility" and the novelist who teaches his protagonist that life is a latent hive of infinite possibilities draw close together in their attempts to find an artistic resolution of the contrarieties of existence.

"Only he can give, who has," wrote Emerson; "he only can create, who is." Experience is the fluxional material from which these all-important values and identities are created, and Emerson's great essays are processive incantations whose ultimate function is to bring identity into being, even as they chant the fundamental fluidity of all forms spontaneously and eternally merging into other forms. When we remember that Emerson once wrote: "A believer in Unity, a seer of Unity, I yet behold two," it may be worth a speculation that the Emerson behind the triumphant artifices of the *Essays* was not a terribly different person from the Invisible Man in the coalpit whose submersion into the lower frequencies had given him an entree to the consciousnesses of all men. This awareness of the absurdity of meaning (and the potential meaningfulness of chaos) is at the heart of Emerson's delight in paradox, his seeming inconsistencies, his "dialogistic" techniques, his highly functional approach to language. "All symbols are fluxional," he declaimed; "all language is vehicular and transitive and is good for conveyance not for homestead." Thus Melville's attempted criticism of Emerson in *The Confidence Man* misses widely the mark; Emerson isn't there when the satire strikes home. Melville, who above all of Emerson's contemporaries should have known better, mistook the Olympian pasteboard mask for a reality and misread the eloquent quest for identity as a pretentious melodrama. For, as Constance Rourke recognized, Emerson is one of our most deft practitioners of the American joke, and the magnitude of his success may be measured by the continued effectiveness of his disguises after more than a hundred years.

But again we must return to the *form* of *Invisible Man* to appreciate [39] how deeply involved Ellison's work is with the most basic American vision of reality. Although it is probably true as some critics have pointed out that the dominating metaphor of the novel —the "underground man" theme—was suggested by Dostoevsky and Richard Wright, it is for our purposes more interesting to note a similar metaphor in Hart Crane's poem, "Black Tambourine":

> The interests of a black man in a cellar
> Mark tardy judgment on the world's closed door.
> Gnats toss in the shadow of a bottle,
> And a roach spans a crevice in the floor.
>
> * * * * *
>
> The black man, forlorn in the cellar,
> Wanders in some mid-kingdom, dark, that lies,
> Between his tambourine, stuck on the wall,
> And, in Africa, a carcass quick with flies.

Invisible Man achieves an expert evocation of that "mid-kingdom," that *demi-monde* of constant metamorphosis where good and evil, appearance and reality, pattern and chaos are continually shifting their shapes even as the eye strains to focus and the imagination to comprehend. The Kafkaesque surrealism of the novel's action, the thematic entwinement of black-white and dark-light, and the psychic distance from the plot-development which the use of the Prologue and the Epilogue achieves posit the moral center of the novel in that fluid area where experience is in the very process of being transformed into value. The narrator, the author, and the reader as well are caught in the "mid-kingdom" which seems to me to be the characteristic and unavoidable focus of American literature. For this mid-kingdom, this unutterable silence which is "zero at the bone," seems to me to be the one really inalienable birthright of being an American. Some Americans following Swedenborg named it "vastation"; others gave it no name and lamented the dearth of an American tradition within which the artist could work; at least one commissioned the sculptor, St. Gaudens, to incarnate it in a statue. One way of attempting to describe the sense of being within this mid-kingdom can be most dramatically seen in "The Castaway" chapter of *Moby-Dick* where Pip is left floundering in the boundless Pacific. And although the techniques of approaching the experience have been richly various, the experience itself, an incontrovertible sense of absolute metaphysical isolation, can be found at the core of the most vital American creations. [40]

"American history," writes James Baldwin in *Notes of a Native Son*, is "the history of the total, and willing, alienation of entire peoples from their forebears. What is overwhelmingly clear . . . is that this history has created an entirely unprecedented people, with a unique and individual past." The alienation, of course, is more than sociological and ideological; it seeps down into the very depths whence the sureties of identity and value are wrought; and it imprisons the American in this mid-kingdom where the boundaries—the distance from the tambourine on the wall to the carcass quick with flies—cannot be measured in either years or miles. The American seeking himself—as an individual, a member of the collectivity, a link in the chain of tradition—can never discover or create that identity in fixed restrictive terms. The past is dead and yet it lives: note Ellison's use of the narrator's grandfather, the yams, the techniques of the evangelical sermon. Individuals are frozen in mute isolation, and yet communication is possible between them: the Harlem riot, the way the narrator listens to music. Ellison's novel is the unique metaphor of his own thoroughly personal experience, and yet it makes a fitting link in the chain of the American tradition.

That Ellison and his narrator are Negroes both is and is not important. From the severe standpoint of art the racial fact is negligible, although there are doubtless areas of meaning and influence in *Invisible Man* which sociological examination might fruitfully develop. From the viewpoint of cultural history, however, the racial fact is enormously provocative. It is strikingly clear that contemporary American writing, particularly the writing of fiction, is dominated by two categories of writers: members of religious and racial minorities, and writers who possess powerful regional heritages. Both groups have an instinctive leasehold within the boundaries of the "mid-kingdom"; the Negro, the Catholic, the Jew, and the Southerner share the immediate experience of living on the razor's edge of time, at the very point where traditions come into desperate conflict with the human need to adapt to change. And, of equal importance, both groups—in varying degrees—are marked out on the contemporary scene as being "different"; both groups cannot avoid the terrible problem of identity, because it is ever thrust upon them whether they like it or not. These are the conditions which in the American past have nourished our spasmodic exfoliations of significant literary activity: the great "Renaissance" of the 1840's and '50's, the Twain-James-Adams "alliance" of [41] the late nineteenth century, the post-World War One literary florescence from which we have just begun to break away. But the Lost Generation was the last generation which could practise the necessary expatriation or "fugitivism" in which these factors—the disseverance from the past and the search for identity—could operate on non-minority or non-regional American writers. Thus Ralph Ellison—and contemporaries like Saul Bellow, Flannery O'Connor, and William Styron—are *inside* the heart of the American experience by the very virtue of their being in some way "outsiders." Like Emerson, himself a royal inhabitant of the mid-kingdom over a century ago, they are challenged to create form, or else succumb to the enveloping chaos within and without.

And the answers which they arrive at—again as with Emerson—are answers which cannot be taken out of the context of their individually achieved forms without being reduced to platitude or nonsense. Form, the creation of a radical, self-defining metaphor, is the one rational technique which human beings have developed to deal adequately with the basic irrationality of existence. The answer which *Invisible Man* gives to the unanswerable demands which life imposes on the human being has something to do with human limitation and a good deal to do with freedom; it has something to do with hatred, and a good deal more to do with love. It defines the human distance between the tambourine and the carcass and it accepts with wonder and dignity the immeasurable gift of life. The black man in the cellar transforms his isolation into elevation without denying the brute facts of existence and without losing his ironic grip on the transiency of the moment. The amorphous ambiguity of the mid-kingdom is for a timeless instant conquered and made fit for habitation. Perhaps tragedy teaches man to become divine, but before man can aspire to divinity, he must first accept completely the responsibilities and limitations of being human. The American experience, cutting away the bonds of tradition which assure man of his humanity, has not allowed a tragic art to develop. But there has developed a rich and vigorous comic tradition to which *Invisible Man* is a welcome embellishment, and it is this art which promises most as a healthy direction into the future. [42]

SIGHT IMAGERY IN *INVISIBLE MAN*
Alice Bloch

Ralph Ellison's *Invisible Man* (Random, 1952), written in the 1940's, seems a preview of today's racial conflict. A young Negro, raised in the South, tells of his attempts to become a leader of his people within a white man's world, and how he is thwarted by the ambitions of Negroes and whites alike. He is first humiliated by the leading whites of his town, then betrayed by the seemingly honorable president of his college, and finally, after moving to New York and becoming the leader of the Harlem branch of the Brotherhood, finds his work sacrificed in the interests of the dictates of the "committee." It is at this point that he *realizes* his invisibility, that he has no personality of his own but is, in fact, shaped by the needs of others. Invisibility, then, emerges as the focal point of the novel. The hero of the story could have been any man—black, white, yellow—but its impact is greater because of the contrast between black and white, a contrast which should enhance individual differences, but instead, emphasizes the rift between the groups. The worth of the novel, then, is not simply its early sensitivity to the crux of today's racial problems, but its perception of the heart of the difficulty: the failure of men to see each other as individuals. Thus most of the people he meets do not perceive the narrator of *Invisible Man* because the "inner eyes" of traditions, racial barriers, and personal desires prevent them from seeing him as an individual. Sight, then, and lack of it, as implied by the word *invisible*, become key images in Ellison's novel.

Lack of sight in a Negro indicates him as an "Uncle Tom," one who accepts and praises the impositions of the whites and insists that he is content with them. The narrator first encounters sightlessness on the campus of the small, Negro college he attends by describing the statue of a man in the act of holding a veil over the face of a kneeling slave. The man depicted, the founder of the college, known for his saintliness and beloved by whites and Negroes alike, is described as having "empty eyes," and the narrator points out that he does not

SOURCE: Alice Bloch, "Sight Imagery in *Invisible Man*," *English Journal*, LV, 1019–1021, 1024. Copyright © 1966 by the National Council of Teachers of English. Reprinted by permission of the publisher and Alice Bloch.

know whether the Founder is lifting the veil so the slave can see clearly or dropping it to impede his sight further.

Miss Susie Gresham, the college's old matron, is another Negro who does not [1019] see clearly. She listens to a speech given in the college chapel with her eyes closed so that she only hears the sounds of the words but does not see who makes them. She listens to a speech by the Reverend Barbee who eulogizes the empty-eyed Founder. The climax of his speech comes, however, not with his description of the Founder's resigned death, but afterwards, when Barbee falls and drops the dark glasses he is wearing, revealing that he is blind. The sightlessness of the "Uncle Tom" Negroes illustrates their inability to perceive the real needs of their people and the true motives of the white men.

In contrast to their empty, closed, and blind eyes are the clear, sharp eyes of Dr. Bledsoe, the president of the college, who can terrorize students and teachers at a glance. His clear sight foreshadows his statement to the narrator in which he reveals that despite his obsequious attitude towards white men, he understands their feelings about Negroes, and that he has consciously humored their beliefs to suit his own ends. It is after this revelation that the narrator goes north to find that Bledsoe has betrayed him.

There, as he matures, he slowly becomes aware of the subtleties of the racial conflict, both in the white's attitudes towards the Negro and in the Negro's reaction to these attitudes. In the first speech he makes for the Brotherhood, he describes his audience as blind in one eye to describe how the whites have treated them and how they have reacted to it: "They've dispossessed us each of one eye from the day we're born. So now we can only see in straight white lines." Half-sight, thus, is used to illustrate the awareness that problems exist, but there is no conception of what causes them or how to react to them.

Half-sight is not an exclusive quality of the Negro; the narrator encounters it in white men also. In them, too, it indicates the inability to perceive true solutions to problems. Brother Jack, the head of the Brotherhood, wears a glass eye in place of the one he lost working for the organization. What he cannot see is that instead of working with Negroes as a "brother," he instead follows the old line of bearing the "white man's burden." Thus, the false eye he wears symbolizes his basic deviation from the ideals of brotherhood. His sight is artificial, then, rather than nonexistent. If he simply saw the Negroes and their problems incorrectly instead of sacrificing them, as he did his eye, to his desire for power, he would undoubtedly be pictured as wearing a patch. The moment when the narrator discovers that Jack wears a false eye emphasizes its significance. The eye suddenly "pops out" of Jack's head at a committee meeting of the Brotherhood where the narrator learns that the people of Harlem are to be sacrificed to an undefined greater goal; where it becomes apparent that the words of brotherly love are only mouthings which hide the aim of stereotyping thought into the one proper pattern. Jack retrieves the eye and puts it in a glass of water where, magnified, it mocks the narrator, and he begs Jack to replace it—so everything will again appear normal; so the goals he so diligently worked towards will again seem honest and real.

Blindness to the truth characterizes white men as well as Negroes, and that blindness is easier for both to bear. The narrator, while attending college, is given the job of chauffeuring Mr. Norton, one of the school's rich, white benefactors. He asks the complacent Norton what he would like to do and is answered, "Let me see . . . ," and he is shown the reality of Southern Negro life: Jim Trueblood, respected by Negroes until in a "dream sin," he commits incest. Then his own people reject him, and he is patronized by the whites. There is the "Golden Day," a saloon [1020] where shell-shocked veterans come to visit the prostitutes, and where Norton hears some frightening thoughts. Reality is too much for him, and he collapses under the strain.

White man's eyes come to symbolize the awe the Negro has of his power. Before the narrator goes to the interview with Dr. Bledsoe, where he first personally feels the effect of the whites' power over him, he sees the full moon rising and describes it as, "a white man's bloodshot eye." The first job he gets when he moves north is with the Liberty Paint Company. Their prime paint is called Optic White. This eye-white paint can cover anything, even the blackness of a lump of coal, just as the power of the white men can override the Negro's greatest efforts. The factory's slogan is, "If it's Optic White, it's the Right White," which the narrator ironically paraphrases into, "If you're white, you're right." He accidentally causes an explosion in the factory and when he awakens in the hospital, the first thing he sees is a white man looking at him out of a "bright third eye," which he cannot rationally explain. Here, too, when the doctors speak of giving him an operation, probably a lobotomy, which may deprive him of his personality, one of the most vivid images in his mind is the bloodshot, bulging eyes of a doctor peering at him through thick glasses. White men's eyes become, in a sense, hypnotic, in that they represent the power of white over black.

When one puts on sunglasses, everything appears darker—closer to black. When the narrator puts on sunglasses to disguise himself, he finally sees his people as they are, the darkness of the glasses brings him closer to them, because, when he wears them, he resembles a man named Rinehart. Rinehart may be looked on as a "universal" Negro, for he is all that the stereotype evokes. He is the hipster, the ladies' man, the numbers runner, the Harlem big man, and, at the same time, a preacher, telling the Gospels to a boogie beat. He is all these characters and more, depending on who sees him. Thus, when the narrator is taken for Rinehart, he comes into contact with all phases of Negro life, the phases which before he had been too wrapped up in empty platitudes to see. His dark glasses have the opposite function of those worn by the Reverend Barbee. He wears them to hide his blindness, symbolically, to hide his inability to see the true status of his dominated people.

Only as there is less and less "white" light does the narrator come to see clearly the dilemma of the Negro as an invisible man in a white society. When, finally, he falls into the darkness of a coal cellar and can literally neither see nor be seen, he understands the fact of his invisibility. Yet when he does see it, he is powerless to act because no one else recognizes his dilemma. To describe his situation, he compares himself to Jim Trueblood's bluejay which was stung by yellow jackets until it was paralyzed everywhere but its eyes and could do nothing but watch the insects sting it to death.

Of course, the narrator does not die, but seeks light so he can see a solution to his problem. Symbolically, then, he illuminates the ceiling and walls of the cellar into which he has fallen; thus, as he adds more light, his understanding increases. He finally comes out of the hole, because he does not want to remain invisible but wishes to be seen by the whites as he wants them to see his people. He wants them to be aware of Negroes as human beings. He as a Negro seeks light for himself and his people so they may see the nature of the white man's domination.

Sight imagery in *Invisible Man* is basic because sightlessness in others is implied in the concept of invisibility. By presenting [1021] characters in the novel as physically unable to see, the author conveys the idea that what people are really unable to see is the harsh reality which lurks behind the platitudes they spout. The reactions of the characters who actually perceive reality emphasize the harshness of it. Mr. Norton falls in a faint; Dr. Bledsoe becomes harsh and cynical; the narrator has a fit of madness. Unlike the others, however, the narrator becomes accustomed to the darkness of the reality and tries to fill it with light. [1024]

WHITMAN AND ELLISON: OLDER SYMBOLS IN A MODERN MAINSTREAM
Marvin E. Mengeling

In recent years literary critics have been eager to examine the conscious technical and thematic adoptions made by modern American writers from the world of eighteenth- and nineteenth-century literature. Already introduced to the world of scholarship have been such seemingly unlikely combinations as Walt Whitman and Allen Ginsberg, Jonathan Edwards and Robert Lowell, William Wordsworth and Theodore Roethke, Edgar Allan Poe and Robert Penn Warren, Poe and Vladimir Nabokov, and Ralph Waldo Emerson and Ralph Ellison. Perhaps the reader will feel that the following note is concerned with an even more unlikely combination.

Personally, I am a strong admirer of Walt Whitman, man and poet. And recently it occurred to me that other admirers of Whitman's poetry might be interested in learning how some of his most successful symbols are still being used by modern authors to comment upon the mainstream of American life and its attendant problems. To partially satisfy such an inquiry we need look no further than the last-mentioned author on the list above, Ralph Ellison, whose electrifying classic *Invisible Man* won the National Award for 1953.

It is in Chapter Five of Ellison's novel that the reader first learns the story behind the founding of a state college for Negroes in a nameless southern state. But more importantly, it is the tale of the institution's Founder and first President, the illustrious leader (never specifically named) who through the processes of formal education would attempt to draw his people out from beneath the white foot of the majority. As expected, such a reverent eulogy is replete with Bible-thumping images of Moses and Christ in the best tent-meeting tradition. The symbols most skillfully and powerfully [67] used, however, are those strikingly unexpected ones, whose close affinity with Walt Whitman's 'When Lilacs Last in the Dooryard Bloom'd' is unquestionably obvious. All the Whitman symbols are there: the lilac, the star, and the thrush—the bells and the funeral train—but, and I do not

SOURCE: Marvin E. Mengeling, "Whitman and Ellison: Older Symbols in a Modern Mainstream," *Walt Whitman Review*, XII, 67–70. Reprinted by permission of Wayne State University Press and the author.

think that this point can be emphasized too heavily, Ellison employs them for almost entirely opposite reasons than did the bard of American poetry. I feel such a critic as Charles Feidelson, Jr. to be correct when he concludes that Whitman was attempting in his poem to measure the potential of the poetic mind within the framework of the death of the great emancipator, Abraham Lincoln. But Ellison is much less concerned with poetic potentials than with more pessimistic ideas, for the reader is quick to recognize that he uses these same symbols of the lilac, star, and thrush to measure the great irony and bitter disillusion of racial betrayal brought about after the death of another great fighter for emancipation, the beloved Founder—Ellison's picture of a black and mythical Lincoln.

The Reverend Homer A. Barbee of Chicago recounts at the college chapel the story of the martyred Founder and his struggle for the educational emancipation of his people: 'Having been preaching in a northern city, he had seen it [the college] last in the final days of the Founder, when Dr. Bledsoe was the "second in command." "Those were wonderful days," he droned. "Significant days. Days filled with great portent."' And then the story of a black Lincoln:

> I'm sure you've heard it time and time again; of this godly man's labors, his great humility and his undimming vision, the fruits of which you enjoy today; concrete, made flesh; his dreams, conceived in the starkness and darkness of slavery, fulfilled now even in the air you breathe, in the sweet harmonies of your blended voices, in the knowledge which each of you—daughters and granddaughters, sons and grandsons, of slaves—all of you partaking of it in bright and well-equipped classrooms.

And after more platitudes:

> You have heard it and it—this true story of rich implication, this living parable of proven glory and humble nobility—and it, as I say, *has made you free.*

So the Founder fought, as perhaps Lincoln did, for the emancipation of the Negro. He was their 'coal-black Daddy' who rose from humble origins, with great humility and an 'undimming vision.' But his enemies had plotted 'to take his life . . . then the almost fatal volley that creased his skull—oh my!—and left him stunned and apparently lifeless.' Unlike Lincoln, the Founder recovered, but only to be struck down a short time later by 'a sudden and mysterious sickness' which left him to die on the train which became his hearse. This is the story heard. But *how* does Ellison want us to hear it?

The reader is quite familiar with Whitman's poem which begins with the 'lilac blooming perennial' in its throbbing message of life [68] and hope. Just so does Ellison's young Negro hero trudge to chapel amid the 'feel of spring greenness,' while all about is the rising 'spring grass' and the air 'restless with scents of lilac. . . .' But any message of life and hope which this scene might have contained has already been muted for this rapidly learning student by the 'sound of vespers' which calls him. They are described as 'somber chapel bells.' They are 'doomlike bells' that lead the reader to thoughts of the sad and 'perpetual clang' of the 'tolling tolling bells' in Whitman's poem.

Also, in Whitman's poem the death of Lincoln is symbolized by the 'great early star dropped in the Western sky.' It was a 'tearful night' for the soul of the melancholy singer of songs when the 'sad orb, / concluded, dropt in the night, and was gone.' Again, this usage is obviously similar to the one Ellison erects in reflecting the death of the Founder, whose 'great north star' slid 'down the cheek of that coal-black sky like a reluctant and solitary tear.'

Finally, there is the thrush, for Whitman a genesis of life and death which is 'warbling a song' in 'secluded recesses.' 'Solitary—withdrawn to himself' this 'gray-brown bird . . . sings by himself a song.' For Whitman it becomes 'Death's outlet song of life,' and the 'voice of my spirit tallied the song of the bird.' But Ellison's thrush, a 'brown girl in white choir robe,' achieves no such genesis for the already despairing hero. Immediately before the story of the Founder is related, this brown-skinned girl 'begins to sing *a capella* . . . in [the] upper rows of the choir.' She seems to be 'singing to herself of emotions of utmost privacy,' almost as though she intuitively suspected the tenor of the eulogy which would soon issue from the lips of the good Reverend. And as Ellison's nameless hero 'sat with a lump in my throat,' her song 'throbbed with nostalgia, regret and repentance.' She sang with a 'controlled and sublimated anguish,' but the 'mood, sorrowful, vague and ethereal' was met with only an 'appreciation of profound silence.' Yet, unlike the others in the audience, the invisible man is silenced not so much out of aesthetic appreciation as he is out of growing numbness which accompanies his ever growing insight into the underlying irony of the entire convocation meeting.

The hope and genesis in Whitman's poem were largely drawn from faith in the potentiality of the unknowable future. But what would be potential and future to Whitman is in a different respect (on the racial question) little more than the dead past to Ellison's hero, speaking here for an author who has seen what he considers an original promise of freedom and equality turn into a grotesque and bitter joke. Yes, Ellison is saying, all promised fulfillments have proved 'vague and ethereal,' hardly worthy of applause.

Just as many Negroes feel they were betrayed by the men who followed Lincoln—men like Andrew Johnson—so does the invisible man feel that the Founder's dream has been betrayed by his [69] successor, Dr. Bledsoe (ironically, a man who 'bleeds' far less than any other)—an 'Uncle Tom' who has compromised with the whites in an attempt to keep the Negro socially and culturally subservient. Further irony is provided when the reader notices the inequity of the laurels Barbee heaps on Bledsoe as being a worthy successor to the Founder, for when he stumbles (appropriately, we feel) over the outstretched legs of Bledsoe and gropes for his opaque glasses on the stage we quickly recognize that Homer A. Barbee is much more blind than his ancient Greek namesake, also a singer of 'mythical songs.'

So it is because Ralph Ellison sees into the injustices of the past rather than into the potentialities of the unknowable future that he has his young hero hurry from the chapel 'past the disapproving eyes of teachers and matrons, out into the night,' there to hear the trilling note of a mockingbird 'from where it perched upon the hand of the moonlit Founder, flipping its moon-mad tail above the head of the eternally kneeling slave.' [70]

RALPH ELLISON'S MODERN VERSION OF BRER BEAR AND BRER RABBIT IN *INVISIBLE MAN*

Floyd R. Horowitz

Mr. Ellison's Invisible Man is an intelligent, young Negro attuned to what he considers the clarion philosophy of the white world—"keep this nigger boy running." At first we find him like a bear, by his own admission, hibernating, unknown to anyone in a Harlem tenement basement. There he reflects upon his past experience, which soon, like Dante's travail to the blinding light of knowledge, is to be recounted. We can meanwhile understand symbolically one of his preoccupations. Around him in this dark basement he has rigged electric fixtures. He has tapped a power line and currently is stealing the electricity that illuminates his hibernation. On the ceiling and walls there are now 1369 lighted bulbs. Such enlightenment metaphorically sets the tone of the book. It is from one frame of reference a psychological study, impressionistically told.

So begins the story. In the South, once, a Negro boy was awarded by the whites a scholarship to a Negro state college. He was to learn the tradition of Booker T. Washington—practical service to the Negro community, humble dignity (at least in public), intellectualized acceptance of white authority. And naively on that foundation he frames his goals, and affixes in the rafters the hopeful branch of religion. Diligently and in innocence he learns to conform. As a reward, in this third year, he is chosen to chauffeur a visiting white trustee of the college.

The day is a disaster. Taking a back road he allows the delicately sensitive trustee to see the Negro in all his squalor. Following a conversation with a farmer who is known to have committed incest, the trustee faints and is carried to the only available haven, a saloon and brothel just then at the height of its weekly business with the Negro ambulatory Vets of a mental institution. Within the day our hero is dismissed from the college of conformity, on the morrow traveling North to the expectation of greater freedom.

In short order, thus upon the verge of manhood, other disillusionments follow. The letters of recommendation which he carries

SOURCE: Floyd R. Horowitz, "Ralph Ellison's Modern Version of Brer Bear and Brer Rabbit in *Invisible Man*," *Mid-Continent American Studies Journal*, IV, 21–27. Used by permission of the publisher.

from the college president prove treacherous. In the North he is economically exploited. Because of his skill as a public speaker he is enlisted by the Communists and later duped. In the shadow of each rebuff he distinguishes his grandfather's enigmatic smile and hears his words: "overcome 'em with yesses." Accordingly, the race of his experience in the South and North exhausts his [21] consciousness of self. He finds that in running he is nowhere. Like a continually endangered Odysseus under the polyphemal white eye of society he is Noman. The whites are blind to him, he is invisible to himself, having failed in a succession of roles. While in itself this is a kind of knowledge by suffering, it is more than he can bear. His self-imposed basement exile is therefore an escape from responsibility, if also from the inequity of a hostile world. The winter of his discontent, he knows, must come to its hibernative end, and he must chance the new spring, yet for the time—and for the emphasis of the novel—his past disillusioning experience must be narrated.

Because the mode of that narration is impressionistic, Ellison takes the opportunity to convey the largest part of the novel's meaning via a quite imaginative, often bizarre range of imagery. In that way the logic of image associations sets out the basis of thematic implication. This may come as a new idea to the historian and litterateur alike, especially because the social and political significance of Mr. Ellison's book seems conclusively to derive from its open drama, colorful vignettes, and frank appraisals. Yet it may not be amiss to demonstrate that there is a good deal more social and political commentary being effected in the work via a highly planned if somewhat covert structure.

This means several things. Such a demonstration is necessarily involved with its own tools, the logic of interpolation as well as the more generally understood judgment of interpretation. Further, the story is not always told literally, but rather is rendered by symbols and images that have something like a life of their own. At an extreme (the Invisible Man's experience while in shock), the literal result takes the form of an impenetrable impressionistic morass, and the reader must agree to witness rather than to understand in the traditional sense. Other times a logical association can be drawn from similar instances: at the beginning of the novel the Invisible Man comes to a southern "smoker" where he will enter the prizefight ring, and while there he sees a nude dancer who has an American flag tattooed on her belly; at the end of the book he is described as a "black bruiser" who is "on the ropes" and "punch drunk" and he scrawls another distortion of another American message across the belly of another nude: "Sybil, you were raped/ by/ Santa Claus/ Surprise." Such devices as these form the texture (albeit an ironic one) of the American meanings which the hero experiences, and which no less importantly the reader is invited to experience with him.

As we do so we may trace the Invisible Man as a Christ-like figure, sacrificed and sacrificing. Many of the symbols by which he is described are distinctly Christian symbols, many of his actions are analogues of Biblical events. Or, psychologically considered, he is the dramatic vortex of Negro neuroticism: so extensive is the imagery here that we must read and interpret with the aid of an unabridged Freud. Historically and politically, too, he is beset by a cavalcade of American symbols and images which are [22] in the wrong places, a sometimes subtle, sometimes raucous debunking of the names and institutions which Americans are supposed to hold so dear: the American flag upon her belly undulates to the shimmy of a nude, the identity of Jefferson is an illusion in the mind of a shellshocked veteran, the Statue of Liberty is obscured in fog while liberty is the name appellate to a corporate enterprise, Emerson is a businessman, the Fourth of July is Jack the Communist's birthday as well as the occasion of a race riot.

Based fairly closely upon the folklore motif of Brer Rabbit and Brer Bear, the line of imagery discussed in this paper is as ironic as such other patterns of meaning, and perhaps even more so because of its Negro origin. Like the novel's fifty or perhaps seventy-five other motifs, it is not especially extensive, nor does it so closely effect an analogy that it admits of no other meaning for its individual parts. Quite the opposite. The bear and the rabbit are sometimes psychologically one in the same, as in Jack the Rabbit, Jack the Bear. But it would seem that the rabbit can be Peter as well. Or he is called Buckeye, which describes Jack the Communist later on. Or he is about to be peppered with BUCKshot. Or there is a pun on bear, so that the hero can not bear his existence. There is, in short, a rich language play which intertwines this motif with many others, which, perhaps too gratuitously on occasion, identifies rabbit with Brer Rabbit, which makes literary explication not the easiest of pursuits. Yet, for all that, the point of Ellison's use of this motif seems plain enough. Though they are sometimes friendly enough, less than kin and more than herbivorous quadrupeds, rabbit and bear are naturally irreconcilable. More, we know from Uncle Remus that soon they will match wits.

This makes for a good metaphor in which to cast the Invisible Man, since, interestingly enough, for Ellison, wit is not the same as intelligence. His protagonist is not a victor. Early in his education the Invisible Man discovers that. While he is chauffeuring Mr. Norton, the trustee of the college, they approach Jim Trueblood's backroad shack. The Invisible Man mentions that Trueblood has had relations with his own daughter. Norton demands that the car be stopped. He runs over to Trueblood, accosts him, wants his story. While the amazed and morally upright Invisible Man looks on, Trueblood complies in full detail. Ellison already has described him "as one who told the old stories with a sense of humor and a magic that made them come alive." And again, as one "who made high plaintively animal sounds." Now this story: sleeping three abed because of the extreme cold, his wife, daughter and himself, as if in a dream well beyond his control, just naturally, incest occurred. The story is a colloquial poetic. Before the act Trueblood has been nothing, but now he freely admits: "But what I don't understand is how I done the worst thing a man can do in his own family and 'stead of things gittin bad, they got better. The nigguhs up at the school don't like me, but the white folks treats me fine."

This irony is the key to Ellison's entire treatment of Brer Rabbit and Brer Bear's relationship. Here the issue is moral. Trueblood, in the middle [23] of the night which he describes "Black as the middle of a bucket of tar," has given his daughter a baby. For this he is rewarded. Norton gives him a hundred-dollar bill. "You bastard," says the Invisible Man under his breath, "You no-good bastard! You get a hundred-dollar bill!" Playing the bear, the Invisible Man is fooled, of course; thrown out of school in a hurry. In vain he objects to the college president: "But I was only driving him, sir. I only stopped there after he ordered me to. . . ." "Ordered you?" retorts the president, "He *ordered* you. Dammit, white folk are always giving orders, it's a habit with them. Why didn't you make an excuse? Couldn't you say they had sickness—smallpox—or picked another cabin? Why that Trueblood shack? My God, boy! You're black and living in the South —did you forget how to lie?"

This is the form of the anecdote. Brer Bear is outwitted by Brer

Rabbit in a first encounter. So the Invisible Man travels to the North. There on the streets of New York City he meets the second rabbit man, in this instance named Peter. Of course, exactly considered, Peter Rabbit is not the same as Brer Rabbit, yet he belongs to the same tradition. He knows how to escape the McGregors of the world. Here in Harlem he looks like a clown in baggy pants, wheeling a cart full of unused blueprints. Says Peter, "Man, this Harlem ain't nothing but a bear's den." The Invisible Man then completes the bridge of logic to the original analogy: "I tried to think of some saying about bears to reply, but remembered only Jack the Rabbit, Jack the Bear." Peter needs no social reenforcement, however. He proffers his key to success: "All it takes to get along in this here man's town is a little shit, grit, and mother-wit. And man, I was bawn with all three." So the friendly side of the rabbit's personality, advising the Invisible Man what to expect from the city, the North, the white world. But it is no use, for the bear must always be tricked—and soon he is.

He has heard of a job at Liberty Paints and hurried to apply. The scene depicts a patriotic devotion to the free enterprise system: flags flutter from the building tops. A screaming eagle is the company's trade mark. Liberty Paints covers America with what is advertised as the whitest white possible, a defective shipment just then being sent out for a Washington national monument. The bear is sent down, down, down, to help the irascible Negro, Lucius Brockway.

"Three levels underground I pushed upon a heavy metal door marked 'Danger' and descended into a noisy, dimly lit room. There was something familiar about the fumes that filled the air and I had just thought *pine*, when a high-pitched Negro voice rang out above the machine sounds." In an image which we may recall, the first rabbit, Trueblood, has already dreamed of such machinery. And his black as tar description is taken up now by the Invisible Man's thought of *pine*, and by Ellison's pun "high-pitched." So the hero encounters Lucius, the next Brer Rabbit, who is described as small, wiry, with cottony white hair, who defends himself by biting, and whose coveralls covered by goo bring the image of the Tar Baby to the Invisible Man's mind.[24]

Against Lucius's grit and mother-wit there is barely any defense. It turns out that Lucius alone has the secret of America's whitest white paint. He and no one else knows the location of every pipe, switch, cable and wire in the basement heart of the plant. Only he knows how to keep the paint from bleeding (whereas Trueblood does actually bleed for his moral smear), only he knows how to mix the base. He has helped Sparland, the big boss, word the slogan "If It's Optic White, It's the Right White." And he knows his worth: "caint a single doggone drop of paint move out of the factory lessen it comes through Lucius Brockway's hands." So in the matter of economics as before with morals, Brer Bear can not win. As Lucius's assistant he tends the steam valves, and when they pass the danger mark, burst, Brockway scrambles for the door and escapes while the Invisible Man attempts to shut them off and is caught in the steam. Again we may remind ourselves that the concepts of machinery and scalding have been united in Trueblood the rabbit's dream. Brer Bear can not win no matter how hard he tries.

In this case, moreover, his efforts are naive, short of the hypocrisy which alone means survival for the natively talented Negro. While he struggles for consciousness and self in the company hospital, that fact of Negro existence is brought out. A card is placed before him: "What is your name?" Under the bludgeoning of experience he has lost his identity, "I realized that I no longer knew my own name. I shut my eyes and shook my head with sorrow." The fantasy of his impression continues. Other cards are submitted, finally the question: "Boy, who was Brer Rabbit?" Soon after, he is released in a daze, finds his way to Harlem and collapses on the sidewalk.

Here Ellison has been portraying the New Negro intellectual. What has this Invisible Man learned?—that in the South, in the course of enlightenment he is pitted against his fellow Negro, farmer and college president alike; that Negro inured to the quasi-slavery practiced by the white. And in the North little better: survival in a slum, a bear in a bear den. Yet defeat is a realization, and a realization is a victory of perspective. In short, he is no simple Brer Bear. It is Ellison's intention to have him learn what the young intellectuals must learn—that as long as narrow self-interest motivates him he can have no peace. His must be the realm of the universal. That becomes the next phase, not with a rush of empathy, but as before, through trial, through defeat, through knowledge of self.

One day, when he has recovered from his ordeal in the paint factory, he comes upon the Harlem eviction of an aged Negro couple. Their meagre possessions on the sidewalk, the wife attempts to return into their apartment to pray. When the marshals in charge refuse permission the crowd riots. Suddenly in the melee the Invisible Man hears himself yelling, "Black men! Brothers! Black Brothers!" His further role as Brer Bear has begun. Under the aegis of his colloquial eloquence the crowd returns the furniture to the apartment. Then, in another moment, the police have arrived and he searches for a way of escape. A white girl standing in the doorway accosts him, [25] "Brother, that was quite a speech you made," directs him to the roof. He hurries across to another building, down the stairs, into the street a block away, across to a far corner. But as he waits for the light to change there comes the quiet, penetrating voice beside his ear, "That was a masterful bit of persuasion, brother." The biggest, most persistent rabbit of all has just tracked him, Brer Jack the Communist, alias Buckeye the one-eyed international hopper. Brer Bear is wanted for the organization. Will he listen over coffee?

Says the Invisible Man, "I watched him going across the floor with a bouncy rolling step." Again: "His movements were those of a lively small animal." And Jack's pitch is short: "Perhaps you would be interested in working for us. We need a good speaker for this district. Someone who can articulate the grievances of the people. They exist, and when the cry of protest is sounded, there are those who will hear it and act." Communism is the answer to his needs, for as many reasons as it is advertised to have. It offers him a cause, social equality and a job. It fulfills what must seem the generic destiny of a Brer.

What informs the Communist policy is the scientific attitude, however; not the man but the mass. To this positivistic philosophy the Invisible Man must immediately be trained, for in the course of change to the new brotherhood, he is told by Hambro, the Communist philosopher, certain sentimental ideas will have to be sacrificed. The very idea of race, that core and defense of Negro unity, must be sublimated. Nor is there place in the Brotherhood's teaching for emotion, for psalm singing, yam-eating, Tuskegee zeal. All is to be logical: the answers to the woman question, the rational youth groups, the organization of labor, even the public rallies. At least this is the theory, and if like Liberty Paints it is myopic and actually tinged with grey, if the women take him to bed to answer their political questions, if the youth are too easily frantic, if the public is still strong for the gospel and labor distrusts the Negro as scab; if these realities, the Invisible Man's idealism draws him into the bear trap, Brother Jack his foil.

His *is* a persuasive skill. Soon he is known, liked, trusted, powerful, confident that the Brotherhood is leading the Negro aright. Now he is willing to fight Ras the Exhorter, leader of the Negro-only movement. But as quickly, the trap springs: the internationally directed Brotherhood changes its Harlem policy. Indefinitely, there will be an interdiction of its plan to better the Negro's social condition. Unless the Invisible Man is willing to sacrifice the trust, the hopes of his fellow Negro, he must renounce identity once more.

In a scene which proves the Brotherhood's shortsightedness—Brer Jack, it turns out, actually has but one eye—there comes the break. But now, unallied, the Invisible Man must reckon with Ras the Destroyer, who in a Fourth of July flash electrifies Harlem as the nationalist leader of a super race riot. This is no time for intellectualism, nor this the place. Pursued, [26] to survive, our hero has no choice but to hide in an underground cavern. There we find him when the novel begins: "Call me Jack-the-Bear, for I am in a state of hibernation." That is the pattern, from rural copse to cosmopolitan forest.[27]

THE POLITICS OF ELLISON'S BOOKER: *INVISIBLE MAN* AS SYMBOLIC HISTORY
Richard Kostelanetz

> Invisible Man *is* par excellence *the literary extension of the blues. It was as if Ellison has taken an everyday twelve-bar blues tune (by a man from down South sitting in a manhole up North in New York singing and signifying about how he got there) and scored it for a full orchestra.*
> ALBERT L. MURRAY

I

In his collection of essays, *Shadow and Act* (1964), Ralph Ellison defines the purpose of novelistic writing as "converting experience into symbolic action," and this phrase incidentally captures the particular achievement of his novel, *Invisible Man*, in which he creates a nameless narrator whose adventures, always approximate and unspecific in time and place, represent in symbolic form the overall historical experience of the most politically active element of the American Negro people.

"It is through the process of making artistic forms," Ellison adds elsewhere, "that the writer helps give meaning to the experience of the group," a statement which, especially in its tactile imagery, echoes Stephen Dedalus's ambition, in James Joyce's *Portrait of the Artist as a Young Man*, "to forge in the smithy of my soul the uncreated conscience of my race." In the major sequences of *Invisible Man*, the narrator confronts a succession of possible individual choices which, as they imply changes in group behavior, have a symbolic political dimension for Negro people. When an alternative seems adequate enough to win the narrator's favor, his acceptance becomes, in effect, a pragmatic test of its viability. After he discovers the posited solution is inadequate to his needs, as all of them are, he samples another. Al-

SOURCE: Richard Kostelanetz, "The Politics of Ellison's Booker: *Invisible Man* as Symbolic History," *Chicago Review*, XIX, No. 2, 5–26. Copyright © 1967 Richard Kostelanetz. Reprinted by permission of *Chicago Review* and Richard Kostelanetz.

though Ellison does not have his narrator confront every known political possibility, the novel is still the most comprehensive one-volume fictional—symbolic—treatment of the history of the American Negro in the twentieth century.

In the opening quarter of the novel, the narrator eagerly tests opportunities for Negro existence within the Southern system, and just as [5] Voltaire's *Candide* innocently embraces philosophical optimism, so the young Negro assumes the notions prevalent in the early twentieth century of how the colored people can best succeed in the South —those of Booker T. Washington. From a vantage point later in time, the narrator remembers that as a young man about to graduate high school, "I visualized myself as a potential Booker T. Washington," who hoped to follow his idol's advice and perhaps emulate his career.[1] The most successful Negroes, he believed, were those who proved themselves essential to white society, either because they had an employable trade or because they helped to keep order within the Negro communities.

The whole future of the Negro rested largely upon the question of whether or not he should make himself, through his skill, intelligence and character, of such undeniable value to the community in which he lived that the community could not dispense with his presence. From this proposition stemmed Washington's major corollary: since the South offered the Negro greater social and economic opportunities, the Southern Negro would be wise to remain where he was born. "Whatever other sins the South may be called to bear," he wrote, "when it comes to business, pure and simple, it is in the South that the Negro is given a man's chance in the commercial world." At the base of Washington's politics, then, was a faith that Southern whites would give the respectable Negro a fair opportunity to succeed, and honor whatever success a Negro achieved for himself.

From these positions, Washington, as history and Ellison's nar-

---

1. What Washington actually believed and said, it should be pointed out, differs slightly from the ideas generally ascribed to him by both followers and enemies. In fact, he spoke out against the grandfather clause, protested lynching, and urged legal action against discrimination. However, since the narrator of Ellison's novel as a high school student subscribes to the prevailing popular image, the following summary deals with the myth, rather than the fact, of Washington. History remembers Washington as having primarily urged his fellow Negroes to lead an honest and industrious life within the framework of Southern segregation.

rator saw him, derived the three major lines of conduct implemented at Tuskegee Institute (which distinctly resembles the college in *Invisible Man*). First, Washington believed that to make himself as appealing as possible to white society, the Negro must be industrious in his work, respectful in his dealings with his white superiors, responsible for his family and to his community, and, perhaps most important, scrupulously clean. In *Up from Slavery*, his most influential book, Washington never ceased proclaiming the advantages of an immaculate appearance. For Tuskegee's students, instruction in hygiene was as important as book- and trade-learning: [6]

> It has been interesting to note the effect that the use of the toothbrush has had in bringing about a higher degree of civilization among the students. With few exceptions, I have noticed that, if we can get a student to the point where, when the first or second toothbrush disappears, he of his own motion buys another, I have not been disappointed in the future of that individual. Absolute cleanliness of the body has been insisted upon from the first. The students have been taught to bathe as regularly as to take their meals. . . . Most of the students came from plantation districts, and often we had to teach them how to sleep at night; that is, whether between the two sheets . . . or under both of them. The importance of the use of the nightgown received the same attention.

Thus, in the daily schedule at Tuskegee, Washington allocated one-half hour for cleaning one's room, and school officials made periodic inspection tours of the dormitories. A central aim of Tuskegee's education was to take a back-country Negro and, metaphorically, soak him with whitewash.

Secondly, if the Negro were to succeed, he must not challenge the system of white supremacy. In Washington's pet phrase, he must campaign for "responsibility," not "equality." A demand for equal rights, he feared, could only violently disrupt the stability of the South; and not only would revolt have little chance of success, but also the cost in Negro lives would be too exorbitant to make it worthwhile. "The wisest among my race understand that the agitation of questions of social equality is the extremist folly," he wrote, for the Negro must, following Washington's own example, "deport himself modestly in regard to political claims." Political rights, he argued, "will be accorded to the Negro by the Southern people themselves, and they will protect him in the exercise of those rights," only if the Negro treads the path of humility, impresses white society with his conscientiousness, and contributes to their material prosperity.

Thirdly, the Negro must measure his success in tokens of recognition from white society, rather than in terms of respect of his own people. This is the major lesson Washington drew from his own life, and in the latter half of his autobiography he catalogues the honors he received from white America. He especially enjoyed lecturing before groups of white Southerners, and he saved his most important speeches for the racially mixed audiences of large Southern expositions. Among his deepest desires was to have the President of the United States visit Tuskegee; and when the possibility arose, he twice journeyed to Washington, D.C., to persuade McKinley to come. Furthermore, few things pleased him more than encountering a group of white people who, like [7] some Georgia men mentioned in his book, "came up and introduced [themselves] to me and thanked me earnestly for the work that I was trying to do for the whole South." (Whether they addressed him by his Christian name or "Mr. Washington," he does not disclose.) What a Negro's peers thought of his own work was not as important as what the white folks judged; again, Washington felt that Negroes could best succeed in America by conforming to the prescriptions of entrenched white authority.

Ellison's narrator so thoroughly and innocently subscribes to the Washingtonian ethic that, when he is selected to give the valedictory address at his high school, he echoes both Washington's ideas and his rhetoric. Telling his Negro classmates to cultivate friendly relations with their white neighbors, the narrator quotes the key line of Washington's Atlanta Proclamation Address, "Cast down your bucket where you are," for, it is implied, if the colored Southerners look for water elsewhere, they may die of thirst. Likewise, the narrator uses the Washingtonian phrase "social responsibility" to define the role the Negro should play in the South. Upon his graduation the narrator believes that he can rise through the Southern system, perhaps becoming, like his idol, an educational leader or, more modestly, a doctor or lawyer in the Negro South.

The narrator, along with other class leaders, is invited to a gathering of the local white dignitaries; and at the occasion, they ask the narrator to repeat his valedictory address. When he arrives at the meeting, he is first directed to join his classmates in a free-for-all "battle royal" that is a feature of the evening's entertainment. Although he instinctively shies away from bodily contact with boys bigger than himself, the narrator consents to the ordeal to please the white audience. Along with the other Negro youths, he is blindfolded with white cloth; when the bells ring, he is pushed into the ring and throughout the fight, the white citizens on the sidelines encourage the Negro school boys to "knock" each other's "guts out." This incident, like most of the major scenes in the book, embodies a symbolic dimension that complements the literal action; that is, the scene stands for something larger in the experience of the Southern Negro. Here, Ellison shows how the white powers make the Negroes channel their aggressive impulses inward upon their own race instead of upon their true enemy, who remains on the sidelines, supervising the fray to make sure the violence is directed away from themselves.

To pay for the "entertainment," the hosts put numerous coins and bills upon a rug and encourage the Negroes to pick up "all you grab." [8] Once this new contest starts, they discover the rug is electrified. The shocks lead the boys to jump and shriek, in animal-like movements, to the amusement of the white audience. "Glistening with sweat like a circus seal and . . . landing flush upon the charged rug," one boy "literally dance[d] upon his back, his elbows beating a frenzied tattoo upon the floor, his muscles twitching like the flesh of a horse stung by many flies." In other words, before the Negro receives the pay he earned, he must overcome unnecessary hazards, often arbitrarily imposed, and publicly make a fool of himself. Between the Negro and the money he earns from white society are, symbolically, all the galvanic terrors of an electrified rug; and the price of the white man's pay is the Negro's debasement of his humanity.

After the other boys are paid their pittances and excused, the narrator delivers his speech. Again, he voices the platitudes of Booker T. Washington, feigning the air of sincerity and accents of emphasis. When he mentions the phrase "social responsibility," they ask him to repeat it again and again, until in a moment of mental exhaustion he substitutes the word "equality." Challenged by the audience, he quickly reverts to the traditional, unrevolutionary phrase. Ellison here illustrates that as the speaker's censor relaxes, his true desires are revealed; but as soon as he remembers the power of Southern authority, he immediately represses his wish. At the end of the meeting, the superintendent of the local schools presents the narrator with a briefcase; in it is a scholarship to the state college for Negroes. Again, the political meaning is that the Negro must publicly debase himself and suppress his true desires before he will receive the rewards of Southern society. Washington's guidance would seem to underestimate the price of Negro success in the South.

In the second sequence of the novel, the narrator discovers what kinds of Negroes receive rewards totally disproportionate to their work. As a student, the narrator is assigned to act as a chauffeur for a white trustee, Mr. Norton (whose name at once echoes "Northern" and Charles Eliot Norton, the first professor of art history at Harvard and heir to a certain kind of New England Brahmin liberalism). Responding to Norton's commands, the narrator drives the old man to the Negro slum down below the "whitewashed" college on the hill. At his passenger's request, he stops the car before the log cabin of Jim Trueblood, who, as his name suggests, represents the primitive, uneducated Negro unaffected by the values of white culture. Norton, discovering to his horror that Trueblood has impregnated his daughter, asks the Negro whether he feels "no inner turmoil, no need to cast out the offending eye?" Refusing Oedipus's response to a similar sin, the Negro uncomprehendingly [9] replies, "My eyes is all right," adding, "When I feels po'ly in my gut I takes a little soda and it goes away." Prompted by Norton's queries, Trueblood tells how the officials at the Negro college responded to his misdeed: "[They] offered to send us clean outta the country, pay our way and everything and give me a hundred dollars to git settled with." To the "whitewashed" Negroes, Trueblood represents that elemental humanity that college education must eliminate; and Trueblood's presence near the campus serves as a reminder of the primitive past the college community wants to repudiate.

To escape their strategy of alternate threats and enticements, Trueblood enlists the aid of his white boss who, in turn, refers him to the local sheriff. That official and his cronies so relish Trueblood's tale of sexual indiscretion that they ask him to repeat all the details, giving him food, drink and tobacco in return for their second-hand pleasure.

> They tell me not to worry, that they was going to send word up to the school that I was to stay right where I am. It just goes

to show yuh that no matter how biggity a nigguh gits, the white folks always cut him down.

In the days following, Trueblood becomes a celebrity, attracting the interest of white people he had never encountered before.

> The white folks took to coming out here to see us and talk with us. Some of 'em was big white folks, too, from the big school way 'cross the State. Asked me lots 'bout what I thought 'bout things, and 'bout my folks and kids, and wrote it all down in a book.

Presumably, these men were Southern scholars who intended to use Trueblood's confessions as evidence of the inherent immorality of the Negro. Moreover, Trueblood reports, the local white people now give him more work. "I'm better off than I ever been before," he says. "I done the worse thing a man can do in his family and 'stead of things gittin bad, they got better." In short, Trueblood's experience contradicts Washington's belief that white society would reward only those Negroes who live by its expressed morality. Instead, they eagerly appreciate a Negro who conforms to the traditional stereotype of the immoral savage in black skin.

After leaving Trueblood, the narrator follows Norton's command to take him to a roadside bar. Here they encounter a group of hospitalized Negro veterans, mostly psychiatric patients, going to the ironically named "Golden Day" for their weekly round of drinks and whores. Their shepherd is the hospital attendant Supercargo who, as his name suggests, functions as their collective super-ego. Not only does he impose the repressive forces of white society upon them, but he also represents [10] obedience internalized into their own consciences. Therefore, as soon as he disappears to fetch a drink upstairs, the men "had absolutely no inhibitions." A brawl ensues, directed largely against Supercargo and the social forces he represents. As the "veterans" air their complaints, the narrator discovers that they are the dispossessed Negro middle-class. One is an ex-surgeon who was dragged from his home by white men and beaten, it is implied, for saving the life of a white person. Another is a composer on the borderline of lunacy, "striking the [piano] keyboard with fists and elbows and filling in other effects in a bass voice that moaned like a bear in agony." A third "was a former chemist who was never seen without his shining Phi Beta Kappa key." The lesson of their experience is that Southern society destroys Negro talent and genuine accomplishment. Once again, Washington's advice on how the Negro should live in the South proves an inadequate guide.

Back on the campus, the narrator is summoned into the office of the college president to be reprimanded for taking Norton down to the slum, for letting him talk to Trueblood, for leading him to the Golden Day, and for allowing the benefactor to hear complaints of the dispossessed Negroes. He blames the narrator for innocently following Norton's commands and, even worse, for honestly answering his queries. The heart of the young man's error, Bledsoe says, is that "You forgot to lie." "But," the narrator replies, "I was only trying to please him. . . ." To this Bledsoe retorts in anger, "Why, the dumbest black bastard in the cotton patch knows that the only way to please a white man is to tell him a lie! What kind of education are you getting around here?" Bledsoe believes, echoing some cynical implications in Washington's thought, that the Negro college should preach the attainment not of dignity and self-achievement but of surface obsequiousness and underlying cynicism. Had not, the narrator remembers, Bledsoe himself been a model of such behavior? Had not he illustrated how the Negro should play the role of the second-class man?

Since Bledsoe's authority within the college is absolute, the narrator decides to accept punishment for the mistakes his innocence engendered—expulsion; and armed with several of Bledsoe's letters of recommendation, the young man heads for New York. He recognizes that his ethics cannot cope with the reality he finds:

> How had I come to this? I had kept unswervingly to the path placed before me, had tried to be exactly what I was expected to be, had done exactly what I was expected to do—yet, instead of winning the expected reward, here I was stumbling along. . . . For, despite my anguish and anger, [11] I knew of no other way of living, nor other forms of success available to such as me.

Rather than succumb to the new reality he discovers, the young man who scrupulously followed the suggestions of Booker T. Washington is forced to disobey his idol's advice and leave the South.

Perhaps the final commentary on Booker T. Washington's ideas is the address given in the college chapel by a Rev. Homer Barbee, a visitor from Chicago. Barbee presents all the optimistic platitudes, predicting the improvement of conditions in the South and greater opportunity for his people to fulfill their worldly ambitions. Instead of bitterness or notions of emigration, revolt and racial conflict, he offers the hope of success within the Southern system—a "bright horizon" through self-improvement. His ideas offer a certain appeal to the narrator and his classmates, until the young man realizes that Barbee wears dark glasses. He is blind, both in the physical sense and in his awareness of political realities. To the Negro in quest of self-fulfillment, the South in fact offers no hope, except to the blind, the immoral, and the cynical. This is the political meaning of the first section of the book.

II

Before he lets his narrator explore much of the North, Ellison introduces a scene which serves as a symbolic portrait of the underlying reality of Negro-white relations in America. Ostensibly, the chapter describes the operation of a paint factory; but the remark that the factory "looks like a small city" indicates symbolic dimensions. The narrator is assigned to mix ten drops of black paint into every can of "Optic White." When he protests that the black would discolor the pure white, his white foreman replies, "Never mind how it looks. You just do what you're told and don't try to think about it." Unaware of the physical principle that mixing small amounts of black paint into white paint actually makes white whiter, the narrator scrupulously follows directions. This process for enriching white paint symbolically parallels the interplay of racial colors in America. The black Negro makes the white world whiter; for since his values and aspirations emulate those of the white world, he reinforces the white American's escatology and, like the black in the can of paint, embellishes the whiteness of American public life. The company's motto is, ironically, "Keep America Pure with Liberty Paints," and, since the paint will be used on a national monument, the passage suggests that all of American history has a similar color composition. Although Negroes have contributed to the American [12] achievement, their effort, like the ten drops, enriches the existing texture. When the narrator inadvertently takes his refill from the wrong tank, the mixture he produces is "not as white and glassy as before; it had a grey tinge." If put on the national monument, it would reveal the heretical truth that American life, underneath the white surface, is, like the color grey, a mixture of black and white. For this mistake, the narrator is removed from his paint-mixing job. If he had likewise revealed the actuality beneath the white-washed surface of America, it is implied, he would have been exiled from the country.

In the second quarter of the novel, the narrator arrives in New York to test the opportunities open to the Negro in the North. He carries seven sealed letters of introduction from President Bledsoe to philanthropic white liberals who are patrons of the college. At six of the offices, the narrator asks to see the man to whom the letter is addressed. The letter is taken from him and delivered; and every time, the secretary returns and informs the narrator that the important man will contact him later. None fulfill his promise; for unbeknownst to the narrator, Bledsoe's letter tells the businessmen that this student has seriously violated some undisclosed rule of the school:

> This case represents one of the rare, delicate instances in which one for whom we held great expectations has gone grievously astray, and who in his fall threatens to upset certain delicate relationships between certain interested individuals and the school.

However, in his concluding sentence, Bledsoe, perhaps disingenuously, asks each recipient to help the young man. The lesson this episode portrays is that the Northern philanthropists will aid "Negroes" in the South, but they will not rescue an individual needy Southern Negro in the North. They suffer from hyperopia: Pain in the distance can be seen clearly, while that close at hand is blurred.

Since one of the businessmen is away from New York, the narrator postpones calling at his office. Finally getting an interview, the narrator meets the son of "Mr. Emerson," an heir to the American liberal tradition. He speaks in platitudes, often using a second platitude that doubles back on the first: "Ambition is a wonderful force," he tells the narrator, "but sometimes it can be blinding . . . . On the other hand, it can make you successful—like my father . . . . The only trouble with ambition is that it sometimes blinds one to realities." He is also extremely self-conscious. "Don't let me upset you," he tells the narrator, "I had a difficult session with my analyst last evening and the slightest thing is apt to set me off." When he makes a slip of the tongue, Emerson stops to ponder its significance. He boasts of the number of Negro [13] acquaintances he has—artists and intellectuals all—and of his regular attendance at an important Negro club. Being, as he says, "incapable of cynicism," he reveals to the narrator the deceitful contents of Bledsoe's letter. However, because he is afraid to disobey his father's wishes, young Emerson does not hire the narrator and warns him not to reveal their conversation to anyone. The Northern Emersonian liberal, the novel tells us, is too torn by neurosis, self-doubt and compromise to help the Negro in need.

Recognizing that those who support him in principle offer him few opportunities in practice, the narrator seeks a job as a laborer at Liberty Paints. He is hired, he later discovers, as a "scab," because the company wants to replace its unionized white workers with cheaper non-union Negro labor. The narrator is assigned to the foreman named Kimbro, described as a "slave driver." Assuming this traditional role, Kimbro instructs his Negro workers in their jobs. When a worker makes an error, as does the narrator, Kimbro exercises an overseer's authority and assigns him to another task. After his mistake in mixing the colors, the narrator is assigned to assist Lucius Brockway in the third sub-basement of the plant. Since his job is to control and service the machines that mix the base of the paint, the whole operation of paint-making depends upon his talents. The company has in the past frequently attempted to replace Brockway with white labor —during Brockway's illness an engineer of Italian ancestry was assigned to the job—but it discovered that no one else could do his work. Fearing that someone else will intrude on his domain, Brockway is fanatically anti-union. Entirely subservient to white authority, he takes a childish delight in the company's dependence on him and his special relationship with the boss. When Brockway retired, the Old Man discovered the paint was losing its excellence and personally persuaded Brockway to return to his job. Underpaid and underpraised, Brockway survives in the industrial system by embracing the existing authority and by having indispensable talents.

One day, the narrator inadvertently enters a union meeting in the locker-room. The white workers, assuming that he is applying for membership, at once suspect that he is a company spy. One member proposes that the narrator prove his loyalty to the union before he be permitted "to become acquainted with the work of the union and its aims." Although the novel does not develop the theme of this encounter, the incident suggests that before the labor movement will accept the Negro, he must go to inordinate lengths to justify his right to belong. Once the union people identify him as suspect, they make no effort [14] to ascertain his actual attitude toward unions. "They had made their decision without giving me a chance to speak for myself." As the narrator departs, the meeting chairman tells him, "We want you to know that we are only trying to protect ourselves. Some day we hope to have you as a member in good standing."

What the sequence illustrates is that to both white industry and white unions the Negro is acceptable only if he is either more loyal or more competent than a white; and business would prefer that his labor be less expensive. "The existence of racial prejudice in both employee and employer groups is of course an indisputable fact," wrote Horace R. Cayton and George S. Mitchell in 1939, in *Black Workers and the New Unions.* "If there were no economic advantages in employing Negroes, most employers would prefer a white labor force." This situation creates what the sociologist Robert Merton christens the self-fulfilling prophecy: "In the beginning, a *fake* definition of the situation [evokes] a new behavior which makes the originally false conception come true." If the dominant majority decides that Negroes are unfit to become union members because, it reasons, their lower standard of living allows them to take jobs at less than the prevailing wage, then the Negroes, as a result of exclusion, will become strike-breakers, accepting the lower wage and, it follows, necessarily adjusting their existence to the lower standard of living. Similarly if an employer rules that the Negroes are incapable of doing important work, then, acting upon their own false belief, they give Negroes only menial jobs. If the Negro, having no other choice, accepts the distasteful labor and handles it competently, then, in the employer's eyes, the Negro has "proved" he is fit only for menial work. Both employers and unions, then, exploit the Negro's second-class position in American society; and neither offers the Negro an acceptable solution. Later in the novel, a misunderstanding, coupled with a difference in attitude, produces a fight between the narrator and Brockway. An explosion occurs, and the narrator finds himself in a hospital. Here he undergoes an unidentified operation somewhat resembling a lobotomy, from which, the doctor promises, he will emerge with a "complete change of personality."

III

In the development of the novel, this chapter and the one following it serve a transitional function; for whereas the narrator once accepted the conventional solutions to the Negro's dilemma, now he is emancipated [15] from this narrow sense of possibility and prepared to sample more radical alternatives. Upon returning to his boarding house, a residence for more ambitious Negroes in New York, he recognizes that his house-mates display the vanities and deceits of those who either failed to climb through the existing system or deluded themselves with artificial tokens of success:

> The moment I entered the bright, buzzing lobby of Men's House I was overcome by a sense of alienation and hostility. My overalls were causing stares and I knew that I could live there no longer, that that phase of my life was past. The lobby was the meeting place for various groups still caught up in the illusions that had just been boomeranged out of my head: college boys working to return to school down south; older advocates of racial progress with utopian schemes for building black business empires; preachers ordained by no authority except their own, without church or congregation, without bread or wine, body or blood; the community "leaders" without followers; old men of sixty or more still caught up in post-Cvil War dreams of freedom within segregation; the pathetic ones who possessed nothing beyond their dreams of being gentlemen, who held small jobs or drew small pensions, and all pretending to be engaged in some vast, though obscure, enterprise, who affected the pseudo-courtly manners of certain Southern congressmen and bowed and and nodded as they passed like senile old roosters in a barnyard; the younger crowd for whom I now felt a contempt such as only a disillusioned dreamer feels for those still unaware that they

dream—the business students from Southern colleges, for whom business was a vague, abstract game with rules as obsolete as Noah's Ark but who yet were drunk on finance.

This complements the lobotomy; for just as the narrator assumes a new identity (the operation having caused him to forget his name), so he emerges from his residence hotel with a different set of inclinations.

Soon after, when the narrator discovers some poor old Negroes being evicted from their flat, he makes a speech on their behalf; and as his efforts attract a Harlem crowd, the narrator is accosted by a red-bearded man who introduces himself as "Brother Jack," who says of the narrator's extemporaneous speech: "*History* has been born in your brain." Jack explains that he belongs to a radical action group; and once the conversation becomes more relaxed the narrator accepts Jack's request to see him in the evening. That night, the narrator is introduced to the "Brotherhood," persuaded to become a salaried organizer for the movement, and assigned to a "theoretician" who will educate him in its aims and method. The "Brotherhood" is the American Communist Party in a thin fictional disguise.

This third major section of the novel portrays the narrator's discovery [16] that this radical movement understands neither his existence nor that of his people. From his opening conversation, Brother Jack speaks a language strange to the Negro experience. Addressing the narrator as "Brother," Jack offers him cheese cake, a white delicacy wholly foreign to Negro taste. Furthermore, he muses on how "history has passed by" the old evicted Negroes who are, he adds, "agrarian types, you know. Being ground up by industrial conditions. Thrown on the dump heaps and cast aside. They's like dead limbs that must be pruned away so that the tree may bear young fruit or the storms of history will blow them away." To this the narrator responds, "Look, I don't know what you're talking about. I've never lived on a farm and I didn't study agriculture." Later with an inappropriateness that is typical of him, Jack predicts that the Brotherhood will transform the narrator into "the new Booker T. Washington." A conciliator like Washington is precisely the opposite of the kind of leader a radical group needs; a reference to, say, Frederick Douglass would have been more appropriate. Moreover, the Brotherhood's images of Negro Americans come from the storehouse of bourgeois stereotypes.

When one "Brother" asks the narrator to sing a spiritual, the narrator replies that he cannot sing. The Brother's reply is, "Nonsense, *all* colored people sing." Yet, although he senses the Brotherhood's lack of understanding, the narrator is flattered enough to cast his lot with them.

From his earliest contact with the movement, the narrator is aware that he must assume a pre-cast role. When he accepts the job, he is outfitted with a new identity—on a slip of paper is written his new name. At a Brotherhood party, he overhears a female leader say, "But don't you think he should be a little blacker," and the statement prompts him to think, "What was I, a man or a natural resource?" Later, the Brotherhood suggests that he move to a new address and discontinue writing to his relatives for a while. When Jack introduces him to the larger circle under his new identity, the narrator notices, "Everyone smiled and seemed eager to meet me, as though they all knew the role I was to play." Though the narrator senses that the Brotherhood's aims and methods may not coincide with his, he accepts the role they thrust upon him for two reasons—because it offers him a key to understanding his experience and "the possibility of being more than a member of a race."

What the narrator fails to see at this point—and what he discovers later—is that "being more" than a member of his race means being less of a Negro. After he joins the Brotherhood, the narrator symbolically attempts to sever connections between himself and his [17] Southern Negro past. In a boarding house in Harlem, he discovers an object of much ulterior meaning:

> The cast-iron figure of a very black, red-lipped and wide-mouthed Negro, whose white eyes stared up at me from the floor, his face an enormous grin, his single large black hand held palm up before his chest. It was . . . the kind of bank which, if a coin is placed in the hand and a lever pressed upon the back, will raise its arm and flip the coin into the grinning mouth.

The figurine represents an aspect of the historical past that the narrator now wants desperately to forget; it has become "a self-mocking image." When the steam pipe of his room emits a clanking sound, the narrator strikes it with "the kinky iron head," cracking the figurine whose parts scatter across the floor. To escape both the landlady's wrath and his own feelings of guilt, the narrator scrapes the parts into the leather briefcase he received from the Southern businessmen. He drops the package in a garbage can outside an old private house; but its owner demands that he retrieve it (and, all that its contents symbolize). He protests, but when she threatens to call the police, he digs his hand into the muck (that lies between him and his Negro past) and recaptures the load. Two blocks later, he drops it in the heavy snow; but a passerby brings it back to him. The narrator cannot dispose of the package or elements of his character its contents symbolize until near the novel's end. He later acquires from another Negro Brother a link from a work-gang chain which he puts into his pocket; whenever he touches it, he is reminded of his heritage. Through these symbolic devices, Ellison makes the point that not even the Brotherhood can separate the American Negro from his past.

These themes are reinforced by the narrator's introspective monologues. During his affiliation with the Brotherhood, he is haunted by fears of "becoming someone else." For example, just before he is to deliver his first important speech for the Brotherhood, he feels "with a flash of panic that the moment I walked out upon the platform and opened my mouth I'd be someone else. Not just a nobody with a manufactured name which might have belonged to anyone, or to no one. But another personality." The problem is not that the Brotherhood forces him to do things against his will, but that this political life is not an organic outgrowth of his own past. His present experience strikes the narrator as a meaningless series of tacked-on events, chance encounters, and sudden fortunes. He becomes aware of two identities in himself:

> The old self that slept a few hours a night and dreamed sometimes of my [18] grandfather and Bledsoe and Brockway and Mary, the self that flew without wings and plunged from great heights; and the new public self that spoke for the Brotherhood and was becoming so much more important than the other that I seemed to run a foot race against myself.

A rigorous schedule prevents the narrator from thinking too much about this split; only when he is transferred to a less demanding job does this awareness of his divided personality oppress him.

If the Brotherhood has little sense of the needs of an individual Negro, it is even less aware of the actualities of American Negro life. Once the narrator becomes an organizer, he quickly rouses a strong, grass-roots movement among the Harlem populace; he makes speeches at public rallies and regularly visits all the important bars. His extraordinary success, however, makes his more experienced Negro Brothers jealous; and one, Brother Wrestum ("rest room"?), accuses him of individual opportunism and dictatorial aspirations. Although one speech earns applause "like a clap of thunder," the narrator is condemned by his Brotherhood superiors, because his talk was "wild, hysterical, politically irresponsible and dangerous, and worse than that, it was *incorrect!*" The emphasis upon the last word suggests to the narrator that, "The term described the most heinous crime imaginable." They criticize him, he discovers, because he neglected to include the ideology that would organize the Negro audience behind the Brotherhood. To prepare him more adequately for future speeches, they assign him to an intensive indoctrination program. It is implied, though not specifically illustrated, that these "correct" ideas and phrases are incapable of moving the Harlem audience. After all, if Jack's favorite clichés sound strange to the semi-educated ear of the narrator, they would be more wholly foreign to the common Negroes. By not correctly gauging the attitudes of Harlem, the Brotherhood also destroys the narrator's usefulness for its cause.

Once he is cleared of suspicions of both disloyalty and personal opportunism, the narrator returns to Harlem to discover that in his absence his personal following has disintegrated. In a symbolic passage, he enters a bar and addresses two old acquaintances as "Brothers." The tall one replies inquisitively, "he is relative of yourn?" His cohort adds, "Shit, he goddam sho ain't no kin of mine!" The first asks the bartender, "We just wanted to know if you could tell us just whose brother this here cat's supposed to be?" Since the bartender claims to be the narrator's "Brother," an argument ensues, the tall one protesting that since the narrator "got the white fever and left" for downtown —revealed that his ultimate loyalties were not to Negroes and [19] Harlem—he was no longer a "brother" of the Negroes. Later, the narrator discovers that in his absence the Brotherhood has abandoned its efforts in Harlem. The work he did, the support he organized, have all disappeared and there seems little likelihood he can retrieve the lost ground. His own labor for the Brotherhood, he deduces, accomplished nothing. "No great change had been made."

In one comic interlude, the novel suggests that the Brotherhood suffered because many of its organizers and sympathizers had motivations quite distant from politics. After he finishes his speech on the "woman question," the narrator is accosted by an extremely sensual woman who questions him on "certain aspects of our ideology." Since the questioning will take a while, she invites him up to her apartment. Innocently, he accepts her hospitality. She explains, as he enters her sumptuous apartment, "You can see, Brother, it is really the spiritual values of the Brotherhood that interest me." As he answers her questions, she moves closer to him and tells him how he embodies a "great throbbing vitality." After he seduces her, he condemns her for "confusing the class struggle with the ass struggle."

The Brotherhood's failure to gauge the Negro's actual needs lies not so much in the confusion of motives exemplified by the seductive women as in the blindness intrinsic in the movement's approach to reality. The movement's ideology contains elements appealing to the impoverished Negroes. It offers colored members equal rights; yet it is unable to empathize with the people's needs and spiritual temper. The novel explains this failure in both symbolic and narrative terms. When the narrator is reprimanded by Brother Jack for not preaching the correct line at the proper time, the narrator retorts that Jack, a white man, cannot know "the political consciousness of Harlem." Jack insists that the committee is the ultimate judge of reality and that the narrator is disobeying its "discipline." The narrator rejoins that Jack wants to be "the great white father" of Harlem, "Marse Jack." A fight seems imminent; but before it starts, Jack snatches his glass eye from its socket. The eye, Jack explains, was lost in the line of duty—by implication, in following the "discipline." The passage suggests not only that Jack is half-blind to the realities of Harlem—with only one eye his perception is limited—but also that he is incapable of seeing Harlem *in depth*. The narrator himself recognizes the second implication: "The meaning of discipline," he figures, "is sacrifice . . . yes, and blindness." Once he discovers this failure of perception, the narrator never again feels total loyalty to the Brotherhood.

Still, he accepts their command to see Hambro, the chief theoretician, [20] who reveals more obviously why the Brotherhood is oblivious to the needs of Harlem. It has deserted its drive to recruit

Negroes, because, the narrator is told, its emphasis has switched from national issues to international ones. When he asks Hambro, "What's to be done about my district," explaining the decline in membership and the threats from the black nationalists, the theoretician authoritatively informs him, "Your members will have to be sacrificed. We are making temporary alliances with other political groups and the interest of one group of brothers must be sacrificed to that of the whole." When the narrator argues that exploiting the Negro people is cynical, Hambro replies, in characteristic double-talk, "Not cynicism—realism. The trick is to take advantage of them in their own best interests." The narrator asks what justifies the sacrifice of unwitting people, and Hambro replies, "the laws of reality." Who determines the laws of reality? "The collective wisdom of the 'scientists' of the Brotherhood" is the reply. However, as the narrator perceives, the Brotherhood's science has little contact with hard facts. All they know is ideas about history's movements on the world stage; instead of trying to see Harlem as an individual entity, they see it only as an interdependent cog in a big machine. To the actual lives and hopes of American Negroes, the scientists are completely insensitive.

In talking with Hambro, the narrator concludes, "Everywhere I've turned somebody has wanted to sacrifice me for my good—only *they* were the ones who benefited." This recognition unlocks the narrator's first general thesis about the relations of white people with the Negro. Both Hambro and Jack, he thinks, are incapable of seeing a human essence either black or white. They believe that only the political part of a man, that segment that could serve the interests of the movement, is worthy of attention; all other problems and aspirations, whether emotional or physical, are ignored. Men could just as well be invisible. "Here I had thought they accepted me," the narrator decides, "because they felt that color made no difference, when in reality it made no difference because they didn't see either color or men." He then recognizes that Jack and Hambro hardly differ from Emerson and Norton. "They were very much the same, each attempting to force his picture of reality upon me and neither giving a hoot in hell for how things looked to me. I was simply a material, a natural resource to be used." As the four white figures blend into one, the narrator discovers the core truth of his relationship with them: "I now recognized my invisibility."

The recognition means that the narrator implicitly accepts the

[21] warning Ras the Exhorter, the black nationalist, offered to him earlier in the book:

> Why you with these white folks? Why a good boy like you with them? You *my* brother, mahn. Brothers are the same color; how the hell you call these white men *brother?* Shit mahn. Brothers the same color. We sons of Mama Africa, you done forgot? You black, BLACK! You got *bahd* hair! You got thick *lips!* They say you *stink!* They hate you, mahn. You African. AFRICAN! Why you with them? Leave that shit, mahn. They sell you out. That shit is old-fashioned. They enslave us—you forget that? How can they mean a black man any good? How they going to be your *brother?*

Ras's point—that all white men, whether enemy or friend, will use the Negro for their own purposes and finally betray him—is supported by the narrator's own understanding of his experience.

Ras himself proffers a political alternative for the American Negro, as he represents those Negro leaders who have espoused a racism that inverts the Manichean color symbolism traditional to the Christian West. Whereas the Western, which is to say American, mythos makes black synonymous with evil, the Negro racist makes black the color of all that is good. He attracts the support of Negroes by making them proud of their blackness. According to one scholar of black nationalism, C. Eric Lincoln,

> All black nationalist movements have in common three characteristics: a disparagement of the white man and his culture, a repudiation of Negro identity and an appropriation of "asiatic" culture symbols. Within this framework, they take shape in a remarkable variety of creeds and organizations.

The most prominent black nationalist in the period covered by Ellison's novel was Marcus Garvey, as the most famous exemplars in recent years are Elijah Muhammed and Malcolm X. However, there is little reason specifically to identify, as some critics have done, any of these figures with Ras the Exhorter. Although Ras is described as having, like Garvey, a West Indian accent, he favors resettlement in

Abyssinia ("Ras" being Abyssinian for prince), whereas Garvey wanted to send American Negroes to West Africa. In this respect, one could say, Ras is closer to the historic Noble Drew Ali, the self-styled leader of the "Moors," who designated Morocco in North Africa as the Negro homeland; moreover, his name evokes a nod to the Ras Tafari movement of colored West Indians. What this multiple reference suggests is that Ras, like other important characters in the novel, is conceived as a fictional prototype embodying a utopian alternative that has been espoused by several historical figures; and sure enough, Ras's group [22] embodies all three of the characteristics Professor Lincoln enumerates as typical of black nationalist movements.

The narrator never allies himself with Ras; for although he knows that Ras is capable of telling the truth about the Negro's relations with whites, the narrator also recognizes that the alternative Ras offers is unrealistic—absurd in everyday practice. Ras advocates a massive return to Africa which—given the costs, the lack of inhabitable space and the difficulties of resettlement—would be too hazardous for an average American Negro. For the United States, Ras preaches counterviolence, which the narrator discovers is ultimately self-destructive.

The Harlem battle Ras eventually wages is most thoroughly characterized by an anonymous Negro who tells his drinking cronies about the riot he has just witnessed. Through this device, Ellison reveals not only the absurdity of the battle itself but also the average Negro's bemused view of the fray:

> You know that stud Ras the Destroyer? Well, man, *he* was spitting blood. Hell, yes, man, he had him a big black hoss and a fur cap and some kind of old lion skin or something over his shoulders and he was raising hell. Goddam if he wasn't a *sight*, riding up and down on this ole hoss, you know one of the kind that pulls vegetable wagons, and he got him a cowboy saddle and some big spurs. . . .
>
> Hell, yes! Riding up and down the block yelling, "Destroy 'em! Drive 'em out. Burn 'em out! I, Ras, commands you—to destroy them to the last piece of rotten fish!" And 'bout that time some joker with a big ole Georgia voice sticks his head out the window and yells, "Ride 'em cowboy. Give 'em hell and ba-

nanas." And man, that crazy sonofabitch up there on that hoss, looking like death eating a sandwich, he reaches down and comes up with a forty-five and starts blazing up at that window—and man, talk about cutting out! In a second wasn't nobody left but ole Ras up there on that hoss with that lion skin stretched out behind him. Crazy, man.

When he seen them cops riding up he reached back of his saddle and come up with some kind of old shield. One with a spike in the middle of it. And that ain't all; when he sees the cops he calls to one of his goddam henchmens to hand him up a spear, and a little short guy run out into the street and give him one. You know, one of the kind you see them African guys carrying in the moving pictures. . . .

Ras rides hard, "like Earle Sand in the fifth at Jamaica," into the mounted police; and although he manages to knock down two with his spear, a third policeman fells him with a bullet. Meanwhile, the onlookers of Harlem are looting the damaged stores. The political point is quite clear: To the typical Harlemite, Ras's actions are ludicrously ineffectual; for he is neither prepared for a modern battle nor [23] able to win the support of the Negro people. Moreover, the violence he creates causes more deaths among the Negroes than the white enemies. In this respect, the riot echoes the battle royal fought at the beginning of the novel; for in both scenes, the Negroes vent their anger not against their oppressor but against their own people.

Against both Ras and Brother Jack is counterposed Rinehart, who represents the possibilities of Harlem life. As Ras's thugs are closing in upon the narrator, he steps into a drugstore and purchases a disguise of dark glasses and a wide-brimmed hat. Advancing down the street, he notices that several passers-by mistake him for a certain "Rinehart"; within moments, he discovers that Rinehart must be a desirable lover, a gambler, a numbers runner, a police briber, a male whore, a hipster, a zoot-suiter, and a self-ordained Reverend—"Spiritual Technologist." The narrator realizes why Rinehart can fill so many roles, for his own dark glasses reveal that the world of Harlem is "a merging fluidity of forms." In contrast to the Brotherhood, and also to Ras, who try to squeeze the world into rigid categories which limit the dimensions of existence, Rinehart sees that the Negro world in the North offers anonymity and possibility:

In the South everyone knows you, but coming North was a jump into the unknown. You could actually make yourself anew. The notion was frightening, for now the world seemed to flow before my eyes. All boundaries down, freedom was not only the recognition of necessity, it was the recognition of possibility. And sitting there trembling I caught a brief glimpse of the possibilities posed by Rinehart's multiple personalities. . . .

This recognition echoes the advice an anonymous veteran gave the narrator back in the Golden Day: "Be your own father, young man. And remember, the world is possibility if only you'll discover it." After this revelation, the narrator perceives that "Hambro's lawyer's mind was too narrowly logical" to understand Harlem.

After hastily departing from Hambro's, the narrator decides "to do a Rinehart," to face life with the most ironic of strategies. Remembering his childhood, he repeats to himself his grandfather's deathbed advice: "Live with your head in the lion's mouth. I want you to overcome 'em with yesses, undermine 'em with grins, agree 'em to death and destruction, let 'em swoller you till they vomit or bust wide open." He decides to master the trick of saying yes and no at the same time, yes to please and no to know. "For now I saw that I could agree with Jack without agreeing, and I could tell Harlem to have hope when there was no hope." To please his Brotherhood superiors he fabricates reports of a nonexistent growth in membership, [24] and at the next Brotherhood gathering he entices Sybil, the wife of an organizational functionary, to come to his apartment. Although he knows that she sees him as just another hypersexual Negro, "expected either to sing 'Old Man River' and just keep rolling along, or do fancy tricks with my muscles," he decides this time to exploit his invisibility. However, when she makes "a modest proposal that I join her in a very revolting ritual," the narrator, sometimes a prig, is repelled by what he interprets as an assault on something deeper than mere sexuality. So, he spends the evening torn between the impulse to throw her out of his bed and wondering how Rinehart would have handled the situation. Though he imitates the motions he imagines to be Rinehart's, seducing the girl who calls him "boo'ful," he cannot play the role with the assurance of the master.

This experience with the Brotherhood, along with his recognition of the vanity of Ras's efforts, leads the narrator to a decisive decision: "I knew that it was better to live out one's own absurdity than to die for that of others." Later, he elaborates on the theme:

> I've never been more loved and appreciated than when I tried to "justify" and affirm someone's mistaken beliefs; or when I've tried to give my friends the incorrect, absurd answers they wished to hear. . . . Oh yes, it made them happy and it made me sick. So, I became ill of affirmation, of saying "yes" against the nay-saying of my stomach—not to mention my brain. . . . My problem was that I always tried to go in everyone's way but my own. I have also been called one thing and then another while no one really wished to hear what I called myself. So after years of trying to adopt the opinions of others I finally rebelled.

In the final sequences of the novel, the narrator confronts the problem of how to face what he takes to be the absurdity of society. In escaping from the police, he jumps through a manhole into a bin of coal. Unable to climb out, he experiences a "dark night of the soul," which includes a nightmare in which Norton, Emerson and Jack castrate him of his "illusions." Wading through the tunnels, he finds a large basement cavern which becomes his underground home; in his own way, the man who had Candide's innocence and questing energy eventually accepts Candide's final dictum, "That we must cultivate our [own] garden." Whereas Rinehart exploited absurdity for personal gain, the narrator as underground man accepts, as an expatriate, the condition through his own non-participation.

However, this escape, he discovers, is not satisfactory either. "I couldn't be still even in hibernation," he thinks, "because, damn it, there's the mind, the *mind*. It wouldn't let me rest." The narrator's [25] conscience inspires him to write a book that will explain his experience. "Without the possibility of action," he thinks, existence takes on a meaninglessness, knowledge is forgotten, and the capacities to love and care are suppressed. The narrator achieves what Ellison described in his essay on Wright as the spirit of the blues: "They at once express both the agony of life and the possibility of conquering it through sheer toughness of spirit. They fall short of tragedy only in that they provide no solution, offer no scapegoat but the self." While he agrees with the wisdom of Louis Armstrong's song, "Open the window and let the foul air out," he also believes another song that says, "It was good green corn before the harvest." It is the latter belief that leads him to resolve to "shake off his old skin," to repudiate his form of expatriation, and to seek in the aboveground society an existence that allows him to live primarily for himself. He concludes his story affirming the desire to affirm. "There's a possibility that even an invisible man has a socially responsible role to play." With all his previous experiences and rejections, this becomes the most positive commitment that Ellison's narrator can justifiably make. [26]

EPILOGUE

BRAVE WORDS FOR A STARTLING OCCASION
Ralph Ellison

First, as I express my gratitude for this honor which you have bestowed on me, let me say that I take it that you are rewarding my efforts rather than my not quite fully achieved attempt at a major novel. Indeed, if I were asked in all seriousness just what I considered to be the chief significance of *Invisible Man* as a fiction, I would reply: Its experimental attitude, and its attempt to return to the mood of personal moral responsibility for democracy which typified the best of our nineteenth-century fiction. That my first novel should win this most coveted prize must certainly indicate that there is a crisis in the American novel. You as critics have told us so, and current fiction sales would indicate that the reading public agrees. Certainly the younger novelists concur. The explosive nature of events mocks our brightest efforts. [102] And the very "facts" which the naturalists assumed would make us free have lost the power to protect us from despair. Controversy now rages over just what aspects of American experience are suitable for novelistic treatment. The prestige of the theorists of the so-called novel of manners has been challenged. Thus after a long period of stability we find our assumptions concerning the novel being called into question. And though I was only vaguely aware, it was this growing crisis which shaped the writing of *Invisible Man*.

After the usual apprenticeship of imitation and seeking with delight to examine my experience through the discipline of the novel, I became gradually aware that the forms of so many of the works which impressed me were too restricted to contain the experience

SOURCE: Ralph Ellison, "Brave Words for a Startling Occasion," pp. 102–6. Copyright © 1963, 1964 by Ralph Ellison. Reprinted from *Shadow and Act* by permission of Random House, Inc.
   Ellison gave this address on being presented with The National Book Award, January 27, 1953.

which I knew. The diversity of American life with its extreme fluidity and openness seemed too vital and alive to be caught for more than the briefest instant in the tight well-made Jamesian novel, which was, for all its artistic perfection, too concerned with "good taste" and stable areas. Nor could I safely use the forms of the "hard-boiled" novel, with its dedication to physical violence, social cynicism and understatement. Understatement depends, after all, upon commonly held assumptions and my minority status rendered all such assumptions questionable. There was also a problem of language, and even dialogue, which, with its hard-boiled stance and its monosyllabic utterance, is one of the shining achievements of twentieth-century American writing. For despite the notion that its rhythms were those of everyday speech, I found that when compared with the rich babel of idiomatic expression around me, a language full of imagery and gesture and rhetorical canniness, it was embarrassingly austere. Our speech I found resounding with an alive language swirling with over three hundred years of American living, a mixture of the folk, the Biblical, the scientific and the political. Slangy in one [103] stance, academic in another, loaded poetically with imagery at one moment, mathematically bare of imagery in the next. As for the rather rigid concepts of reality which informed a number of the works which impressed me and to which I owe a great deal, I was forced to conclude that reality was far more mysterious and uncertain, and more exciting, and still, despite its raw violence and capriciousness, more promising. To attempt to express that American experience which has carried one back and forth and up and down the land and across, and across again the great river, from freight train to Pullman car, from contact with slavery to contact with a world of advanced scholarship, art and science, is simply to burst such neatly understated forms of the novel asunder.

A novel whose range was both broader and deeper was needed. And in my search I found myself turning to our classical nineteenth-century novelists. I felt that except for the work of William Faulkner something vital had gone out of American prose after Mark Twain. I came to believe that the writers of that period took a much greater responsibility for the condition of democracy and, indeed, their works were imaginative projections of the conflicts within the human heart which arose when the sacred principles of the Constitution and the Bill of Rights clashed with the practical exigencies of human greed and fear, hate and love. Naturally I was attracted to these writers as a Negro. Whatever they thought of my people per se, in their imaginative economy the Negro symbolized both the man lowest down and the mysterious, underground aspect of human personality. In a sense the Negro was the gauge of the human condition as it waxed and waned in our democracy. These writers were willing to confront the broad complexities of American life and we are the richer for their having done so.

Thus to see America with an awareness of its rich diversity and its almost magical fluidity and freedom, I was forced [104] to conceive of a novel unburdened by the narrow naturalism which has led, after so many triumphs, to the final and unrelieved despair which marks so much of our current fiction. I was to dream of a prose which was flexible, and swift as American change is swift, confronting the inequalities and brutalities of our society forthrightly, but yet thrusting forth its images of hope, human fraternity and individual self-realization. It would use the richness of our speech, the idiomatic expression and the rhetorical flourishes from past periods which are still alive among us. And despite my personal failures, there must be possible a fiction which, leaving sociology to the scientists, can arrive at the truth about the human condition, here and now, with all the bright magic of a fairy tale.

What has been missing from so much experimental writing has been the passionate will to dominate reality as well as the laws of art. This will is the true source of the experimental attitude. We who struggle with form and with America should remember Eidothea's advice to Menelaus when in the *Odyssey* he and his friends are seeking their way home. She tells him to seize her father, Proteus, and to hold him fast "however he may struggle and fight. He will turn into all sorts of shapes to try you," she says, "into all the creatures that live and move upon the earth, into water, into blazing fire; but you must hold him fast and press him all the harder. When he is himself, and questions you in the same shape that he was when you saw him in his bed, let the old man go; and then, sir, ask which god it is who is angry, and how you shall make your way homewards over the fish-giving sea."

For the novelist, Proteus stands for both America and the inheritance of illusion through which all men must fight to achieve reality; the offended god stands for our sins against those principles we all hold sacred. The way home we seek is that condition of man's being at home in the world, which is [105] called love, and which we term democracy. Our task then is always to challenge the apparent forms of reality—that is, the fixed manners and values of the few, and to struggle with it until it reveals its mad, vari-implicated chaos, its false faces, and on until it surrenders its insight, its truth. We are fortunate as American writers in that with our variety of racial and national traditions, idioms and manners, we are yet one. On its profoundest level American experience is of a whole. Its truth lies in its diversity and swiftness of change. Through forging forms of the novel worthy of it, we achieve not only the promise of our lives, but we anticipate the resolution of those world problems of humanity which for a moment seem to those who are in awe of statistics completely insoluble.

Whenever we as Americans have faced serious crises we have returned to fundamentals; this, in brief, is what I have tried to do. [106]

BIBLIOGRAPHY

Primary Material

To keep pace with the ever-increasing critical discussions of Ralph Ellison and *Invisible Man* check the yearly bibliographies of *PMLA* and *American Literature*.

"Slick Gonna Learn," *Direction* (September, 1939), 10–16.

"Afternoon," *American Writing*, ed. Hans Otto Storn & others, pp. 28–37. Reprinted in *Negro Story* (March–April, 1945).

"Mister Toussan," *The New Masses*, XLI (November 4, 1941), 19, 20.

"That I Had the Wings," *Common Ground*, III (Summer, 1943), 30–37.

"Flying Home," *Cross Section*, ed. Edwin Seaver (New York: L. B. Fischer, 1944), pp. 469–85.

"In a Strange Country," *Tomorrow*, III (July, 1944), 41–44.

"King of the Bingo Game," *Tomorrow*, IV (November, 1944), 29–33.

Invisible Man (New York: Random House, 1952).

"Did You Ever Dream Lucky?" *New World Writing* #5 (New York: The New American Library, 1954), pp. 134–45.

"A Coupla Scalped Indians," *New World Writing* #9 (New York: The New American Library, 1956), pp. 225–36.

"And Hickman Arrives," *The Noble Savage I*, 1956.

"It Always Breaks Out," *Partisan Review*, XXX (Spring, 1963), 13–28.

"Out of the Hospital and Under the Bar," *Soon, One Morning: New Writing by American Negroes*, 1940–1962, ed. Herbert Hill (New York: Alfred A. Knopf, 1963), pp. 243–90.

Shadow and Act (New York: Random House, 1964).

"Song of Innocence—Excerpt from a Novel in Progress," *The Iowa Review, I* (Spring, 1970), 30–40.

Secondary Sources

Allen, Michael, "Some Examples of Faulknerian Rhetoric in Ellison's *Invisible Man*," *The Black American Writer*, I, ed. C. W. E. Bigsby (Deland, Fla.: Everett/Edwards Inc., 1969), pp. 143–51.

Anon., "Ralph Ellison—Fiction Winner," *Crisis*, LX, 154–56.

———, "Ralph Ellison and the Establishment," *Negro Digest*, XVI (August, 1967), 49–50.

Baumbach, Jonathan, "Nightmare of a Native Son: Ralph Ellison's *Invisible Man*," *Critique: Studies in Modern Fiction*, VI, 48–65. Reprinted in *The Landscape of Nightmare* (New York: New York University Press, 1965).

Bennett, John Z., "The Race and the Runner: Ellison's *Invisible Man*," *Xavier University Studies*, V, 12–26.

Bloch, Alice, "Sight Imagery in *Invisible Man*," *English Journal*, LV, 1019–1021, 1023.

Bluestein, Gene, "The Blues as a Literary Theme," *Massachusetts Review*, VIII, 593–617.

Bone, Robert, *The Negro Novel in America* (New Haven: Yale University Press, 1958), pp. 196–212.

———, "Ralph Ellison and the Uses of Imagination," *Tri-Quarterly*, VI, 39–54. Reprinted in *Anger and Beyond*, ed. Herbert Hill (New York: Harper & Row, 1966), pp. 86–111.

Brown, Lloyd W., "The Deep Pit," *Masses and Mainstream*, V (June, 1952), 62–64.

———, "Ralph Ellison's Exhorters: The Role of Rhetoric in *Invisible Man*," *CLA Journal*, XIII, No. 3 (1970), 289–313.

Christian, Barbara, "Ralph Ellison: A Critical Study," *Black Expression*, ed. Addison Gayle, Jr. (New York: Weybright and Talley, Inc., 1969), pp. 353–65.

Clarke, John Henrik, "The Visible Dimensions in *Invisible Man*," *Black World*, XX (December, 1970), 27–30.

Clipper, Lawrence J., "Folkloric and Mythic Elements in *Invisible Man*," *CLA Journal*, XIII, No. 3 (1970), 229–41.

Collier, Eugenia W., "The Nightmare Truth of an Invisible Man," *Black World*, XX (December, 1970), 12–19.

Corry, John, "Profile of an American Novelist," *Black World*, XX (December, 1970), 116–25.

Ford, Nick Aaron, "The Ambivalence of Ralph Ellison," *Black World*, XX (December, 1970), 5–9.

———, "Battle of the Books: A Critical Survey of Significant Books by and about Negroes Published in 1960," *Phylon*, XXII, 119–34.

———, "Four Popular Negro Novelists," *Phylon*, XV (March, 1954), 29–39.

Fraiberg, S., "Two Modern Incest Heroes," *Partisan Review*, XXVIII (1961), 646–61.

Geller, Allen, "An Interview with Ralph Ellison," *Tamarack Review*, XXXII, 3–24.

Girson, Rochelle, "Sidelights on Invisibility," *Saturday Review*, XXXVI, 20, 49.

Glicksberg, Charles I., "The Symbolism of Vision," *Southwest Review*, XXXIX, 259–65.

Goede, William, "On Lower Frequencies: The Buried Men in Wright and Ellison," *Modern Fiction Studies*, XV, 483–501.

Griffin, Edward M., "Notes from a Clean Well-Lighted Place: Ralph Ellison's *Invisible Man*," *Twentieth Century Literature*, XV, 129–44.

Hassan, Ihab, *Radical Innocence: Studies in the Contemporary American Novel* (Princeton: Princeton University Press, 1961), pp. 168–79.

Heermance, J. N., "The Modern Negro Novel," *Negro Digest*, XIII (May, 1964), 66–76.

Horowitz, Ellin, "The Rebirth of the Artist," *On Contemporary Literature*, ed. Richard Kostelanetz (New York: Avon Book Division of the Hearst Corp., 1964), pp. 330–46.

Horowitz, Floyd Ross, "The Enigma of Ralph Ellison's *Invisible Man*," *CLA Journal*, VII, 126–32.

———, "An Experimental Confession from a Reader of *Invisible Man*," *CLA Journal*, XIII, No. 3 (1970), 304–14.

———, "Ralph Ellison's Modern Version of Brer Bear and Brer Rabbit in *Invisible Man*," *Mid-Continent American Studies Journal*, IV, 21–27.

Hyman, Stanley Edgar, "The Negro Writer in America: An Exchange," *Partisan Review,* XXV (1958), 197–211.

———, "Ralph Ellison in Our Time," *Standards: A Chronicle of Books for Our Time* (New York, 1966), pp. 249–53.

Isaacs, Harold R., "Five Writers and Their African Ancestors," *Phylon,* XXI, 243–65, 317–36.

Jackson, Ester Merle, "The American Negro and the Image of the Absurd," *Phylon,* XXIII (Winter, 1962), 359–71.

Kaiser, Ernest, "A Critical Look at Ellison's Fiction and at Social and Literary Criticism by and about the Author," *Black World,* XX (December, 1970), 53–59, 81–97.

Kent, George E., "Ralph Ellison and Afro-American Folk and Cultural Tradition," *CLA Journal,* XIII, No. 3 (1970), 265–76.

Killens, John O., "*Invisible Man,*" *Freedom,* II (June, 1952), 7.

Klein, Marcus, *After Alienation: American Novels in Mid-Century* (New York: The World Publishing Co., 1964), pp. 71–146.

Klotman, Phyllis R., "The Running Man as Metaphor in Ellison's *Invisible Man,*" *CLA Journal,* XIII, No. 3 (1970), 277–88.

Kostelanetz, Richard, "The Negro Genius," *Twentieth Century,* Vol. 175, No. 1033: 49–50.

———, "The Politics of Ellison's Booker: *Invisible Man* as Symbolic History," *Chicago Review,* XIX, 5–26.

———, "Ralph Ellison: Novelist as Brown-Skinned Aristocrat," *Masterminds* (New York: Macmillan, 1969), pp. 36–59.

LeClair, Thomas, "The Blind Leading the Blind: Wright's '*Native Son*' and a Brief Reference to Ellison's *Invisible Man,*" *CLA Journal,* XIII, No. 3 (1970), 315–20.

Lee, L. L., "The Proper Self: Ralph Ellison's *Invisible Man,*" *Descant,* X (Spring, 1966), 38–48.

Lehan, Richard, "The Strange Silence of Ralph Ellison," *California English Journal,* I, 63–68.

Levant, Howard, "Aspiraling We Should Go," *Mid-Continent American Studies Journal,* IV, 3–20.

Lewis, R. W. B., "Ellison's Essays," *New York Review of Books* (January 28, 1964), 19–20.

Ludington, Charles T., Jr., "Protest and Anti-Protest: Ralph Ellison," *Southern Humanities Review*, IV (Winter, 1970), 31–40.

Margolies, Edward, *Native Sons: A Critical Study of Twentieth-Century Negro American Authors* (Philadelphia: J. B. Lippincott Co., 1968), pp. 127–48.

Mason, Clifford, "Ralph Ellison and the Underground Man," *Black World*, XX (December, 1970), 20–26.

McPherson, James Alan, and Ralph Ellison, "Indivisible Man," *The Atlantic*, 226 (December, 1970), 45–60.

Mengeling, Marvin E., "Whitman and Ellison: Older Symbols in a Modern Mainstream," *Walt Whitman Review*, XII, 67–70.

Nash, R. W., "Stereotypes and Social Types in Ellison's *Invisible Man*," *Sociological Quarterly*, VI (Autumn, 1965), 349–60.

Neal, Larry, "Ellison's Zoot Suit," *Black World*, XX (December, 1970), 31–52.

O'Daniel, Therman B., "The Image of Man as Portrayed by Ralph Ellison," *CLA Journal*, X, 277–84.

Olderman, Raymond M., "Ralph Ellison's Blues and *Invisible Man*," *Wisconsin Studies in Contemporary Literature*, VII, 142–59.

Randall, John H., III, "Ralph Ellison: Invisible Man," *Revue des Langues Vivantes*, XXXI, 24–44.

Rodnon, Stewart, "Ralph Ellison's *Invisible Man*: Six Tentative Approaches," *CLA Journal*, XII, 244–56.

Rovit, Earl H., "Ralph Ellison and the American Comic Tradition," *Wisconsin Studies in Contemporary Literature*, I, 34–42.

Sanders, Archie D., "Odysseus in Black: An Analysis of the Structure of *Invisible Man*," *CLA Journal*, XIII, No. 3 (1970), 217–28.

Schafer, William J., "Irony from Underground—Satiric Elements in *Invisible Man*," *Satire Newsletter*, VII (Fall, 1969), 22–28.

———, "Ralph Ellison and the Birth of the Anti-Hero," *Critique: Studies in Modern Fiction*, X, 81–93.

Singleton, M. K., "Leadership Mirages as Antagonists in *Invisible Man*," *Arizona Quarterly*, XXII (Summer, 1966), 157–71.

Stanford, Raney, "The Return of the Trickster: When a Not-Hero Is a Hero," *Journal of Popular Culture*, I (Winter, 1967), 228–42.

Thompson, James, Lennox Raphael, and Steve Canon, "'A Very Stern Discipline': An Interview With Ralph Ellison," *Harpers*, 234 (March), 76–95.

Tischler, N. M., "Negro Literature and Classic Form," *Contemporary Literature*, X (Summer, 1969), 352–65. Reply with rejoinder T. A. Vogler (Winter, 1970), 130–35.

Turner, Darwin T., "Sight in *Invisible Man*," *CLA Journal*, XIII, No. 3 (1970), 258–64.

Vogler, Thomas A., "*Invisible Man*: Somebody's Protest Novel," *The Iowa Review*, I (Spring, 1970), 64–82.

Waghmare, J. M., "Invisibility and the American Negro: Ralph Ellison's *Invisible Man*," *Quest*, 59: 23–30.

Warren, Robert Penn, "The Unity of Experience," *Commentary*, XXXIX (May, 1965), 91–96. (Review of *Shadow and Act*)

West, Anthony, "Black Man's Burden," *The New Yorker*, XXVIII (May 31, 1952), 79–81.

Williams, John A., "Ralph Ellison and *Invisible Man*: Their Place in American Letters," *Black World*, XX (December, 1970), 242–57.

Wilner, Eleanor R., "The Invisible Black Thread: Identity and Nonentity in *Invisible Man*," *CLA Journal*, XIII, No. 3 (1970), 242–57.

POSSIBLE DISCUSSION QUESTIONS OR RESEARCH TOPICS

For the sake of convenience I have divided these topics according to the major divisions of the book. In each division the topics proceed from the simple to the complex—from those requiring merely the casebook and the novel to those requiring additional reading and research. This list is by no means exhaustive, but it does offer some basic topics for both instructor and student to build on.

I. The Historical Tradition: The Racial Heritage

Booker T. Washington

1. Discuss Ellison's use of Booker T. Washington's "Atlanta Exposition Address" in the opening chapters of *Invisible Man*.
2. Compare the ideology in Washington's speech with the ideology of the Founder.
3. Compare the visions of black identity present in *Up from Slavery* (New York: Doubleday, Page, and Co., 1901) with Barbee's myth of the Black Horatio Alger.
4. Discuss the theme of Ego (or the individual vs. the group) as it appears in *Up from Slavery* and Ellison's picture of Bledsoe.

W. E. B. DuBois

1. Discuss W. E. B. DuBois' criticism of Washington as it compares with the educational experience of the narrator.
2. Discuss the Veteran's criticism of the Washington ideology as compared with the criticism of DuBois.
3. Discuss the ways in which DuBois' "three responses" provide a key to the behavioral patterns of the novel.
4. What are the potential dangers in DuBois' philosophy? What would Mary Rambo think of DuBois? Compare the visions of black

identity apparent in DuBois and in the character of Bledsoe with
E. Franklin Frazier's analysis in *Black Bourgeoisie* (New York:
The Free Press, 1957).

Alain Locke

1. Compare Locke's idealism about the Northern black experience
   with the narrator's experience.
2. How is Locke's contention about the positive impact of the modern
   industrial North on the black man in need of qualification? Read
   Ellison's "Harlem Is Nowhere" in *Shadow and Act* (New York:
   Random House, 1964).
3. Compare Locke's expectations for Harlem and the black community with James Weldon Johnson's *Black Manhattan* (New York:
   Atheneum, 1968) and Gilbert Osofsky's *Harlem: The Making of
   a Ghetto* (New York: Harper & Row, 1963).
4. Compare the impact of modern Northern industrialism on the narrator of *Invisible Man* with the historical account of that experience
   portrayed in Julius Jacobson's *The Negro and the American Labor
   Movement* (New York: Doubleday, 1968).
5. Compare Locke's expectations for a Harlem Renaissance in the
   twenties with the analyses of that period by Langston Hughes in
   The Big Sea (New York: Hill and Wang, 1940), Claude McKay
   in *A Long Way from Home* (New York: Harcourt, Brace & World,
   1970), and Harold Cruse in *The Crisis of the Negro Intellectual*
   (New York: William Morrow and Co., 1967).

Marcus Garvey

1. Compare Ellison's portrait of Ras with Marcus Garvey as he is
   revealed by his speech.
2. Compare Ras with a larger portrait of Marcus Garvey. Consult Edmund D. Cronon's *Black Moses: The Story of Marcus
   Garvey and the Universal Negro Improvement Association*
   (Madison: The University of Wisconsin Press, 1955).
3. Compare Ellison's criticism of Ras with Harold Cruse's criticism of
   Garveyism in *Crisis of the Negro Intellectual*.
4. Compare Ellison's view of black nationalism with those of Malcolm
   X in his *Autobiography* (New York: Grove Press, 1964) and
   Eldridge Cleaver in *Soul on Ice* (New York: Delta, 1968).

Richard Wright

1. Discuss the similarity of Wright's and the narrator's experience with the communist party.
2. Compare and contrast Ellison's criticism of the party with that of Harold Cruse in *The Crisis of the Negro Intellectual*.
3. Discuss the historical accuracy of Ellison's portrait of the party by comparing it to Wilson Record's analysis in *The Negro and the Communist Party* (Chapel Hill: University of North Carolina Press, 1951).

II. The Historical Tradition: The Artistic Heritage

Ralph Waldo Emerson

1. Discuss the ways in which knowledge of any one of the following essays by Emerson gives us a key to *Invisible Man*: "Self-Reliance," "Fate," "Circles."
2. Discuss Ellison's preoccupation with his Emersonian heritage in "Hidden Name and Complex Fate" in *Shadow and Act*.
3. Discuss the ways in which Ellison may be viewed as Emerson's "poet."

T. S. Eliot

1. Discuss the theme of the historical tradition as it appears in Eliot's essay and Ellison's essay "The World and the Jug."
2. Discuss the theme of the dichotomy of citizen and creator as it appears in the essays of Eliot, Ellison, and Howe.
3. Discuss either of the above themes as they may be traced through *Invisible Man*.

Sterling Brown

1. Discuss the appearance of Brown's stereotypes in *Invisible Man*.
2. Discuss the problem of stereotyping in black literature. See, for example, Blyden Jackson's article "The Negro's Negro in Negro Literature," *The Michigan Quarterly Review*, IV (1965), 290–95.

Irving Howe

1. Compare James Baldwin's analysis of Richard Wright in "Everybody's Protest Novel" in *Notes of a Native Son* (Boston: Beacon Press, 1955) with Ellison's analysis in "Richard Wright's Blues" in *Shadow and Act*.
2. Howe asserts that violence is at the heart of the black experience. Discuss the theme of violence in *Invisible Man*.
3. Howe says Baldwin and Ellison have tried to go beyond naturalism. To what extent is the technique of literary naturalism employed in *Invisible Man*?
4. Howe says "willed affirmation" alone is not enough. How satisfactory is the narrator's willed affirmation in the Epilogue?
5. Discuss the concept of the black hero as it is revealed by Ellison's narrator, Richard Wright's Bigger in *Native Son*, and James Baldwin's Rufus in *Another Country*.
6. Consult Robert Bone's *The Negro Novel in America* (New Haven: Yale University Press, 1958), David Littlejohn's *Black on White* (New York: Grossman, 1966), Edward Margolies' *Native Sons* (Philadelphia: J. B. Lippincott Co., 1968), and the essays in Leroi Jones and Larry Neal's *Black Fire* (New York: William Morrow & Co., 1968). Then try to formulate a definition of black American literature that confirms either Howe's or Ellison's side in the controversy.
7. To what extent does *Invisible Man* match the aesthetic principles enunciated in "The World and the Jug"?

III. Critical Approaches to the Novel

A. Short Papers

1. Discuss the function of the Epilogue in *Invisible Man*.
2. Discuss the symbolic function of names in *Invisible Man*.
3. Discuss the relationship of the complete lyrics of the song "What Did I Do to Be So Black and Blue" to the novel.
4. Attempt a definition of Rinehartism.
5. Discuss Trueblood's story as an example of the slave narrative. See in particular Gilbert Osofsky's introduction to *Puttin' On Ole Massa* (New York: Harper & Row, 1969).

POSSIBLE DISCUSSION QUESTIONS OR RESEARCH TOPICS

6. Frederick Douglass is alluded to in the Brotherhood section of the novel. Compare Douglass' relationship to the Abolitionist movement with the narrator's relationship to the Brotherhood. See Benjamin Quarles' *Frederick Douglass* (New York: Atheneum, 1969).

B. Longer Papers

1. Discuss the problem of "point of view" in the novel.
2. Discuss the theme of sight imagery in the novel. Can you expand on Miss Bloch's analysis? Consult the bibliography for other critics who have written on this theme.
3. Discuss the symbolic function of the various stage props that show up in the narrator's brief case.
4. Discuss the function of oratory and speech-making in the novel.
5. Discuss the novel as "blues." Begin by consulting the "Music" section in Robert Bone's essay on "Ralph Ellison and the Uses of the Imagination."
6. Discuss the grandfather's riddle as the central enigma of the novel. How valid are the answers offered to the riddle by the narrator in the Epilogue.
7. Consult Richard M. Dorson's "American Negro Folktales" (New York: Fawcett, 1956) and Langston Hughes and Arna Bontemps' *The Book of Negro Folklore* (New York: Dodd, Mead & Co., 1958). Then discuss Ellison's use of folklore in *Invisible Man*.
8. Discuss *Invisible Man* as an existentialist novel.
9. Discuss the theme of the "white woman" in the novel. Begin by reading Eldridge Cleaver's "The Primeval Mitosis" in *Soul on Ice*.